Also by Gay Courter

Fiction
The Midwife

River of Dreams

Code Ezra

Flowers in the Blood

The Midwife's Advice

Healing Paradise

The Girl in the Box

Nonfiction
The Beansprout Book

I Speak for This Child: True Stories of a Child Advocate

How to Survive Your Husband's Midlife Crisis
(co-author with Pat Gaudette)

Dedicated to
the fourteen souls who lost their lives,
the 712 men and women who suffered with COVID-19,
the 1045 officers and crew led by Captain Arma, gladiators all,
and with love and gratitude to
our children—Blake, Joshua, and Ashley—who helped bring us home,
and Philip, without whom survival is meaningless

Contents

PROLOGUE

I still believe that if your aim is to change the world, journalism is a more immediate short-term weapon.

—Tom Stoppard

I heard a loud double knock at the door of our mini-suite on the *Diamond Princess* cruise ship.

"Can you get that?" I shouted to my husband as I stepped out of the shower.

Phil didn't respond. I put on my robe and peered out but didn't see him. It's hard to lose someone in 354 square feet. I felt a breeze and realized he was on the balcony filming the chaos on the pier below. We were docked in Yokohama, the port for Tokyo. It was the evening of February 9, 2020. Four days earlier, the Japanese Ministry of Health had ordered us to quarantine in our cabins. The ship had been exposed to a virulent new pathogen, the same one that in just a few weeks had caused cases of a respiratory illness in China to balloon to forty thousand, with more than eight hundred deaths, well surpassing their 2002–2003 SARS epidemic statistics. In a bizarre coincidence, a man from Hong Kong, who

1

had joined the cruise with us on January 20 and left on the 25th, had tested positive for the coronavirus after leaving the ship. Now, instead of enjoying the rest of our Asian vacation, we were among more than thirty-seven hundred passengers and crew who had just completed a dazzling cruise celebrating the Lunar New Year and awakened one morning to learn that we were marooned on a modern-day plague ship.

As soon as we heard about the man from Hong Kong and realized we were at the mercy of the Japanese health authorities, I emailed a friend who had been an ABC news producer. "Guess where we are?" I wrote. By the next day, we were blindsided by a barrage of interview requests. Texts and emails were coming in so fast we barely had time to reply, let alone schedule appointments for audio, print, and television in time zones that circled the globe.

This whole experience—which began with the announcement about the disembarked passenger on February 3, the evening before our scheduled departure—was our first taste of a media frenzy. Helicopters whirred around the ship. A red-carpet's throng of reporters was kept at bay by a police cordon. Behind them was a phalanx of satellite vans. But who was giving them information about what was happening on the ship? The captain? The Japanese authorities? Princess PR? We just knew that every day, more and more of our fellow passengers were contracting this terrifying, yet-unnamed coronavirus that wasn't a cold or the flu. Ten cases among the passengers were announced the morning of February 5, at the same time the quarantine was imposed. When our daughter, Ashley, heard this news, she jumped into the Twitterverse to gather more information. The next day another ten people were sent to local hospitals. She called her brothers: Josh in Oregon and Blake in Massachusetts. "They're so vulnerable," she sobbed. "That's twenty-one total. We have to get them off that ship!"

"Chill, Ash," Blake told her. "You'd expect one infected person to have that many contacts."

"It's flu season," Josh said, "and you know Mom is a maniac about all of us getting flu shots."

When there were no new cases announced on February 7, Blake wrote a group email telling everyone to relax and that "Mom is probably using the time to plan her next cruise." Of course, he didn't know that we were sublimating our panic by telling our story to whoever would listen while simultaneously sending the kids upbeat emails and asking for pictures of our seven grandchildren to cheer us up.

We were not strangers to the media. I'm a bestselling writer who's been on many book tours. I've appeared on all the morning shows and done other national television for both novels and nonfiction. Phil is an award-winning documentary filmmaker who is far more comfortable on the other side of a camera, but he knows what producers want in terms of sound bites and succinct messaging. As boomers in our seventies, we fit into the grandparents-on-holiday niche; and while hardly influential enough to attract a wide social media following, we were—as they say—relatable, and at that point, the journalists wanted to know how it felt having our dream trip interrupted and how we were handling being cooped up involuntarily. They were especially interested in what the ship's kitchen was giving us to eat.

Ashley's Twitter and Instagram friends thought we were lucky to be getting a "free cruise" out of Princess, which infuriated her because she felt we were in danger. We understood why she was so fearful. She had spent ten years in foster care before we adopted her at age twelve, and her emotional dependence on us was far more intense than that of the older boys.

Everything changed on February 8 with the announcement of forty-one new passenger cases, a total of more than sixty in less

Our 354-square-foot mini-suite and its balcony, for which we were grateful.

than a week. Any vestige of denial on our part dissolved. Our health was at risk—and possibly our lives.

When I phoned Blake, he immediately asked, "How many new victims?" and when he heard the answer, his tone turned from light-hearted to serious. Blake has the classic engineer personality and a reputation for solving complex problems. He's thoughtful, precise, executes plans flawlessly with as little emotion as possible—and always meets his objectives.

"What can I do to help get you out of there?"

I told him how the media was descending fast and furious and we couldn't do both the organizing and the interviews. "And frankly I'm creeped out. How are more and more passengers getting sick when nobody has been out of their cabins? They aren't telling us what's really going on. We aren't safe here. We have to find a way to get the hell out of this—this posh penitentiary."

"Why can't you go ashore, where you won't be around whatever is making everyone sick?"

"It's the Japanese Ministry of Health. They don't want us contaminating the population."

"What about our State Department?"

"We get daily messages from the consulate here in Tokyo. They say we're safest 'sheltering in place.' I get it," I said. I'd not only studied Japanese history in college, I'd lived in Japan as a child. "It's an island mentality. They totally control who they let in—or out."

Blake said we should send everything to him and he'd organize it like a business campaign.

"But you're so busy—"

"Hey, that's my problem, not yours."

✦ ✦ ✦

Today was the second day of Blake's media schedule, which started with a pre-dawn call that woke us from a deep sleep. "I'm sorry but you have to get up. You have someone FaceTiming in half an hour. Put Dad on speaker."

"I'm here," Phil said in a hoarse voice.

"Today it's going to be morning to midnight," Blake said, "but you get a break in the middle of the day. Everyone in the U.S. and Europe is sleeping when it's two in the afternoon in Tokyo, so you can catch a nap then."

"If the disease doesn't kill us, this will," Phil chimed in.

Blake's voice deepened. "Hey, I'm trying to get you prime time in New York, London, and Tokyo. You have to look at the big picture. There are people from all over the world on that same ship. The only way we're going to get you out of there is with international coverage. If the U.S. doesn't rescue you first, maybe the Brits or the Aussies will come for their folks. We just need somebody to break the ice."

"I don't see how—" I said, yawning.

Blake sighed like a parent trying to get a toddler ready for preschool. "Listen," he told us, "nothing happens unless the whole world is watching. That's what we're trying to do here. You have to make everyone see what's really going down, what's at stake, and that these are real people, not just statistics." His voice was steely yet filled with compassion.

"But how?" I asked.

"Mom, don't you realize what a powerful list of media you've already compiled? And we haven't even touched the surface. We know people who know people. We'll call in all our cards. People are dying from this disease. It's a potential worldwide epidemic."

"I wouldn't go that far," Phil replied. "But we'll do what we can." I hung up the phone and lay back in bed. Phil rubbed my arm. "Blake's right about putting pressure on Washington. It won't look right if they come for the French and not for us."

"What about the crew? Who's going to come for them? They're much more at risk because they have to serve us. Let's mention them to everyone today. How about…"

Phil grabbed a notepad and scribbled a note. He handed it to me. I read it back. "Our mission is to liberate every single soul from this posh penitentiary." I smiled. "I love it."

Blake was right about the day's schedule. Between giving interviews and sending photos of the view from our balcony, we barely had time to eat, let alone take a nap. I had just grabbed a shower so I could look decent for the next round of interviews.

Another knock. Dinnertime. I slipped on my surgical face mask and opened the door. As had become the routine, the corridor was filled with room-service carts. A server handed me two salads and cutlery wrapped in a napkin. I set the plates on the ledge of a suitcase placed upright in the entryway for this purpose. The person pushing the next cart passed me two unwrapped dinner rolls. I plopped these on top of the salads. My right foot kept the heavy door propped open while I wiped my dripping hair away from my face. "Phil!" I called again. Luckily, he heard me this time, because the next maneuver required four hands: The waiter wasn't permitted to step inside our room, nor could we step out. I lunged for one main course platter, passed it to Phil, and accepted the other. I waited at the threshold for the dessert plates, then traded places with Phil, who reached for the Cokes.

Just as we sat down to eat, Phil's phone beeped with a text message. "Kenneth Stewart, Sky News, London. Wants to know if you have Skype working."

"Not yet. I'm having to create a whole new account. Can't he do FaceTime?"

"You have Skype on your phone."

"It's an old version because I always use the one on my desktop," I said, feeling cornered.

"You told Blake you'd reinstall it."

I slammed my glass on the table. "I'd like to see him or his brainiac Princeton friends figure out how to do live television interviews on a cruise ship halfway around the world with two iPhones and one iPad."

"Hey, it's my fault," Phil said to appease me. "I can't believe this is the first trip when I've left my editing laptop and camera at home. I don't know why, but I thought we were on vacation."

I took a bite of the salad while Phil checked his email. "Here's a request from a local station in DC."

"For tonight?"

"Really late, because it will be their morning. Blake said the more we do in the capital, the better." I swallowed but choked and began coughing. "It's someone your sister arranged."

"Phil, this is getting crazy."

"Getting?" He waved his phone. "I was talking to Blake while you were in the shower. He's sent a draft of tomorrow's press release—he's keeping 'posh penitentiary,' but also wants you to use some fresh talking points in your interviews tonight."

"You mean today's release—it's early in the morning in Boston, right?" I rubbed my temples. If it was 6:30 p.m. in Japan, that would make it 4:30 a.m. in Boston. Blake had started writing a press release about us daily. "That means that we're doing a morning show in London, right? Is it February eighth or ninth there?" I checked my watch. "Gotta get ready."

"You need to eat..." Phil said, but I'd already turned on the hair dryer.

BEST LAID PLANS

The world is a book, and those who do not travel only read one page.

—St. Augustine

Phil and I had been planning a second trip to Japan for more than a year. When I was six, in the early 1950s, my father transplanted our family of three from suburban New York to Taiwan and later Japan because of his business dealings related to the Korean War. I hadn't gone back till October 2017, when Phil and I crafted a trip that would be both a vacation and a peek into my past.

"As long as we're going that far, we should stay for at least a month," I said to Phil, who is not quite as keen on travel as I am. To sweeten it, I suggested a two-week cruise around Japan on the *Diamond Princess* because I was researching my next novel, a murder mystery set on a cruise ship. "Let's call it the Ultimate Sushi Tour." I give every trip a name.

"Sold," Phil replied. Sushi is his favorite food.

In the end, a month was not long enough and we tried to find a time to return. We wanted to see more of Tokyo and stay in some traditional inns, called *ryokans,* in the Japanese countryside.

An email from Princess Cruises the following fall highlighted a 2020 Lunar New Year's cruise from Japan that was stopping in Hong Kong for the celebrations. There was a sale on the fare and I knew from experience that the best deals are found the farther out you reserve.

"Phil," I said in a teasing voice. "I'm going to book another trip to Japan unless you say no."

"You had me at 'Japan,'" he said. "We've been raving about the last trip for so long. Why don't you see if anyone wants to go with us?"

Several friends and family members had said they'd love to travel with us if we ever went back, so I sent a few emails. We heard right away from Jerry and Cathy Giambalvo, who live in Dallas. We'd first met them eight years earlier at a pre-cruise dinner in Venice. Our travel style is similar. We're planners, list makers, and prefer independent excursions, which involve complex arrangements with guides and tours that are both cheaper and more bespoke than the large ones the ship sponsors. I'm an uber-organizer, and Jerry, retired from corporate human resources, is precise about costs and currency exchange; thus, our styles complement each other. He and Cathy have been on nineteen cruises and spent 197 days with Princess. She has a brilliant packing spreadsheet as well as both flair for what clothes to take and an eye for which boutique will have the perfect scarf or souvenir. After watching several YouTube videos of Hong Kong fireworks, they signed up.

Vana Mendizabal and I have been friends since our children were in preschool together in Crystal River, the town on Florida's Gulf Coast, where we've lived since the 1970s. She's a retired school nurse, and her husband, Mario, is our long-time family physician. It turned out that Jerry, Mario, and I were all having milestone birthdays right before the trip, and Mario, who had always wanted to go to Japan, decided to take more than two weeks off from his practice, which he had never done. We'd taken a Baltic cruise with Vana and Mario several years earlier, as well as spent a long weekend in Cuba with them. Game for almost any experience, the Mendizabals were happy to leave the details to Jerry and me.

Our group planned to spend the first five days in Tokyo, allowing us to adjust to the fourteen-hour time difference as well as tour the city before boarding the *Diamond Princess*. The other couples would head home the day after docking. Phil and I would end the trip with another five days at *ryokans* and two final nights in Tokyo. Or so we thought.

✦ ✦ ✦

Email from Terry, January 9, 2020
Chinese researchers say they have identified a new virus behind an illness that has infected dozens of people across Asia, setting off fears in a region that was struck by a deadly epidemic 17 years ago. There is no evidence that the new virus is readily spread by humans, which would make it particularly dangerous, and it has not been tied to any deaths. But health officials in China and elsewhere are watching it carefully to ensure that the outbreak does not develop into something more severe.

—*New York Times*

Five of our grandchildren, all age six or under, were visiting at Christmastime. We loved having them but keeping up with their shenanigans was exhausting, as was the cooking and general chaos. "I'm more than ready for a cruise," I said, thinking of a month without any responsibilities.

Where others our age have retired, we've decided to keep on chugging for as long as we can, which keeps us quite busy. Phil is the quintessential Renaissance man: He builds furniture and musical instruments, creates kinetic sculptures, and can fix anything. He maintains our home and cars, walks more than ten thousand steps a day, and still makes films for select long-time clients. (I, on the other hand, spend most of my time writing, glued to my computer.) Phil likes cruising because it's the only time he reads more than an article here or there and takes videos and stills for his own satisfaction. What he most enjoys is that all he has to do is show up. I often ask him what he would prefer for excursions or restaurant reservations, but he would rather not make any decisions. "Just don't forget to take me along" is his only request.

When his friend Terry asked about the trip, Phil said he looked forward to seeing more of Tokyo and the fireworks in Hong Kong's harbor. Retired from consulting for corporate owners, Terry has a second career curating internet content for an impressive roster of people in high places. Unfailingly modest, Terry almost whispers when he drops a name during one of his recollections of visits to various power enclaves—like the Hoover Institution or the all-male Bohemian Grove—where he hobnobbed with prominent business leaders, elected officials, and media executives. His early association with GOPAC, an organization founded in the late 1970s to develop the next generation of Republican officeholders, led to long-term and ongoing friendships in Washington.

Terry's health issues preclude travel and he asked if we'd share our itinerary—I'd named this trip "Seventy-five and Still Alive"— so he could "follow along" using his virtual-reality headset and Google maps.

He called Phil after reading it. "I don't want to burst your bubble," he said, "but you're not going to see the fireworks."

"We're there on the twenty-fifth. That's their Lunar New Year's Eve."

"I double-checked several sites. The big celebration is on the twenty-sixth."

When Phil broke the news, I said, "Maybe he's wrong."

"Terry's always right."

"At least in politics," I replied, jokingly, because Terry skews as far right as we do left. Whatever our differences, we both respect Terry's open yet analytical mind and his eclectic friends, some of whom Phil has met, who represent every side of an argument.

Phil and I each receive distinct streams of daily emails from Terry and they are always right on the mark. Mine usually involve writing, publishing, storytelling, rare diseases, or psychology, and they speak to some of my quirky interests, like meteor showers.

Phil's are even more varied. Many years ago, Terry introduced Phil to agronomist and Nobel Peace Prize winner Norman Borlaug, who became the subject of one of our documentaries, which is why he receives the latest famine and hunger reports. Terry sends the latest TED Talks, political commentaries from the left and right, and hints on things that guys are supposed to know, like how to catch a frog with a flashlight. Terry's selections don't echo social media trends, and they are often targeted with exquisite accuracy. Leading up to our trip, for example, there was insightful information on Asian politics. Even though I began to think his curiosity about our trip was over the top, I never imagined that his inquisitiveness would eventually help save our lives.

Just after New Year's 2020, Terry started emailing us stories about an "unusual viral pneumonia outbreak" in China and how nearby Asian destinations had "stepped up their surveillance of travelers." I barely paid attention. On January 9, Phil forwarded another one of Terry's emails, a *New York Times* story datelined Hong Kong, January 8. "Terry seems to think we'd be interested in this," he said. "Do you think it's anything to worry about?"

I scanned the article. "'First known death from a new virus… central Chinese city of Wuhan…seven patients in severe condition…'" I read aloud. "It just sounds like a new strain of flu—many of which originate in Asia for some reason. And, anyway, it says, 'There is no evidence that the virus can be spread between humans.' They think it's linked to a market that sells live fish, birds, and other animals, and thus far, none of the people—including medical workers—who came in contact with the patients have come down with it, and no additional cases have been found."

"Terry asked me if we're considering postponing."

"Really? He's such a worrywart. Remind him that we're not going to China, let alone Wuhan, wherever that is."

"Hong Kong is China," Phil reminded. "And he just sent another link about coronaviruses."

"The common cold is a coronavirus. Ask Terry whether he's had his flu shot this year—that's what he needs to be concerned about."

I'm not only a great believer in the flu vaccine, I bully my family and friends into getting their shots early every fall. In August 2016, I was hospitalized with influenza after we got home from a Princess cruise in Alaska we took with Josh, his wife, Giulia, and their toddler. In the ER they performed tests related to my heart and lungs but couldn't find the culprit.

At my bedside, Phil called Dr. Ken Rand, a friend who specializes in infectious diseases. "Have they checked her for flu?" he asked.

"It's not flu season."

"Right, that just means she hasn't had the flu shot yet."

I tried to signal Phil but broke into a painful coughing spasm. Finally, I got his attention. "The Aussies—" I croaked. "W-winter there."

Ken overheard me. "Did you spend any time with people from Australia?"

"Yes, the last day we had lunch with some nice folks—one of them had a really bad cough."

"Ask for a flu test. Should only take a short while to rule it out."

Indeed, I had a particularly virulent strain of flu. It was a harsh reminder that when you travel, you are exposed to a variety of pathogens from whoever is in the restaurant or airport or on your plane or train—or cruise ship. The doctors couldn't offer me much except supportive care with oxygen and IV fluids. Phil was prescribed Tamiflu prophylactically and he only got a bad cold.

"Terry's just sharing information."

"I know, and he's a sweetheart. Why don't you ease his mind? Tell him we're only going to be in Hong Kong one day," I said, "plus Jerry has hired a guide to pick us up and return us to the ship. She'll know how to avoid the holiday crowds and the demonstrators, who are much more likely to be a problem."

Just in Case

Fall down seven times; get up eight times.

—Japanese Proverb

Right after New Year's Vana, Cathy, and I compared packing strategies. We expected everything from freezing temperatures in Japan to semi-tropical ones in Vietnam. "Take everything you think you'll need," I said. "It's against my principles to travel light." In the end, Vana had the most suitcases while I had the most diverse "just in case" supplies, including two face masks in case anyone on the plane was coughing. I had picked them up the last time we were in Japan.

On January 14, Jerry, Cathy, Phil, and I took an early airport shuttle from the Houston hotel where we had all stayed overnight. (Vana and Mario were taking a different route and would meet us in Tokyo.) They had enough frequent-flier points to travel in business class on the way over; we had a few more so we scored first class both ways. When we arrived at the ANA check-in just before 8 a.m., a rope held us back. Next thing we knew, all the agents on that shift lined up in front of the counter. At the stroke of eight, a uniformed man welcomed us in both English and Japanese and then all the agents bowed simultaneously. Jerry whispered to Cathy, "This is going to be amazing."

Once checked in, the four of us were dispatched to United's Polaris Lounge, available for upgraded passengers on ANA. There was both a sit-down restaurant and a buffet. Because we had plenty of time, we chose to be waited on. "Order whatever you want from the menu," our server told us. "Everything is no charge, of course."

"Of course," Phil echoed under his breath. I watched him begin to unwind.

After breakfast, we settled into a cozy arrangement of four leather chairs back in the lounge and plugged our phones into the built-in charging stations.

At the buffet, Jerry found some small pastries and a cup of coffee. I checked my watch. Since we still had an hour before boarding, I made a cup of tea and brought back a raspberry tart and two forks.

"Happy Squab Day, honey," I said, bending to kiss Phil's cheek.

He grinned. "Fifty-two!"

Cathy looked up quizzically.

"It's our anniversary," Phil said with his little winky-twitch that I adore.

"Well, not really, but this is the one that counts," I said. "In 1968, I was a writer-producer for a documentary film company in New York and we were hiring a director/cameraman. Phil wanted the most money, but I said he was going to be worth it." Cathy and Jerry laughed. "The boss insisted we get together on a weekend before he was supposed to start, so we could go into production immediately. To sweeten the deal, I offered to make dinner, but there was a blizzard and he called to say he was stuck in Pennsylvania and hoped it 'wouldn't be a problem' to reschedule."

Jerry raised his bushy eyebrows. "Oh, boy!"

"Gay's exact words were 'Actually…it would.' I risked my life to get there because the new job would be hell if she was pissed off. She made this fabulous meal: crab bisque, squabs, hearts-of-artichoke salad, and apricot chiffon pie."

"And he never went home—ever. We've never had a date."

"That's amazing," Cathy said.

"Time to board," Jerry announced.

Three flight attendants bowed and showed us to our spacious seats in a cabin for only eight. We had chosen the single seats by the windows, with Phil in front of me. I handed him the package of disinfectant wipes. We have morphed into germaphobes when we travel, following the strict protocol our travel agent recommends for cruise cabins as well. "Sanitize! Sanitize!" she preaches and swears her methods will prevent everything from pink eye to Ebola. Thus far—except for my flu episode—we've avoided viral illnesses when traveling.

Then the nonstop service began. The chief purser came by to tell us our flight to Narita airport would be just under fourteen hours. Krug Grande Cuvée Champagne was poured. Phil leaned into the aisle and saluted me. "I feel very lucky," he said.

The doors were slammed shut and we began the pushback. I tucked a pillow behind my head and closed my eyes. Everything had gone perfectly so far. After all, what could go wrong?

✦ ✦ ✦

Email from Terry, January 15, 2020

Japan has reported a novel coronavirus infection in a traveler from Wuhan, the second country to report a case outside of China, raising more questions about how easily the virus is spreading among people.

—Center for Infectious Disease Research
and Policy, University of Minnesota

"That was the most fantastic flight of my life," Phil said as we deplaned on January 15.

"How did you sleep?"

"Better than at the hotel. Of course, all that premium *sake* didn't hurt." He grinned. "They brought me a different one to match every course. I wonder if they change the selections on the way back."

"Why don't we just stay on the plane and skip the rest of the trip?" I asked. Phil did a double take. "I'm kidding, but I'm really looking forward to the return flight."

We caught up with Cathy and Jerry in the baggage area. Their business-class seats had been in the compartment right behind ours. "How did you like it?"

"I'm never going that far again in a regular seat," Cathy said.

I had one tense moment as we rolled our luggage carts past the customs inspectors. The Japanese have strict drug laws and prohibit many prescription and over-the-counter medicines that Americans consider routine. Technically, I should have obtained a *Yakkan Shomei*, an import certificate, for a few of our meds. Luckily, we were just waved through and I exhaled.

We had a seamless transfer to the Prince Gallery, where we met Vana and Mario. We had never stayed there, but it came highly recommended as one of the more reasonable five-star hotels in Tokyo. I wanted our friends to experience the view from a room in one of the soaring towers that pierce the skyline of the most populated metropolis on Earth. As a surprise, I'd told the concierge about our birthdays, feeling sure that management would put cards and treats in each room, and they did. This was an expensive and complex trip for all of us and I was determined everything would be perfect.

The hotel's lobby is on the thirty-sixth floor, but our three rooms along the same corridor were several floors below. We had not expected all the electronic wizardry. A pad beside the bed controlled not only the blinds and curtains but various lighting combinations, the temperature, and the signs for privacy and housekeeping. A tablet on the opposite nightstand allowed you to order room service, read newspapers in various languages, and look up information on the hotel and the city. As for the bathroom: Enclosed in a translucent glass box, it looked like you could watch someone taking a shower or luxuriating in the separate tub—but with the touch of a button, the wall magically turned opaque. Of course, it also featured a state-of-the-art toilet with a seat set at an ideal temperature and sprays in different positions and different strengths, not to mention a gentle blow-dry. One of the joys of Japan is finding these in every bathroom—from train stations to convenience stores to private homes to crowded temples—and each one is spotless.

Waiting in each of our rooms was a rented portable high-speed Wi-Fi router, which works with mobile phones anywhere in the country—even on a ship if it's near enough to land—and offers unlimited data (though not voice) access. Besides connecting us to our email accounts and texting, it allowed us to use mapping apps and other navigational and translation aids. Once we were quarantined, we were able to use the pocket router to bypass the ship's maddeningly slow and congested service. Without it, we could never have reached out to the media for interviews and uploading videos and photographs.

Phil turned on the device, and like automatons, we checked our email. Up popped several from Terry, including the most recent coronavirus news on Phil's. "They have a case of the new virus in Japan," he remarked.

"How many?"

"Just one."

"I bet there are thousands of flu cases."

"Now they're saying it might be spread between people."

"It shouldn't be a problem in Japan because almost everyone wears medical masks here anyway. Besides, they're fanatics about cleanliness," I said. "I don't know what time it is at home, but I'm starving."

The hotel was housed in Tokyo Garden Terrace, a large complex with offices on the lower floors and residences on the higher floors of a second building. The lowest level was a convenient Metro station—another line was across the street—and the street level had dozens of restaurants, a grocery store, pharmacy, and shops. "It's like a vertical cruise ship," Phil commented as we looked for a place to have a light supper and begin adjusting to the drastic time difference. We settled on a casual restaurant that offered tempura and soba noodles. By the time we had almost finished our first meal in Japan, we all were drooping.

Though it was only nine, we couldn't wait to try out the bed, which was turned down and festooned with chocolates, slippers, and cotton Japanese pajamas. We popped some melatonin because it was only 8 a.m. the same day in Florida.

✦   ✦   ✦

In our attempt to adjust to the time change, we had asked our tour guide, a man named Aki, to meet us at 9 a.m. One lesson learned about traveling is that if you are going to have a unique experience, you will do far better with someone who can navigate for you, because no matter how hard you try, you will miss an essential task. As independent as we like to be, we know not only when we are at a disadvantage but how to equalize it.

That first day, Aki taught everyone how to buy Metro tickets and use them to both enter and leave the station. Our first stop was the Imperial gardens, where thousands of irises swayed along the margins of the Emperor's palace. At Ozu Washi, a shop selling the famous traditional paper, which has been in the same location for 360 years, we tried our hands at making *washi* by scooping pulp onto a screen, then shaking it to spread the fibers evenly. After a typical salaryman's lunch of miso soup and *tonkatsu* pork cutlets, we took the monorail to TeamLab Borderless, a cutting-edge digital light display museum that lived up to our high expectations.

One of the highlights of our 2017 trip to Japan had been various sushi experiences, starting with a pre-dawn visit to Tsukiji, the largest fish market in the world, with master carvers slicing 500-pound tuna with sword-length blades and exacting buyers placing orders for more than four hundred species of seafood. The market has since moved to a more modern facility, but the area around the old market is still a foodie's paradise and Jerry especially wanted to see the food stalls, so that's where Aki took us the second day.

Without Aki we would have been lost in the narrow lanes with shops selling kitchen equipment—especially the famed knives. When we passed Sushi Zanmai, Phil insisted we order a platter of three grades of tuna to compare and contrast.

"It's almost impossible to get this quality outside Japan," Phil said, pointing to the fattiest, called *otoro*. *"It's melting in my mouth."*

If Phil and Jerry had their way, we would have had sushi for every meal—yes, even breakfast. In fact, though we enjoyed all the sights Aki showed us—from Tokyo's oldest Buddhist temple to the avant-garde artist Yayoi Kusama's homage-to-herself museum in a stunning five-story metallic-clad building—the most anticipated experience for our group (Cathy being the lone hold-out) was dinner at an haute sushi establishment. The complicated reservation process required a Japanese-speaking intermediary. By emailing two months in advance with the concierge at the Prince Gallery, we had secured a reservation at Sushi Kokoro. I assured the concierge that we would be on time, which means fifteen minutes early to the Japanese, and that we knew not to make typical *gaijin*—foreigners'—mistakes. I had to sign a form promising to keep the reservation or pay the full price, with my credit card information as a guarantee.

Our trip to Sushi Kokoro on Saturday, January 18, turned into an adventure, entailing not only a subway ride but a mistaken address, a thunderstorm, two separate taxis, and a serious risk of being late. Vana exclaimed at one point, "This is the worst thing I can imagine."

"Welcome, welcome," Chef Tsutomu Oba said with a wide grin once we arrived, only ten minutes late.

Chef Oba spoke wonderful English and not only announced each dish, he pointed out what he was doing at every step. His fluid fingers were as agile as those of an origami master. "Monkfish liver pâté."

Almost in unison, we each popped the whole piece, chewed, smiled, bowed and wowed.

"Grilled amberjack. Number one with wasabi; number two with soy sauce."

"*Oishii desu*," several of us said in unison, using the Japanese term for "It's delicious."

Hot scallops in a seaweed wrap, squid with sea urchin and caviar, abalone—on and on the tastes flowed with peaks and ebbs. Three kids of tuna, sardines, fish roe, and then the chef paused and waited till he had our attention. "Fugu? It's okay?"

For some reason he stopped in front of my seat, waiting for me to respond. "Ah, pufferfish?" I asked. He nodded.

"Is that blowfish?" Jerry asked.

The chef nodded. "You try?" he asked only me.

The truth was I had always wanted to taste this fish that people said was so delicious it was worth risking their lives. Blake had bragged about having had it several times. "A chef who serves fugu has to train for about ten years before he can get a license and then has to eat all the dishes he prepares for a final exam," he said. I did a rapid risk assessment. Surely it was safe to eat fugu presented by this renowned chef.

"I would love to try it," I said, "because if I die tonight, I die completely happy."

Everyone laughed. He set a frothy dish in front of me. Jerry and Phil also assented. Mario and Vana held up their hands, declining. I admit my heartbeat quickened with a surge of adrenaline before I ingested the light, creamy delicacy, without a hint of anything fishy or briny. Subtle, sublime, and otherworldly—it was like nothing I had ever tasted before.

"*Fugu shirako,*" the chef said.

The chef's wife, who had just poured more tea, whispered in my ear. "Fugu sperm."

"*Oishii desu,*" I said, truthfully.

The next course—miso soup with little clams—was at my place. I decided to wait to tell Phil what we'd actually consumed until we were back in our hotel room.

"Sperm?" Phil laughed. "No wonder people are afraid of fugu."

"Well, it didn't kill us, did it?" I said, assuming that we had just survived the most dangerous part of our trip.

THE ZEN OF CRUISING

The fishermen know that the sea is dangerous and the storm terrible, but they have never found these dangers sufficient reason for remaining ashore.

—Vincent Van Gogh

We couldn't wait to board the *Diamond Princess*. Our love of cruising surprises people who have tried it—usually in the Caribbean—and scorn the concept or others who also disparage timeshares or *If It's Tuesday, This Must Be Belgium* bus tours. If we question anyone's knee-jerk negativity, they often cite their tendency to seasickness, which may be a factor on small boats but less often affects people on modern, stabilized ships. Others are daunted by the idea of being confined on a vessel with thousands of other people without being able to leave at any moment. "It's like Disney World and Las Vegas conceived a hideous baby and you can't escape its howling and puking" was one acquaintance's description. The most famous cruise curmudgeon was David Foster Wallace, who wrote the quintessential anti-cruise essay "A Supposedly Fun Thing I'll Never Do Again."

Our whole family loves boats, from canoes to ocean liners. Once, when sailing between Jamaica and the Cayman Islands, we were in a sixty-foot trimaran facing a rollercoaster of twenty-foot swells for several days on end. The passage was more wearying than sick-making since we're all pretty good sailors. Still, the takeaway was that we just had to persevere. "There's no remote control to turn this off," Phil told Blake and Josh, then in their teens. "Sometimes you have to see it through minute by minute and hold tight—literally—until things calm down." This is a metaphor that we still mention in difficult moments. "Rough passage" is a family password for making the best of a difficult situation.

The Mendizabals, Giambalvos, and Courters represent different subsets of typical cruisers. One works full-time, two are semi-retired, and three are retired. Mario is originally from Bolivia and Vana is from Canada. They travel at least once a year internationally and more frequently in this country to visit their five children, but Mario's being a working physician limits how much they can be away. The Giambalvos, both retired from a major communications company, prefer cruises to other vacations. Princess offers the sweet spot of affordable luxury, and as frequent cruisers, Princess gives them a better deal than booking with other lines. Cathy and Jerry are more interested in the itinerary than fancy amenities and the cuisine meets Jerry's high culinary standards. In recent years they've seen the world one port at a time, including many in the Mediterranean, South America, and the Baltics. Any attempt to fly to these countries and stay in hotels would be costly and exhausting. Some travelers may scoff at short port visits, yet they fail to realize how much time can be wasted getting from place to place, settling into new accommodations, and learning the lay of the land.

Nothing makes me happier than being on a ship. I inhale sharp, salty air as if it has medicinal properties, which I call Vitamin Sea.

I never sleep as well as I do on a ship in a rolling sea, mimicking the womb, soothing all aches, muffling every sound. Even though I live on the water, I cannot reproduce the effect unless I'm on a moving vessel. Apparently, it involves Delta waves, the slowest yet loudest brainwaves, which rumble in low frequency and penetrate like the beat of a drum. The undulating motion of a ship, even with modern stabilization, may heighten Delta waves and be the reason serial cruisers are addicted. Many people mention the silence of the sea, when, in fact, ships are quite noisy. Because of my severe hearing loss, I never trust my sense of sound. Phil, who has acute hearing, once said, "There's some combo of engine vibration and sea swell that muffles our awareness of all the 'noise'— which includes ambient noise and also the chatter in our heads."

"Like when you chant 'om' or some other mantra?"

"Or relaxing music—whatever takes you away from your physical or mental aches and pains."

"Water music…." I said to Phil, who knew just what I meant.

✦ ✦ ✦

Email from Terry, January 20, 2020

Governments around the world have always struggled to stop the spread of disease, from the deadly swine flu which struck the globe in 2009, to ongoing attempts to rein in Ebola in West Africa. No health authority has ever tackled the challenge currently faced by China, however, as the country grapples with a new coronavirus just as hundreds of millions prepare to travel during the Lunar New Year period—the largest annual human migration on Earth… people from across the country will cram themselves into homebound trains, buses and planes for family reunions. Others will take advantage of the time off to holiday overseas. Last year, close to 7 million Chinese tourists traveled

abroad for Lunar New Year....The holiday—the most
important in the Chinese calendar—comes at the worst
possible time for health authorities racing to contain the
outbreak which has put the rest of Asia on alert.

—CNN

On January 20, the six of us piled what then looked like an obscene
amount of luggage into a hired van outside the Prince Gallery and
set off on the forty-four-kilometer ride to Yokohama to board the
Diamond Princess.

Cathy was the most animated I'd seen in several days. "This
is my favorite part of a cruise," she said. "I love unpacking in a
familiar stateroom."

Phil laughed. "It's like moving into a summer cottage. Everything goes back into its place."

"I've brought everyone the latest and greatest in disinfecting
wipes—they're better than bleach," I said. "They're called SONO.
They're supposedly the only one that kills noroviruses as well as the
2009 H1N1 flu virus."

"Nobody cleans a cabin the way Cathy does," Jerry boasted.

"Vana's a nurse," I said. "Her house is fastidiously clean. I'm
not fussy at home, but I turn into a regular Lady Macbeth as soon
as I get on board a plane or boat. There are people bringing pathogens from all over the world for which we haven't developed any
immunities."

"Is anyone else worried about that new bug in China?" Vana
spoke so softly I almost didn't hear her.

"Not really," I said.

"Did you read Terry's latest email?" Phil asked me.

"The one about how the Chinese are worried about wider
transmission because many families travel over New Year's?" I
asked. "Apparently, it's like our Thanksgiving," I said. "Families go
to a lot of trouble to be together."

"I worry about H1N1—the swine flu—coming back," Vana said. "It killed a lot of people in Asia ten years ago."

"It's covered in this year's vaccine," Mario said.

"Did all of you get the high-dose senior shot?" I asked. Everyone nodded. "They should make it mandatory for winter cruising," I said.

"I noticed they didn't ask us to fill out health questionnaires before we boarded our last cruise," Phil said.

"You know why?" Jerry asked, then answered his own question. "Because everyone lies." He checked his phone. "Hey, this Wi-Fi device is working. I can see where we're going on the map."

"How much longer?" his wife asked.

"We're on the outskirts of Yokohama."

"Then we have plenty of time to visit the CUPNOODLES factory," I said. Everyone groaned. I had been lobbying for this stop because an acquaintance told me how much she enjoyed designing her own cup at the museum honoring the inventor of instant ramen. "You get to select your favorite stock and then add your choice of ingredients. There are more than five thousand possibilities."

"All I want to do is get on board and sail away," Cathy said.

"I'll just be happy not to have to lug anything for at least two weeks," Phil said.

I opened a copy of the English-language *Japan Times* that I had taken from a stack in the hotel's lobby. There was a long article about the coronavirus. I knew that the word referred to a large group of viruses known to affect birds and mammals, including humans. "Corona" means "crown" in Latin and refers to the spiky projections on the surface of the organism that resemble a crown. Out of the hundreds of coronaviruses, only seven affect humans, and they mostly cause mild cold- or flu-like symptoms. In recent years several more virulent strains have appeared, including Severe

Acute Respiratory Syndrome (SARS), which had popped up in Asia in 2002–2003, and Middle East Respiratory Syndrome (MERS), originally called Camel Fever when it first appeared in 2012. Still, I wasn't fazed by the news. Both SARS and MERS had been contained and did not spread worldwide. Also, not every coronavirus is deadly; that's why there was no reason to assume this new strain was especially contagious or dangerous. The *Japan Times* article mentioned the virus was in four countries: China had 278 cases; there were two in Thailand and one each in Korea and Japan. Big deal. Every country has its share of other contagious diseases. I was more worried about the children my grandchildren went to school with whose parents were anti-vaxxers.

I tucked the newspaper away. No point in alarming anyone. Before leaving home, Mario had mentioned the "new pneumonia" to Vana and she asked me whether we should cancel the trip. "It's flu season, right?" I'd replied. "We know that our vaccinations won't protect us from all the variations, and that's not stopping us."

As we drove by the industrial outskirts of Yokohama, I Googled flu data. According to the Centers for Disease Control and Prevention (CDC), in 2019, there had been almost thirty-four thousand deaths in the U.S. alone, with an estimated half a million worldwide. The chances of coming in contact with any of the three hundred contagious people in the world who had this rare virus were statistically infinitesimal.

As we arrived at Daikoku Pier, I was feeling a bit smug. Thanks to a prescription from Mario, we had brought some Tamiflu in case we caught a strain of flu that wasn't covered by this year's vaccine.

Jerry spotted the *Diamond Princess* first. "There it is!" He checked his watch. "Perfect timing. We should be able to board right away because we're Elite." The more you travel with Princess, the higher you move on their loyalty scale, with Elite being the top tier in the Captain's Circle.

"We'll be Elite after this trip, but we still get priority boarding with our Platinum cards," I said.

"I guess we'll line up with the riff-raff," Vana joked.

"No worries," Phil said. "Since we're traveling as a group, we can board together."

To Phil and me, since we had sailed on the *Diamond Princess* in 2017, this moment was a homecoming. The others had never been on the ship, which is uniquely bilingual (Japanese and English). Of the 2666 passengers, 1281 were Japanese. The passengers and crew came from 56 countries and passengers included 428 Americans, a fair number of Chinese and other Asians, plus strong contingents from Australia, Canada, and Europe. These days, with some cruise ships accommodating as many as six thousand passengers, the *Diamond* is considered medium-sized, with 1337 guest cabins. Still, at 205 feet high—with eighteen decks—and 952 feet long, painted gleaming white with a royal blue sea witch logo, it seemed like a high rise tilted on its side. Princess, owned by the Carnival Corporation, is one of the more affordable cruise brands but its ships feel luxurious. Their newer and renovated ships are as glossy and classy as they come. The *Diamond* is a bit older and dowdier than some, but the food is superb and the crew runs a first-class operation. There is a wide choice of accommodations: windowless inside cabins can be as small as 160 square feet, while the most prestigious real estate is the suites, which range in size up to 1,329 square feet. The Grand Suite even has its own dining room. A two-week cruise can range in price from under $1,000 a person to over $6,000, depending on the size and location of the cabin, and the season.

As we entered the bustling terminal, I said to Phil, "Look for Katherine." I pointed to the section reserved for continuing passengers, who could be differentiated because they had lanyards with their cruise cards around their necks and weren't rolling luggage or wearing overstuffed backpacks.

"Who's that?" Vana asked.

"She's an Aussie we met on a cruise in 2013," Phil said. "She has an incredible, dry wit."

"Since she and her friend Marlene boarded in Singapore and have been on for two weeks already, they'll have everything scoped out," I said.

"They're spending a whole month on board?" Vana said.

I laughed. "You make it sound like a prison sentence. We did it once for a Med cruise," I said. "That's where we met Jerry and Cathy."

When the Elite and Platinum guests were called, far more people than usual rushed to get in line. "Ow!" I said reflexively as someone elbowed past me to fill a gap in the line ahead.

Phil's eyebrows arched. "Really?" He backed off. "There's no early bird special."

"They're sure as hell not Japanese." I turned to Vana. "If they were, they'd be bowing and trying to let everyone else have the honor of going first."

There was a lot more pushing and shoving as we moved to various stations to get our cruise cards and immigration completed. Sidestepping the eager crew photographers, we crossed the threshold into the atrium, where a string quartet was playing the "Spring" movement from Vivaldi's *Four Seasons*. Cathy gave an exaggerated sigh.

"Home," I mouthed to Phil. He put his free arm around me and hugged me close.

✦ ✦ ✦

Our sunset departure from Yokohama was picture perfect. The conic outline of Mount Fuji was wreathed in the same hot orange as one of Yayoi Kusama's bulbous mosaic pumpkins—minus the polka dots—and faded to coral and then pink as the sky darkened. In the ship's wake, the city lights blended into the starry night. All our mini-suites were midships—the most stable position on any ship—on Deck 9, also known as Dolphin Deck. Since the decks above and below contained only guest cabins, we wouldn't be disturbed by scraping deck chairs or clatter from a casino or cocktail lounge. The Mendizabals were next door, and Edwin, the cabin steward for both our rooms, unlocked the door in the barrier between our balconies so we could share the outdoor space. Jerry and Cathy were ten cabins toward the aft, also on the starboard side of the ship, which we had picked strategically because we wanted to face land for most of the voyage.

Phil and I are not too fussy about cabin size or position on the ship. We've weathered very rough seas without a touch of seasickness and actually like a bit of heaving and bucking. Our requirements include a balcony, a sofa, and desk space. Because Phil and I are crowd-adverse, we spend a good portion of our sea days in our cabin cocoon. We were even happier about our choice once we were quarantined, since being stuck in a more constricted space might have resulted in claustrophobia.

Traveling Club Class gave us access to a dedicated dining room where we weren't restricted to a particular mealtime, as well as various other perks and amenities. By the time the six of us met in the Santa Fe dining room for the first dinner on board, we had retired our city clothes for a brighter palette and had an extra glow as we anticipated a seamless holiday. Tokyo had taken a toll. We tried to keep up with Aki's brisk pace as we walked many miles each day. We had run to catch trains and endured being squeezed in rush hour crowds. Ship life, on the other hand, was effortless. You could find precisely what you wanted to eat any time of the day or night. Your private bathroom was an elevator ride away. And a bed was available whenever you were in the mood to rest for a few minutes or hours.

During dessert—where we all ordered our particular Princess favorites: crème brûlée and mint tea for me, cheesecake and an Irish coffee for Phil, and a flurry of chocolate delicacies for the others—we reiterated how we would interact for the rest of the cruise.

"We agreed that we're not going to be joined at the hip," I began. "As much as we'd enjoy having meals together, some of us might prefer to eat more quickly at the buffet in the Horizon Court, have just a pizza on deck, or order room service. But what shall we do if we want to meet up?"

"Why don't we each call the other two and say what we're doing, then we won't have to wonder?" Jerry said. "Just leave messages by six."

Each couple had a cohesiveness that had made traveling together stress-free so far. While we came from disparate backgrounds, each marriage was respectful, with no petty bickering and only light-hearted banter. Even though we had traveled with each couple separately, I had worried a little before we left. Would our two sets of friends get along? I was relieved when they realized that, in many ways, they were more like each other than like us, especially in terms of spirituality and world view. So far, we had been a compatible group. I exhaled. Nobody needed me. I shut down the executive function switch in my brain and fired up the pleasure-seeking neurons.

What next? I thought, not caring what that might be.

SAILING ON DENIAL

Anyone can hold the helm when the sea is calm.

—Publilius Syrus

Email from Terry, January 21, 2020

A man in Washington State is infected with the Wuhan coronavirus, the first confirmed case in the United States of a mysterious respiratory infection that has killed at least six people and sickened hundreds more in Asia, the Centers for Disease Control and Prevention announced on Tuesday. Federal officials also announced expanded screenings for the infection at major airports in the United States.... The infected man... developed symptoms after returning from a trip to the region around Wuhan where the outbreak began.

—*New York Times*

"I'll say one thing, Terry is persistent with his emails. Is he trying to ruin our trip with his doomsday scenarios?" I asked Phil after checking my Inbox before getting dressed on our first day at sea.

"His point is that it's also in the United States."

"Right, but the guy was actually in Wuhan, China, not Japan, and he wasn't on a cruise ship." I groaned dramatically. "Besides, it's not the sort of news I want to wake up to."

"Terry really cares about us...."

"Just tell me what I need to know."

Phil changed the subject and flipped an imaginary coin. "Breakfast in the buffet or dining room?"

"The buffet will be faster. I want to get to trivia early to find a team." Trivia is my favorite shipboard pastime, but it's of no interest to Phil. "What are your plans?"

"To go where the spirit moves me," he said with a grin. We decided to meet in the cabin before going to lunch.

Trivia is a big deal on cruises. This is a team sport with no more than six in a group—and it is deadly serious, with games taking place at various times of day and some people forming teams before leaving home. On long cruises, the scores may accumulate, resulting in one grand prize winner. On a month-long Mediterranean cruise, Phil encouraged me to try out for the "mastermind" contest, and by some stroke of luck, I tied for top honors with a former Jeopardy grand champion. On this cruise, I never became part of a hardcore team. Our Aussie friends Katherine and Marlene often showed up at the 4:45. I also regularly played with Karen, an accountant from California, and a Malaysian couple who lived in Australia. Later, Karen would be the only person I knew who was stricken with the coronavirus on the ship—and the only person with whom I had close contact just before she developed symptoms.

✦ ✦ ✦

Email from Terry, January 22, 2020

The death toll from a new flu-like coronavirus in China rose to nine on Wednesday with 440 confirmed cases, Chinese health officials said as authorities stepped up efforts to control the outbreak by discouraging public gatherings in Hubei province...As China also vowed to tighten containment measures in hospitals, the World Health Organization (WHO) was due to hold an emergency meeting to determine whether the outbreak of the new coronavirus constitutes a global health emergency.

—Reuters

Once again, we were up early, since we had a rendezvous with our friends to disembark at 8:30 a.m. Our first port stop was Kagoshima, at the southwestern tip of Kyushu island, off the beaten path of even Japanese travelers. It's not easy or inexpensive to travel around the five main islands (out of almost seven thousand) that make up the Japan archipelago.

Phil checked his email while I went over the going-ashore checklist.

"Really?" Phil muttered.

"What?"

"Terry's latest."

"Some Chinese health minister is saying that it's a 'global health emergency,' even though they've only had nine deaths."

"Nine out of how many billion people hardly sounds alarming."

"But it's spreading all over Asia, including Taiwan and Japan."

"At least we're not taking any planes. That's the fastest way to catch diseases. All that recirculated air in a metal tube for hours." I opened the curtains. "Look, we're just coming into port."

After a quick breakfast in the Horizon Court, we headed to the atrium. "Don't say anything to the others about the virus being in Taiwan and Japan," I said. You know Vana's already thinking of the worst-case scenario. Statistically, there's no chance it will affect us."

Phil waved to Vana and Mario as they stepped off the elevator. Jerry and Cathy approached from the other direction. One reason we like traveling with both couples is they are punctual. We wanted to be on time for our Japanese guide. Most passengers had signed up for a Princess tour, which cost $170 per person and included a visit to a sake distillery with a sampling room. On our last trip, we discovered the Systematized Goodwill Guide Groups. Their members are locals eager to show visitors around—for free— in exchange for the opportunity to practice their language skills. Since our previous Goodwill Guides acted like newfound friends, I was excited to find one in Kagoshima. All we were expected to cover was our guide's fares, admission fees, and lunch.

In Kagoshima, as with many ports, Princess provided a shuttle to the town center, and we managed to get on one of the first buses. As we waited for it to fill, I leaned against the window and fell asleep, only waking when we arrived at the meeting point.

Phil shook me awake. "Are you okay?"

"Just can't shake the jet leg."

I looked up and saw a woman in a flamingo-pink jacket waving at me. I recognized Kyoco, a graphic artist who works at the Sakurajima Volcano's visitor center and is studying English, from her Facebook page. We bowed and hugged like old friends. "First, the ferry," she said, and we followed her a few blocks. Even though she kept apologizing for her English, she spoke very well as she explained that Kagoshima is sometimes called the Naples of the eastern world because its bay location is also formed by a caldera and Sakurajima is a stratovolcano built up by lava and ash, just like Vesuvius.

We took a bus that wound its way up the mountain via numerous hairpin turns. In front of the observatory was a sign written in chalk that read: "Most recent eruption—November 12, 2019"—a little more than two months earlier. "This is the most active volcano in Japan—and we have many hundreds," Kyoco said. She pointed out the many monitoring sites and said that scientists went up all the time to take readings. "They have thousands of small explosions every year and the ash can blow as high as a few kilometers above the mountain. At home we have evacuation drills and shelters where we go if there are falling rocks."

Kyoco bent down and began sweeping the ash that littered the pathway into a pile, then she picked up a large pinch and began rubbing her fingers together.

"Come see!" I called to the others, who were taking pictures of the south and north peaks from different angles. I'd seen Kyoco's artworks online. They looked like charcoal drawings, but now I realized they were fine lines of the volcanic ash she dribbled from her fingers. I marveled at how she controlled this flyaway medium. In a few minutes she'd drawn a ship at sea and written "Bon Voyage." After we all took pictures, she swept up her ephemeral creation, which blew away in the stiff breeze.

We took the ferry back and had lunch at a restaurant that specialized in grilling prime meats at your table. Afterwards, Kyoco checked the time and asked if we minded taking taxis to our next stop. "Sounds good," I said. I wasn't feeling up to a long walk. Cathy saw the ship's shuttle bus. "I'm heading back," she said. Jerry walked his wife to the bus. When he returned, he said, "Mary Lou—that's Cathy's mom—isn't doing well. Cathy wanted to talk to her brother before he went to bed."

The Senganen Garden was the highlight of my day. The summer house by the seashore in Japan where I'd stayed as a child had a similar landscape with small ponds, shrines, and a bamboo grove. Vana loved the cat shrine since she gets up before sunrise at home to care for Crystal River's feral cats. I thought I spied cherry blossoms, which would be amazing in January. "No, they're plum trees," Kyoco said, "but we have early *sakura* too because we are so far south. If you love cherry trees, you can see them for several months by following the festivals from the beginning of February in Okinawa to the end of May in Hokkaido."

"We're going to be in Okinawa, but I never expected to see the trees in bloom."

Kyoco bent near a stream and picked up a leaf and folded it. "This is a special place," she said. "They have poetry competitions." She dropped the leaf in a stream that wound around a small garden. "They drop a sake cup in the water right here and the goal is to compose a haiku by the time it floats around the circular area."

We strolled down a lane of traditional shops. Jerry popped into one and came out with a bag of soy candies. I lagged behind, pecking away at my mobile phone. When the rest of the group ducked into a pottery gallery, I waved to Kyoco. "I just sent you an email."

Up popped a picture on her phone of the arched bridge made of lava stone that we had just crossed. She looked at me with a puzzled expression. I motioned for her to scroll down to read the haiku I'd just composed.

Plum blossom opens
Lava stone makes a curved bridge
Goodwill unites friends

Just before getting on the shuttle bus, Jerry, Vana, and I handed Kyoco a fancily wrapped package, an *omiyage*. This is the traditional way to show gratitude, especially when tipping would be inappropriate or as an extra special thanks. The gift itself should be of nominal value, representative of where you are from, and the wrapping is more important than what's inside. Usually it contains a local candy and other souvenirs of your hometown. It's always presented with two hands and a bow. Kyoco was delighted and we promised to stay in touch.

"That was a fantastic day," Jerry said once we settled on the shuttle.

I sighed with relief. After having dragged four friends halfway around the world, I felt responsible for their happiness with the trip. Now, as we look back on that lovely, low-stress day, we are more thankful to Kyoco than she knows because otherwise, we would have taken the ship's tour. And that would have been a tragic mistake.

ROGUE WAVE

What would an ocean be without a monster lurking in the dark? It would be like sleep without dreams.

—Werner Herzog

Email from Terry, January 22, 2020

President Donald Trump told CNBC on Wednesday he trusts the information coming out of China on the coronavirus, which has killed nine people and sickened nearly 500 others in that country…"We have it totally under control," Trump said …in an interview from the World Economic Forum in Davos, Switzerland. "It's one person coming in from China. We have it under control. It's going to be just fine."

—CNBC

Two whole sea days before Hong Kong! After Kagoshima I was too exhausted to dress for dinner or see the juggler in the theater. At breakfast the next morning, the freshly squeezed orange juice burned my throat. I went back to the room and riffled through my cold medications and popped extra vitamin C and added echinacea and zinc, then headed to trivia. Since nobody I knew was there, I joined a team with Carole, a Joan Didion lookalike. Later, over tea in the café, we discovered we had both adopted children from the foster care system and enjoyed the same authors. This was the type of short-but-sweet encounter that can be so enjoyable on a cruise.

I touched base with Phil in the cabin before lunch.

"The Wheelhouse Bar is serving their pub lunch today. Want to have fish and chips with me?"

"A bit too heavy," I said. "Just going to have some soup upstairs."

"Sounds good," Phil replied. After many years living and working together, we both enjoy the many ways to be alone on a ship and have no expectation of one person going along just to keep the other company.

At the elevator bank, I punched UP for me with my index finger's knuckle, then DOWN for Phil. When the door opened, I used the same technique to press fourteen. The next person on said, "Five, please." After I obliged, she nodded in recognition that frequent cruisers use a variety of techniques to avoid touching potentially contaminated surfaces such as door handles, railings, and buttons. I always have a handkerchief in my pocket just for this purpose and use only disposable tissues for colds. If I have nothing between my hand and a bathroom doorknob, I will use the hem of my shirt. It's not just on ships, I do this in all public places when we travel.

This was my first visit to the make-your-own *udon* soup station at the buffet. A server handed me a large bowl of *kakejiru* soup made with *dashi* (a broth made from dried kelp and bonito fish flakes), soy sauce, and mirin, a sweetened wine. To that I added wheat noodles and garnished the bowl with grated ginger, green onion, tempura flakes, and black sesame seeds. I carried my lunch back to an empty table. Within a few seconds, a waiter took my order for an Arnold Palmer and I opened my Kindle to Lisa See's *The Tea Girl of Hummingbird Lane*. I have been reading novels about China ever since elementary school, when I first read Pearl Buck's *The Good Earth*. Right then, I decided I'd be a novelist too.

After the meal, I headed to the Skywalker Lounge—the highest point on the aft of the ship. I settled into a billowy chair with a view of the roiling wake. The story set in a remote mountain village in China was perfect for our Asian travels, as was the mother/daughter adoption theme, and the backdrop of tea farming. Even though I'd written about Indian tea plantations in my novel *Flowers in the Blood*, I knew almost nothing about the trending—and wildly expensive—fermented tea called *pu'er*. I looked up from my reading as the milky froth spilling off the ship's propellers extended out to the unblocked horizon and then seemed to melt into the winter sky. The next thing I knew, I woke to someone rubbing my shoulders. "I thought you might be here," Phil said, kissing my forehead. "You okay?"

I rolled my neck. "A bit stiff and just...no energy."

"I hope you're not getting the 'dreaded cruise crud.'"

That night was the first formal dinner, and I decided to go, even though I was tired. In the multi-story atrium, all the levels were filled with guests in their finery and officers in their dress uniforms. Complimentary Champagne flowed from a pyramid of more than a hundred flutes stacked to create a bubbly waterfall. Captain Gennaro Arma, a devilishly handsome mid-fortyish Italian, gave a welcoming speech and introduced the senior officers, who had been circulating through the crowd. The dresses of the Asian women who were wearing Western clothes seemed more fashion-forward than the "internationals," as the rest of us were called. They also wore more fine jewelry, some of which I imagine came from boutiques on the ship. Many Japanese men and women wore exquisite kimonos.

Photographers had set up backdrops with professional lighting. Two popular spots were the spiral staircases descending to the atrium's marble mosaic floor. Multi-generational families were posed on steps with what appeared to be revered great-grandparents, grandparents, parents, and tiny children all traveling together to celebrate the new year.

Phil handed me a glass of Champagne. "I know what you're thinking."

"Yes, I'd love to travel with the grandkids, but not until they're a few years older."

We clinked glasses. We do more than finish each other's sentences, we can communicate without speaking.

Phil steered me toward the dining room, where Faith, the hostess, greeted us by name. "Your smile could power this ship," Phil complimented her. She has a charismatic quality that should take her far in the hospitality world.

My appetite was off, so I ordered three small appetizers: asparagus soup, rillettes with toast, and shrimp rolls.

"Anyone going to the production show tonight?" Jerry asked. "It's their rock and roll extravaganza. They even bring a pink Cadillac on stage."

"I've seen it," I said, "but Mario and Vana, you'd love it."

Neville, from India, who was maître d' for the entire ship, stopped by to check on our table. The day before, Jerry politely mentioned that one of his Princess favorites had been a disappointment. "I have that on order for you tonight, if you would like to try it again."

Jerry nodded his approval. When Neville was still within earshot, Jerry said, "That's what I love about Princess."

"Mario," Cathy began in a husky voice. "I'm beginning to worry that the Chinese virus might be spreading. Just before dinner, Fox reported that they've closed public transportation in Wuhan and Beijing is canceling all major events, even the New Year's celebrations."

"Does that include Hong Kong?" Vana asked.

Jerry put down his fork. "I hope not!"

"We're missing the fireworks by a day anyway," Phil said, "but someone I met today said there might be some smaller shows around the bay. He also told me the best places to view the digital light show."

"They must suspect it's highly contagious," Mario replied.

"The newscaster said it's behaving like Mars," Jerry said.

Mario nodded and, as usual, thought before he spoke. "I think you mean SARS, although there was another virus in the Middle East called MERS—they're both also in the coronavirus family, as are most colds."

"Isn't the seasonal flu a different sort of virus?" I asked.

Mario paused and sipped some wine. "SARS—it stands for Severe Acute Respiratory Syndrome—popped up as what they call a 'novel' virus—one that had never been seen before—around twenty years ago. Mostly, it stayed in China. We worried about it, but then there were only a few cases in the United States and it was eradicated quickly. It's likely to be the same with this one. I wouldn't get too worked up yet."

Phil nodded. "Don't forget the Chinese will be ruthless about containment. They can send an edict and close that whole province instantly. Chalk one up for despotic governments."

"Yes," Vana said, taking the role of a Debby Downer, "but everyone travels and half the people on this ship are Asians celebrating together. Some of them could have come from that Hub-something province."

"Hubei," I said. "I've wanted to go there. You can take a Yangtze River cruise and see the massive Three Gorges Dam."

"Honey, that's the last place on earth we're going," Phil said.

Vana smoothed the tablecloth in front of her. "The point is that some of the passengers could have traveled from there over a week ago, before it became widely known."

"It's possible," I said.

"I've seen it happen in the school system. Kids come in with regular sniffles and coughs or don't have any symptoms at all, and the next thing we know, they spike temps and then we have a flu epidemic."

"Right, and lots of people on this ship could be shedding the flu virus." I looked at Mario. "Statistically, don't you think that's far more likely?"

"I don't know enough yet," Mario said, ever the cautious clinician.

After dinner, Phil and I walked the Mendizabals to the Princess Theater entrance on the Promenade deck and said our goodnights. Phil pulled open the outside door that was buffeted by the wind. "How about a little fresh air?" We took our usual postprandial stroll. I leaned over the railing and gulped some sea air. I coughed once and then couldn't stop. "Isn't it a bit early in the trip for cruise cough?"

"I just swallowed wrong." Still, I was worried. Upper respiratory viruses are a common cruise-ship scourge.

When we got back to the cabin, there was a note on the pillow to turn back the clock one hour. "That extra hour of sleep is what we both need," Phil said.

The bed's silky sheets and the cradling sea blotted any cares of diseases that intensify in crowded, unsanitary cities. There was absolutely nothing to worry about. Tomorrow was going to be another dazzling day to do anything…or nothing at all.

✦　✦　✦

Email from Terry, January 24, 2020

The novel coronavirus spread to more countries in the Asia Pacific region as China reported a surge in deaths and new cases due to the outbreak.

The virus has killed at least 41 people in China, with media reports citing chaotic scenes as hospitals in the city of Wuhan turned away people who were unwell. The U.S. plans to close its consulate in the city temporarily and evacuate some Americans from the area.

—Bloomberg

I didn't wake up until twelve hours later. Phil had already been out and brought me back a cup of tea and a glass of orange juice. "How are you feeling?"

"Lazy." I decided to watch the news in the cabin, then joined the Mendizabals in the Kai Sushi restaurant for lunch.

We looked at the menu. "No fugu!" I said with fake shock. "Darn."

There was a sudden, odd shuddering of the ship. Vana blanched.

"What's happening?" Mario asked. Before Phil could answer, Captain Arma came on the intercom. He explained that we'd been hit with a high, rogue wave and what we felt was the stabilizing system compensating. There was nothing to worry about.

"The minute someone tells me there's nothing to worry about," Vana said, "that's when I begin to worry."

"Some rogue waves can do a lot of damage," I said. "YouTube has some shots of furniture flying around on a cruise—"

Phil kicked me under the table. Because of my tendency to blurt out whatever comes to mind, our children have nicknamed me "No-Filter Mom." He changed the subject. "Did you hear they're sending a plane to evacuate the Americans in the Wuhan consulate?"

"I think that's because they're isolating the city for the rest of the holidays and closing the airport to commercial flights," I said.

"I heard that," Vana added. "They're also starting to do temperature checks at a few American airports for people coming from

China," she said. "I'm considering staying on the ship tomorrow and not going into Hong Kong."

Phil furrowed his brow. "That's fine, but how will you feel after two thousand people who've been touring in Hong Kong get right back on the ship?"

"Besides," I said, "Jerry arranged a private guide with a van. At that point we were worried about staying away from the pro-democracy demonstrations, but it should also keep us away from crowded public transportation."

"Did you see the bulletin about what to wear tomorrow?" Mario asked. "We're not supposed to wear white or black, because that's what identifies the protestors."

"Can you imagine being caught up in a police sweep?" Vana's voice was serious.

"No worries," I blurted. "We have insurance for that!"

"How is that possible?" Vana asked.

"We bought a supplemental annual policy from CrisisFlite, that company we have an annual membership with. I was worrying about being trampled by a rhino on the safari we're going on in April. For a few dollars more, I added coverage for crisis response."

Phil saluted me with his bottle of Kirin beer. "That's Gay for you. She thinks of everything."

I noticed Vana hadn't touched her sushi. "Are you feeling okay?" The seas were the roughest yet and not everyone was as immune to seasickness as we were.

"Just not hungry."

"That's how I was for the past few days, but I'm making up for it today." I munched one of the cookies they had served with matcha ice cream.

After lunch, a guitar duo was serenading in the atrium. Mario plays guitar and they decided to listen for a while. Phil was anxious to get back to Mary Kingsley's *Travels in Africa*, one of the books suggested by our safari outfitter. He kept stopping to tell me about how she went off to Africa alone in the 1890s, her droll sense of humor, and various insights.

"How did Mary Kingsley die?" I asked as we settled on opposite ends of the sofa with our Kindles.

"How many authors write about their own deaths?"

"Right, stupid question," I said, "although if anyone can pull that off, it would make for a compelling story!"

I Googled Mary Kingsley. "She died of typhoid fever before she was forty."

"Didn't we have that vaccine last year?"

"Yes, for South America. All these anti-vaxxers and people who don't travel have no idea how much disease there is in the world." I clicked on my Kindle. "Remember when Josh caught typhoid in China?" I looked out to sea. "Two people we know died from malaria and we know four people who've had it. And my cousin had dengue fever in Fiji."

"Aren't you a barrel of laughs?" Phil looked up. "What's the takeaway?"

"Get vaccinated, take prophylaxis, or stay home."

"That too, but also that it's dangerous to be friends with us." He smiled and clicked to wake up his Kindle. We read in companionable silence until it was time for me to meet Vana and Cathy.

✦   ✦   ✦

Only Vana and I showed up in the Explorers Lounge for one of the shared multi-cultural activities. Clothes racks with summer kimonos called *yukatas* were on the stage. Baskets held colorful *obi* sashes and folded fans. Two Japanese women approached each of us, bowed, and led us up front. One appraised my very American body and told the other which size to get. I looked over at Vana.

Her helpers laughed as they pulled and tucked the extra fabric into the bands. "I had no idea this was so complicated!" she said.

We were handed fans and told to put on the *zori* sandals, the precursor to flip-flops.

Everyone took pictures of each other separately and together. "*Domo arigatō gozaimashita.*" I thanked them formally with a deep, respectful bow.

We headed back to our adjoining rooms. At the door, I asked, "Are you sure you don't want to go to Hong Kong tomorrow?"

"You know me, I just get anxious."

Phil opened the door. "Mario's with me." We followed him into our room. "Did you hear the news? Hong Kong has canceled New Year's."

"Can we still go ashore?" Vana asked.

"Yes, but it's going to be way less crowded. Besides the fireworks—which wouldn't have been tomorrow anyway—there won't be the parade or the carnival."

"Where did you hear that?"

"Jerry called. Cathy's bummed because Stanley Market is also closed. It seems like overkill, though. Even though they've only had a couple of confirmed cases, they're closing the border and stopping flights from several mainland cities as well as rail travel."

"That's better for us, actually. I really wanted to go up to Victoria Peak, but that would have been impossible with holiday crowds."

"Jerry said they're only pinpointing people who have high fevers and other obvious symptoms," Phil added.

"If they were actually testing everyone coming from Wuhan, there would probably be a lot more." Vana turned to her husband. "Right, Mario?"

He nodded.

"Even if there were a hundred cases, there are seven million people in this city," I said. "Statistically, we're more likely to..."

"Be bitten by a rat?" Phil filled in.

I gasped.

"It's a joke! You know, the Year of the Rat..."

"What do you get from a rat bite?" I asked.

"Ratatouille," Vana answered, and this time, we all laughed.

WHERE IS MR. WU?

You can leave Hong Kong, but it will never leave you.
   —Nury Vittachi, *Hong Kong: The City of Dreams*

Email from Terry, January 25, 2020

The repercussions from a mysterious virus that has sickened hundreds of people began reverberating far from its epicenter in central China on Saturday, as Hong Kong closed its schools for several weeks, Beijing began restricting buses in and out of the capital, and the country's travel association suspended Chinese tour groups heading overseas. The new measures, coming on top of previous travel restrictions that had effectively penned in tens of millions of people in Hubei, the province at the heart of the outbreak, are certain to further dampen celebrations of the Lunar New Year, which began on Saturday.

   —*New York Times*

Three versions of Hong Kong churned in my subconscious: scenes from my childhood of sampans in the harbor and the views from Victoria Peak; the center of the opium trade at the end of the eighteenth century, which I wrote about in *Flowers in the Blood*; and the mighty, modern metropolis of *Crazy, Rich Asians*. I hoped for clarity instead of the hazy images seen through the blurred lens of memory and embroidered by my imagination. What I hadn't expected, though, was that the day would be laced with a frisson of fear.

"I'm putting two masks in my backpack," I told Phil as we prepared for the day on shore.

"Where'd you get those?"

"Last time we were in Japan. I brought them in case anyone on the plane was coughing."

"I don't need one."

"Even with some of the festivities canceled, there are bound to be crowds at the temples and markets. I don't care to be sprayed with a new strain of crap from coughs or sneezes."

Vana and Mario had decided to come after all, and the six of us got in line to disembark into the terminal. It was slower than usual because port officials were pressing thermometers to each passenger's forehead.

"I thought they were only interested in people coming from the mainland," Jerry said as he led us to the curb to meet the guide he had arranged.

"They're probably doing all points of entry, which would include ports," Phil replied.

Jerry looked down at a text. "She's over here." We followed him to where Amy, a Brit living with her family in Hong Kong, was standing by her van.

"I can't believe how light the traffic is," she said. "We're going to be able to do far more than I thought."

A few minutes later, she dropped us off at the entrance to the Wong Tai Sin Temple in Kowloon. Celebrants were converging from every direction and circled the exterior. Guards attempted to funnel everyone through the main gateway. As we followed Amy, we exchanged nervous glances. I kept my elbows out to prevent being jostled. Most of the visitors were wearing face masks and carrying gold-and-red pinwheel decorations and long bundles of incense sticks. Many seemed to be carrying groceries.

"What are the pinwheels for?" Cathy asked.

"In Chinese, the word *spinning* means change, so the pinwheel can change your luck from bad to good," Amy said as she kept our little group from being split up by a family of line-cutters. "Stay close to me."

I fumbled in my backpack for our masks. For the first time, I felt the mask could be important protection. I reached into my pocket for one of my Japanese handkerchiefs and held it to prevent my bare hands from touching the walls. *Tenuguis* are pieces of printed cotton fabric about twelve by thirty-four inches. They're used for everything from gift wrapping to towels. Because their public restrooms, as pristine as they are, rarely have paper towels or a hand dryer, the Japanese use them for drying their hands.

People with bundles of incense sticks pushed their way to the braziers at various altars and then walked around shaking the burning sticks in order to move through the protective smoke.

"What's unusual about this shrine is that there are three sections: one for Taoism, one for Confucianism, and also Buddhism," Amy said.

Huge Chinese lanterns alternating in yellow and red were hung from wires between the buildings. Part of the temple was built around a vast courtyard that was filled with worshippers—mostly older women—who knelt on red cushions while bowing and gesticulating to the heavens. Many held up burning incense in supplication.

Vana indicated mats heaped with fruit pyramids, roast pork, and cooked chickens. "Why all the food?"

Visiting Hong Kong January 25 despite the cancelation of Lunar New Year festivities: Mario and Vana, Cathy and Jerry, and Gay and Phil. *Credit: Amy Overy*

"Sacrifices."

"What are those cylinders?"

Amy walked over to a shelf and brought one to show us. "This is *kau chim*," she explained. "They're filled with sticks." She shook it until one stick popped out and fell to the ground. She picked it up and read the number and matched it with a list in her phone. Then she walked over to what looked like an old-fashioned phone book. "Usually, you consult one of the fortunetellers, but that would be impossible today, so I'm matching the number to the hundred written oracles." She found the spot. "Not my lucky day," she said and handed the cylinder to me. I went through the same process. "Sorry, Gay, not going to get your wish." In fact, nobody received a good fortune.

"We're doomed," Phil said. I laughed because Phil always takes the most pessimistic view.

After a short ride, Amy pulled the van to the curb by the entrance to the Star Ferry. "This is the best way to get from Kowloon to Hong Kong Island," she said, handing us the tickets she had already bought. "I'll take the bridge and pick you up on the Hong Kong side."

I had taken my mask off in the van, but seeing lots more wearing theirs on the ferry, I put it back on. We made our way to the bow. Although Hong Kong had been transformed since I was there as a girl, the outlines of the hills and piers struck a familiar chord. I reached for Phil's hand and grasped it as tightly as I had my mother's.

Once we reached Hong Kong Island, Amy led us to an office building with a glitzy interior. We took an escalator up to a floor with restaurants. "I can't imagine trying to navigate Hong Kong on our own," Vana said to Amy. "You're making this easy."

I smiled. "Glad you decided to come?"

"I'm loving every minute," Vana said, "although I just don't seem to have my usual energy."

"You're probably coming down with the crud I had. At least it didn't last long."

We ducked under a red banner into a dim sum restaurant. The seven of us were seated at a round table with a glass lazy Susan in the middle. The extensive menu was overwhelming, so we asked Amy to orchestrate ordering the house specialties. Most of the dishes served in bamboo baskets looked Instagram-ready. The barbecued pork buns were shaped like cartoonish pig heads with pink ears and snout and the molten custard buns had emoji faces. Little bird dumplings were served in a real bird cage.

Vana spun the turntable around to reach the teapot. "The tea is delicious here," Amy said. "Actually, the restaurant's name, Yum Cha, means to 'drink tea.' In Hong Kong, it's synonymous with eating dim sum."

After a trip to the iconic Victoria Peak, Amy drove us to Stanley Market, which turned out to be only partially closed. I told her that one of the reasons we had wanted a guide with a vehicle instead of using public transportation is that we were worried about the protests. "Were we overreacting?"

"Absolutely not. They've been escalating. Since the locations change daily, I have to keep checking so I can alter my routes if necessary," she said. "This time of year is called *Chunyun*. It's like Christmas on steroids. Family members fly across the world to be together and more than four hundred million people travel during the two months. This is Hong Kong's make-it-or-break-it period, that's why there's a lot of criticism about the travel restrictions."

"Are you worried about this virus?"

"There are only a few corona cases here and Hong Kong needs to contain them so we can continue with commerce and international tourism. No question that the epidemic on the mainland is going to hurt business here, but China has more than its share of epidemics."

"Like swine flu and SARS," Phil said.

"If anyone can control an outbreak, it's the Chinese," Amy said. "One order and it's done. I've heard brutal stories about the SARS quarantine. It was dictatorial, but it saved countless lives."

It was drizzling and beginning to get dark as we arrived at the market. Many shops were closed and others were bringing goods in from the sidewalk stalls. Cathy's eyes lit up as she scanned the array of garments, costume jewelry, scarves, toys, and appealing souvenirs.

Phil pointed to a stack of embroidered pillowcases. "These have your name on them." I have a collection of decorative pillowcases from our travels, which are lightweight and pack flat. Amy gave me hints on bargaining and then went to help the others pick out silk bathrobes. There was a display of the *pu'er* tea I had been reading about near the checkout counter and I bought some to try. The owner turned off the lights as soon as I walked out the door.

"Great timing," Phil said to Amy. "If we'd come here first, we'd never have dragged these ladies away."

I held up my hands. "Guilty as charged."

We passed a pharmacy and I held up my finger to signal I'd be back in a minute. I returned in less than that. "Apparently they've sold out every mask in Hong Kong."

"We already have some," Phil said.

"I wanted to get them for all of us."

"You're not going to wear one on the ship, are you?" Jerry looked dismayed.

"We might run into more crowds like the one at the temple this morning."

Jerry opened the door of the van for me. "Count me out."

✦   ✦   ✦

Email from Terry, January 26, 2020

Chinese coronavirus infections, death toll soar as fifth case is confirmed in U.S.

The Chinese government struggled Sunday to cope with a worsening coronavirus epidemic as its official number of infections soared and the death toll rose to 80, while additional cases appeared in the United States. The government in Beijing broadened an extraordinary quarantine to more than 50 million people—roughly equal to the population of Spain—enforcing a travel ban on 16 cities in central Hubei province, where the lethal virus first appeared.

—*Washington Post*

Our ship was supposed to depart Hong Kong at 11:59 p.m. The late hour was so passengers could attend the various holiday events and had, of course, been scheduled more than a year in advance. I supposed the odd time was so the cruise line would not be charged port fees for another day.

As soon as we got back to the cabin, I tossed my backpack and packages on the sofa and peeled off my clothes and left them in a heap on the floor. We had been going strong for fifteen hours and I couldn't wait to lie down. Phil had beaten me to bed.

"*Gong xi fa cai*, darling."

"Happy New Year, honey." Phil snuggled toward me. "Thanks for planning a fantastic day, as usual."

I was almost asleep when we heard an announcement over the loudspeaker in the corridor. "What's going on?"

"They're calling the names of passengers who aren't accounted for."

I groaned. "If they're not back, how are they going to respond?"

"Maybe they didn't scan their cards properly."

Ten minutes later, I heard them calling again. "Now what?"

"Sounds like they're looking for someone with a name like Wu or Lu."

"It's their own fault if they're late. YouTube is filled with pictures of tardy passengers waving frantically as their ship pulls away without them."

"Remember Cannes?" Phil asked.

"How could I forget! We were with Jerry and Cathy and the Israeli couple." I remembered the six of us renting a car and driving to several *villages perché* (hilltop towns)—in Provence. We thought we had plenty of time but had not factored in rush-hour traffic. The guys dropped the women off to "hold the ship" while they returned the car. If we had had a flat tire or taken the wrong turn, we would have missed the boat. We all had travel insurance that covers "trip interruption," which would have covered flights to the next port, but we were happy to avoid that hassle.

"It's comforting to have insurance, but who wants to go through the trauma that activates it?"

"We're lousy risks," Phil said. "We've been reimbursed for six hurricanes and floods. We've totaled an airplane and lived to tell the tale."

I was walking back to bed from the bathroom when there was another muffled announcement. I opened the door to the corridor to hear it more clearly. "This time they called out cabin numbers and several names ending in Wu." Even though that was the last announcement, I lay awake anticipating the next one. I didn't fall back to sleep until the ship was underway, with or without Mr. Wu or his family.

We would not hear that name again until we were home and had no idea whether he was aboard or not. Eventually, the mystery was solved, but his absence haunted me.

✦ ✦ ✦

The next morning we settled into our sea day routine of sleeping late and having a leisurely breakfast in the dining room with our friends. "Anyone have plans?" Jerry asked.

"Nothing besides trivia in the morning and afternoon," I said.

"There's a lecture on navigation that looks interesting," Phil said.

"Sorry," I said. "I forgot to bring the *Patter*." Jerry handed Phil his copy of the ship's newsletter.

"I'm quite organized at home," I said, "but I become a scatter-brain at sea."

"Letting go of control is good for you," Phil said.

"That's why Jerry's in charge of finances," I said. He kept track on his elaborate "Who Owes What to Whom" spreadsheet.

Phil looked up from the listings. "This is cool. There are going to be some lion dancers from Hong Kong performing in the atrium. I'll want to film that for the doc."

"You're making a film?" Cathy asked.

"Just a home movie. I enjoy editing one for every trip. Remember I sent you the one from the last time we were on this ship?"

"I'd hardly call that a home movie," Jerry said.

Phil and I planned to meet up for the lion dancers. I arrived fifteen minutes early to get us seats but there was hardly a place to stand. The atrium starts on the Plaza deck (the fifth floor) and soars to the Promenade Deck (the seventh floor). There is some seating on the lowest level, but never enough. The audience was already two deep around the brass railings on the upper floors, jostling for a view. Late arrivals commandeered the steps of the two circular staircases for stadium-style seating. I gave up and sat cross-legged on the icy inlaid floor, which turned out to be the best "seat" in the house.

The lion dancers who came from Hong Kong to entertain *Diamond Princess* passengers. Inset: Entertainment Director Karolyn Desbuquois and Captain Gennaro Arma

To the beat of drums, the two gold-and-red lions burst into the atrium—each with one acrobat at the head, a second at the rear—and rushed up to a pile of oranges on the floor and "gobbled" them before offering them to members of the audience. When a lion reared up on his back legs, an acrobat was jumping on the shoulders of another. They were very nimble and everyone clapped at their shenanigans. At one point, Captain Arma stepped out and "fed" an orange back to the lion to much applause. The lions danced over to the audience to be petted—which brings luck—and dropped an orange in my lap. Since I didn't see Phil anywhere, I did my best to film the scene. At least nobody was blocking my view.

At trivia later, Marlene and Katherine were holding our usual front-row spot. Katherine introduced me to a couple they'd met from Queensland.

"I'm outnumbered." I held my hands up in surrender.

"Is that a problem, my dear?" Katherine said in a tone that was teasingly snotty.

"Did you hear that they're finding people who flew into Sydney feeling fine but came down with the virus a few days later and tested positive?" the woman said to Marlene.

"That's the problem with coronaviruses," Marlene, who works for a doctor, said. "People can be infectious before they show symptoms."

"Australia might shut down before America," Katherine said. "It's our summer holiday so we all travel, plus everyone comes to us for milder weather."

"I always forget about the seasons being different Down Under. A few years ago, I caught the flu from Aussies on an Alaskan cruise in August."

Marlene chuckled. "Try and say that three times."

"Here's an idea," Katherine said. "Let's all sign up for a few more weeks on the ship. If we stay on board, we won't have to worry about anything."

✦   ✦   ✦

Everyone in our group had been given specialty restaurant vouchers by our travel agents and had saved them for an evening at sea. Jerry had reserved a table for our group at Sabatini's, the Italian restaurant on every Princess ship. Knowing that the main course servings were overly generous, I decided to have a salad and two appetizers instead.

Marco, the waiter, frowned. "No *secondi piatti*?"

"No, *grazzi mille*," I replied in an accent I hoped wouldn't make Giulia wince.

Marco sighed. "Here, there are no extra charges. I will bring you anything else you would like to taste."

I weakened. "What would you suggest?"

"*Lombata di vitello al forno*," he said. "Rack of veal with a Barolo glaze." I threw up my hands in surrender.

"Phil, shall we order the Châteauneuf-du-Pape we liked at the wine tasting?" Jerry asked.

"Okay, I'll get the second bottle: the Kim Crawford Pinot Noir."

Cathy and I had our usual: Coke for her and Pellegrino with lime for me. Jerry started a toast. I dipped my fingers in Phil's wine and flicked a drop in my glass.

"Why did you do that?" Vana asked.

"Giulia," I said, referring to my full-blooded Italian daughter-in-law, "insists it's bad luck to toast with plain water."

Marco poured golden olive oil into a ceramic plate with a Tuscan design and then mixed in herbs to make a dipping sauce for the warm bread. "What's the gossip?" I asked Cathy, who smokes and is required to go to the designated room. She's always the first in our group to know what's happening.

"Remember the people they were trying to find last night?"

"That *was* annoying," Vana said.

"At least one family never did make it back."

"What if they were in an accident?" I wondered. Nobody else was interested in speculating with me.

Mario mentioned that he'd been researching everything he could find about the virus. "The Chinese doctors are trying different combinations of medicines to help with the symptoms or shorten the course."

"Like what?" I leaned in because Mario has such a soft speaking voice.

"Statins."

"Gay and I both take them, as you know. How do they help?"

"Apparently, patients who regularly take statins are having fewer symptoms and shorter hospital stays."

"Maybe we should increase our doses," Phil suggested.

Mario was thoughtful before he spoke. "Not until you have symptoms." He took a sip of his beer. "Don't take any Advil or Motrin. For now, only Tylenol, because there's some evidence that ibuprofen may worsen chest infections."

"I'm glad I packed some antibiotics because I have some chronic respiratory issues," Cathy said.

"Won't help with this virus," Mario said. "They're testing malaria drugs, an HIV combo therapy, and one of the new influenza meds that they use in Russia but not in the U.S."

"We brought Tamiflu, as you know," Phil said. "And wouldn't our flu shots give us some protection?"

"Hard to say."

"Okay," I said. "But if one of us had flu-like symptoms, we could take one of those rapid flu tests and at least eliminate the flu as the problem?"

Phil furrowed his forehead. "Couldn't someone have the flu *and* this new virus?" His question was met with silence.

"Stumped the panel," I said.

Phil nodded for the headwaiter to bring the Pinot Noir. "Now that's my idea of a vaccine," he said.

The American War

Travel is fatal to prejudice, bigotry, and narrow-mindedness.
—Mark Twain

Phil and I had mixed feelings about visiting Vietnam and avoided dwelling on them till we arrived at Chan May, the port for Hue and Da Nang. Our prevailing emotion was deep sadness. The figure of fifty-eight thousand lost Americans is etched in our minds, as it is with our Boomer-generation contemporaries.

"I had no idea how many Vietnamese people—civilians and military—perished," I said as I stood on our balcony as the *Diamond Princess* glided through the silky, dawn-dappled harbor.

Phil slid his arm around my waist. "I assume you looked it up."

"Way more than we were ever told, perhaps as many as two million men, women, and children from the north and south, plus another million soldiers. And for what?"

Phil reminded me about two of his college buddies who served. "Once they returned," he said, "we had nothing in common."

And I reminded him about one of my closest high school friends, Roberta. We both vehemently opposed the war. "Her brother, Lloyd, had a Nixon poster in his room and was gung ho about stopping the communist threat. And then he was drafted."

"Yes, you've told me about him." Phil left me with my thoughts and went to finish dressing.

Lloyd survived the unthinkable. In one explosion, he lost both arms, both legs, and one eye. He married his college sweetheart, who wrote a book about him and his work on veterans' rights. Roberta died of a heroin overdose. I corresponded with Lloyd and Roberta's mother until she died.

✦　✦　✦

Email from Terry, January 27, 2020

The U.S. State Department has ordered personnel working at the U.S. Consulate General in Wuhan to depart for the United States, a State Department official told CNN in a statement. Priority has been given to US citizens who are "most at risk for contracting coronavirus" if they stay in the city. "The Department of State procured a chartered flight for U.S. government personnel in Wuhan. As space is available, seating will be offered to U.S. citizens on a reimbursable basis…." All passengers will be subject to a CDC screening, health observation and monitoring requirements.

—CNN

"We're still celebrating Lunar New Year," Jerry N., our guide, told us as we drove toward Hue, once the country's capital. Situated in the central part of the now-united country, Hue is located on both banks of the Perfume River. Jerry Giambalvo had made the arrangements for the day, and we were just going with the flow.

Phil pointed to a road sign in both Vietnamese and English. "Da Nang. Wasn't there a U.S. airbase near here?"

"I take American veterans there all the time. Did you want to see it?" our guide asked. Nobody spoke up.

"I had a low draft number," Phil said, "but I flunked my physical because I almost lost my foot in a motorcycle accident when I was sixteen."

"When I graduated college in 1971, the draft was still going on," Jerry said. "I was called up but rejected. Several guys from my high school were killed in action."

"I lived in Canada," Vana said, "and Mario was in Bolivia."

"Cathy wasn't even born yet," Jerry quipped because she was the "baby" of our group.

"More like grade school," she corrected.

I had been weighing whether I should bring up the war with our guide, who appeared to be in his late forties. Our friends had varying political views, and I assumed it would be best to stick to noncontroversial subjects, as we usually did. Still, I wondered whether Jerry N.'s family had sided with the north or south. Did he resent the Americans who returned as tourists? My gnawing questions overrode my better judgment. I leaned forward from the van's second row. "What happened to your family during the war?"

"Do you know anything about the camps?" he asked.

"Not really."

"My father was an officer in the South Vietnamese army. He was sent to what they called a re-education camp for nine years. There wasn't enough to eat and the conditions were brutal—plus, they worked them very hard. Relatives were allowed to visit every three months and they provided almost all the food. My father didn't like to talk about it, which is why I don't know many details."

"Must have been such a terrible time," Vana said.

"He was lucky because his sister had connections. She discovered that he could be released sooner if he had points for good behavior. But it was really about who you knew and how much someone paid. His sister was able to get him out early, which probably saved his life. After that, he wasn't allowed to have an exit visa, get government rations, or send his children to school. Many who left the camps were so desperate they became the boat people. That's why many ended up in the United States."

Jerry N. suddenly pulled over and stopped the van. I feared a flat tire or mechanical problems, but then he said, "Nobody takes tourists here, but I wanted to show you a real fishing village."

Small sampans and fishing boats were tied up along the bank. Phil filmed a fisherman pushing away from the muddy bank with a long oar. "I wonder whether they still hate Americans," Phil mumbled so only I could hear.

"In Vietnam, they call it the American War."

Phil said, "That makes sense, since we were the invaders."

We returned to the van and I kept my roiling thoughts to myself as we continued north. Jerry N. explained that Hue is just south of what had been the DMZ, the demilitarized zone that divided North Vietnam from South Vietnam. "This is the best day of the year to visit the Citadel and Royal Palace because it's Tet— the name for our New Year."

All the visitors to this former home of emperors were wearing holiday finery. The buildings and gardens were decorated with lavish floral displays. As the others wandered off to explore the splendid throne room, I spoke softly. "The Tet Offensive must have happened around this time of year."

"Yes."

"Was it anywhere near here?"

"Exactly here. The Viet Cong, they came and breached these stone walls."

I nodded. "Nineteen sixty-eight." Jerry N. seemed surprised I knew that, but actually, it was the only date from the war I was sure about. Phil and I had our first Squab Day on January 14, 1968. Two weeks later, we had watched news of the attacks on television together.

"What happened after that?" I asked.

"The north captured Hue but were pushed out in a few weeks—after destroying most of the city." Our guide swept his arms around. "There were more than a hundred and sixty buildings here. Less than a dozen survived." I could only shake my head at the loss of lives and heritage.

We made a quick stop at the Linh Mu Pagoda, a graceful seven-story temple first built in 1601. Most of the locals were wearing face masks. "Are the masks usually worn or a new thing?" Vana asked.

"Both," said Jerry N. "In the cities, they help with bad air and infections in crowded trains; in the country, they protect from dust and sun—especially on motorcycles. Now, they are saying it may be a requirement."

Our tour included lunch at an open-air restaurant. Pouring rain began just as we took our seats under cover. A few of the more particular eaters in our group were wary of the unfamiliar dishes but found the crispy noodles and lemongrass-infused chicken tasty. Vana asked Jerry N. about health and education, which I thought were free, but actually aren't. Most of his stories showed the futility of working hard. "If you make a farm prosperous, the state can take it from you."

After lunch, the rain finally ended as Jerry N. parked the van by a misty dock. A brightly painted dragon boat appeared as though emerging from a low cloud. Our guide secured a ladder in the muddy bank and a man and woman on board helped us climb over the gunwale and onto the bow.

"This family lives on the boat," Jerry N. said. "When they don't have tourists, they fish."

I heard a sound behind me and the head of a smiling toddler peeked out. I waved. His mother rushed to keep him quiet. As soon as she settled him, a smaller baby sat up. Jerry N. pointed out various temples and tombs as we cruised down the river, and the couple served glasses of tea and some nuts and fruit.

As we drove back to the ship, motorcycles loaded with parents, children, and packages whizzed past, sending up arcs of muddy water. Most everyone wore raingear. We noticed children and babies swathed in plastic with just their noses poking out.

Just before we went through security, I spotted some souvenir stalls. "I'll be right back," I said to Phil, who reminded me that we didn't have room for anything else. I handed the clerk five American dollars. He gave me back six gray surgical masks.

✦ ✦ ✦

Email from Terry, January 28, 2020

Thailand has reported 14 cases of infection; Hong Kong has eight; the United States, Taiwan, Australia and Macau have five each; Singapore, South Korea and Malaysia each have reported four; Japan has seven; France has four; Canada has three; Vietnam has two; and Nepal, Cambodia and Germany each have one. There have been no deaths outside China.

—*New York Times*

Our second stop in Vietnam, the next morning, was Cai Lan, the port for Ha Long Bay in the north, not far from the Chinese border. Most come-hither ads for southeast Asia feature iconic images of the bay's otherworldly rock formations that seem to be floating in an emerald sea.

Since Mario and Vana decided not to come on the seaplane ride we had arranged, it was just us and the Giambalvos. There was some confusion about which bus to take to the seaplane port and we ended up at the wrong place to meet their van. Jerry made some phone calls and solved the problem, but he was out of sorts.

"Everything okay?" Phil asked.

"Not really. Cathy's very upset. She just heard that her mother is fading fast."

Last we knew her mother wasn't doing well but this sudden downturn was a shock. I decided not to say anything, just to be around in case Cathy wanted to talk, but she sat apart from us in the flight tour waiting room. I walked over to a map of where we would be flying. It showed three bays—Ha Long, Bai Tu Long, and Lan Ha—that were part of the Gulf of Tonkin. I waved Phil over and pointed to the label.

"As in the Tonkin Resolution?" Phil asked.

"I can see why they leave the name off the tourist brochures. It still triggers bad memories."

"I didn't follow the news while I was in college at Bob Jones," Phil admitted.

"It spurred the first antiwar protests when I was a sophomore at Antioch in nineteen sixty-four." I lowered my voice. "President Johnson used the incident to expand the scope of America's involvement in Vietnam without having to formally declare war."

"What kind of a plane is that?" Jerry said, pointing out the window.

Phil turned. "Oh, that's a Cessna Grand Caravan!"

"Is that good?" Jerry asked.

"You're looking at least a million, a lot more with the floats."

Our pilot was a burly Canadian, a veteran of bush flying in Canada and Alaska. He chatted with Phil as he did the pre-flight inspection, then turned to us, introduced his Vietnamese co-pilot, and did a safety briefing for the nine of us aboard. Since all the Asian passengers were wearing masks, I pulled ours out of our backpack.

"Vana gave me two," Cathy said as she handed one to Jerry.

He shrugged. "When in Rome—or wherever we are."

Phil took a window seat and I scrunched in next to him. The woman behind me had a rusty cough. I turned, grateful she was wearing a mask. My own was annoying because my glasses fogged up and the elastic tangled with my hearing aids. I wondered whether the mask was more effective in protecting the wearer or those in the vicinity of someone who was infected. If cruisers wore them, would cruise cough disappear? Still, it made sense in this tightly packed plane during flu season. My musings were interrupted as the plane rolled out of the parking lot and then down a ramp and started bobbing in the bay. The engine revved and we started moving faster in small increments that reminded me of a swan flapping its wings to launch itself into the air. Once we were aloft, I was transfixed by the aerial views, from the sky-piercing limestone pinnacles to what looked like gigantic animal forms carpeted in green velvet. Jagged inlets led to secret lakes. Others were punctuated by mysterious caves. An astonishing array of watercraft— from junks with two red sails that had fan-folded pleats to tour boats with multiple decks, tiny sampans, kayaks, and fishing and speed boats—competed for space in the narrow channels. Modern condos and luxury hotels, which I later learned were financed by mainland Chinese entrepreneurs, crowded the horizon.

On the way back to the ship, I looked up the Gulf of Tonkin and what exactly had provoked the war's escalation. Historians now referred to the "alleged incident" and said the "attacks" were the results of "overeager sonar operators" and the radar was really detecting the waves and not an enemy. Later, though, the U.S. Navy had placed explosive mines in the bay—now a UNESCO World Heritage Site and tourist mecca.

✦　✦　✦

Email from Terry, January 29, 2020

As the case count in China's new coronavirus outbreak eclipsed those reported in the 2003 SARS outbreak on Wednesday, the United States evacuated 200 Americans from the center of the epidemic. Overnight, the number of cases of the 2019-nCoV coronavirus in China shot from 4,515 to 5,974, while the death toll climbed to 132. There were 5,327 cases and 348 deaths reported in China during the SARS outbreak, with more than 800 deaths reported worldwide.... Late Tuesday night, a flight chartered by the U.S. State Department to evacuate American government workers and private citizens landed in Anchorage, Alaska. After refueling, it headed for the March Air Reserve Base near Riverside, Calif.

—*U.S. News and World Report*

There were two sea days before we reached Taiwan. I looked over the *Princess Patter* at breakfast. "Phil, you're not going to want to miss the glockenspiel class."

"I'll pass."

"Phil and Mario should enter the Mister Sexy Legs competition by the pool" was Vana's suggestion.

"Okay, but you both have to go to the hula dance class," Phil said.

"I have a conflicting appointment." I grinned naughtily. "Vana, come on. You'll be glad you did."

"No way I'm going naked in a public pool," Vana said.

"I can't believe you're the same person who went to Woodstock."

I teased, but I didn't expect to sway her. The *onsen* experience is not for everyone. While I was disappointed that none of the women I knew on the ship was even slightly interested in going with me to the Izumi Japanese bath, I knew there is no point trying to overcome anyone's layers of shame and modesty instilled by parents, religion, and culture. I was just lucky to have had the experience of living in Japan as a girl and going to several of these heated baths, including *konyoko*, mixed baths heated by hot springs, with my mother.

The *onsen* has rules and rituals. Even though I had been to the bath on my first *Diamond Princess* voyage, I worried more about making a mistake than about what someone might think of my aging body. I arrived promptly for my appointment and the attendant admonished me: "No bathing suits."

"I understand. I've been here before."

She sniffed the air as if that would root out any deception, then took my cruise card hostage and handed me a large towel and a washcloth. I hadn't seen this many nude women since the communal showers in my college dorm when we were all nubile and beautiful. Now most of us were *obachans*—grandmothers who had given birth, breastfed, raised families. Time had added padding to our hips and butts and our breasts drooped. We were all moving in the same direction: riding the same waves, immersed in a pool of communal water, and getting irrevocably older. I stared out the window-wall where the glittering sea and flawless sky calmed my pulse and silenced my chattering thoughts. Sea and rocks…a Zen saying…Ha Long Bay…pebbles of the Gods…. The waves undulated with "white horses," a poetic way of referring to the foamy crests. Just watching them lifting, falling, waxing, waning—was mesmerizing. I closed my eyes. The jumbled words rearranged themselves: In the confrontation between the stream and the rock, the stream always wins not through strength but through persistence.

✦ ✦ ✦

Email from Terry, January 30, 2020

The World Health Organization declared a global health emergency on Thursday as the coronavirus outbreak spread well beyond China, where it emerged last month. The move reversed the organization's decision just a week ago to hold off such a declaration. Since then, there have been thousands of new cases in China and clear evidence of human-to-human transmission in several other countries, including the United States. All of which warranted a reconsideration by the W.H.O.'s emergency committee, officials said. The declaration "is not a vote of no confidence in China," said Tedros Adhanom Ghebreyesus, the W.H.O.'s director-general. "On the contrary, the W.H.O. continues to have confidence in China's capacity to control the outbreak."

—*New York Times*

The afternoon of our second sea day, Vana and I decided to skip lunch and have afternoon tea, served at three in the dining room.

"Tea is my favorite meal," I said as the waiter passed a tray with a variety of crustless sandwiches.

Vana buttered a flaky scone. "I'm about ready to go home."

"I'm not," I said. "We think the *ryokans* may be the high point of the trip."

Katherine and Marlene walked into the room and I waved at them. "Do you mind if they join us?" I asked, perhaps a bit late to turn them away.

"No, of course not."

We ordered another pot of tea and the two nurses—Vana and Katherine—began discussing the virus.

"Now the Wuflu has an official name," Katherine said. "They're calling it two thousand nineteen hyphen, lowercase N, capital C, lower case O, capital V."

"Well, that sure is easy to remember," I said.

Marlene groaned. "Just say 'two thousand nineteen n... co...V.'"

"Anyway, it's similar to SARS, which was SARS Co Vee Two."

"Wuflu is a lot easier to remember." Marlene looked at me. "Did you get the form?"

"About what?"

"A health advisory about coronavirus. It should be in your mailbox." Marlene unfolded the one she had tucked into her *Patter* and passed it to me.

I read a few highlights aloud about 2019-nCoV. "First detected in Wuhan City, Hubei Province…risk to our guests is very low…coordinating with CDC and WHO…China has canceled public gatherings…airport screenings. They're adopting measures to keep us safe…pre-boarding health reporting, screening for persons from affected areas…evaluation for patients who present to the medical center for respiratory disease…environmental sanitation with non-toxic disinfectant…and then the routine instructions about washing hands often for twenty seconds and covering coughs. Just sounds like a flu warning."

"A bit more than that," Katherine said. "The World Health Organization finally decided to declare coronavirus a global health emergency."

"I thought they decided not to do that last week," Vana said.

"Yeah, well, since then, there have been thousands of new cases including evidence of human-to-human transmission in several other countries, including the United States, so they reversed that decision."

"Did you hear the good news?" Marlene said.

"We sure could use some," Katherine said with a mischievous wink.

"Well, the World Health Organization also announced that domestic canine animals cannot carry coronavirus and should no longer be kept in quarantine." Marlene looked from me to Vana expectantly. "In other words, WHO let the dogs out!"

I started laughing before Vana, but soon both of us were covering our mouths to prevent pastry bits from flying out. "Got me!"

"Me too!" Vana dabbed her tearing eyes. "But seriously, are you worried about catching it?" Vana asked Katherine.

"We arrived in Singapore exactly a month ago and except for two days in Hong Kong on the first leg and then on the twenty-fifth, we haven't been anywhere near China, let alone Wuhan."

"Even if it is spreading in Asia," Marlene said, "we'll be home in a week. The only cases in Australia are one or two who came directly from China."

"That's about the same situation as the States," I said.

"I've had a bad feeling about it even before we left home." Vana turned to me. "Now Gay's going to say 'however, statistically…'"

"You know me too well," I said. "I admit that I'm beginning to rethink our trip to Africa in April because Ebola and AIDS spread so fast there."

"As did the swine flu in 2009," Katherine said.

Marlene put down her teacup with more force than she meant and the tea puddled in the saucer. "I'm trying not to get carried away with speculation. The cruise is almost over. Just Taiwan tomorrow, Okinawa, and back to Yokohama."

"She's right. There's only the most remote chance that we would have exposure to anyone contagious." Katherine spoke in a clipped, authoritative way that left little room for argument.

I noticed that she directed the last bit to her roommate. This trip was Marlene's reward for finishing chemotherapy and she was still dealing with some side effects—and a compromised immune system.

"Oh, I can't resist," Marlene said to the white-gloved waiter carrying a tray of miniature cream puffs and strawberry tarts.

"Meanwhile," Katherine chirped in a different tone, "what's your next adventure, Vana?"

"Let's see if we survive this one first," she said. We all chuckled for a second and then fell silent.

MEMORIES AND
MONUMENTS

Man cannot discover new oceans unless he has the courage to lose sight of the shore.

— André Gide

Email from Terry, January 31, 2020

The Trump administration announced a ban on foreign national travel for those who have been in China within the last 14 days, Health and Human Services Secretary Alex Azar announced Friday. The United States, Azar said, is "temporarily suspending the entry into the United States of foreign nationals who pose a risk of transmitting the 2019 novel coronavirus." Azar noted that any US citizen who has been in the Hubei Province in the last 14 days will be subject to up to 14 days of mandatory quarantine upon return to the United States. US citizens returning from the rest of mainland China who have been there in the last 14 days will undergo screening at US ports of entry and up to 14 days of self-monitoring. The basis for the temporary

ban, Dr. Anthony Fauci told reporters, is "the unknown . . .
aspects of this particular outbreak."

—CNN

I hadn't been to Taiwan since 1952. Because I wanted to see some
of the places I remembered, I volunteered to handle the tour and
had hired a guide named Tom. He warned me that Taipei is now
a modern city—with one of the tallest skyscrapers in the world—
and bears no resemblance to the quaint village of my childhood.

"Not too much traffic today," Tom said as we drove from the
port of Keelung to the city, "because of the New Year."

We climbed a steep hill. Going around a curve, my heart
skipped a beat. "The Grand Hotel!" We had lived there for a
few weeks when I was a six. I imagined a towering gold-and-
red structure glistening in the sun, with massive columns and a
vast gilded roof, but I girded myself for a letdown because places
remembered from childhood inevitably shrink to the adult's eye.
The Grand Hotel, though, did not disappoint. Yes, the lobby
really was as lofty as a cathedral. If anything, it was far more mag-
nificent than I remembered, but with a better heating system. We
had arrived in late February, the same season. The old building
was quite drafty; I stayed warm snuggling inside my mother's
mink coat.

"Take a picture of me," I asked Phil as I posed by the reception
desk. "I remember my mother standing right here."

Vana waved us over to a small gift shop. She held up some children's Chinese dresses. "Gay, you *have* to get these for the twins."

I handed my credit card to the clerk. "Unfortunately, you have
impeccable taste." I bought them without looking at the price—a
mistake—but they were absolutely adorable.

Phil rounded us up and we continued to the obligatory temples
that were crowded with New Year's celebrants. I didn't recognize

the Confucius Temple, but the Lungshan—with its colorful drag-ons on the peaked roof—brought back memories.

"I think we lived near here," I said, then showed Tom the address.

"Yes, not far at all. One of the best neighborhoods." He pointed out a section of the temple that had been rebuilt after it was bombed by Americans in 1945. "This was during a period of Japanese rule and it was rumored that they were hiding armaments here. Many precious works of art were lost."

"That's horrible," Vana said.

"What do you know about the history of Taiwan?" Tom asked us.

"Not much," Vana admitted.

Tom turned toward me. "Everyone my parents knew were nationalists," I said. "My father had some business connections with Madame Chiang Kai-shek during the civil war with the communists. Mao's army was much stronger, which is why they retreated to Taiwan."

"That was in 1949," Tom said. "Following the defeat of the Japanese, the Allies gave Chiang Kai-shek control of Taiwan because it is strategically placed. Many in the West applaud him because he was anti-communist and a strong leader who stayed in power for forty-six years—but they forget he was also a dictator who imposed martial law." Tom parked the car. "Come, you will find this most interesting."

He pointed to a brick building and said it was a former radio broadcasting station. A guard wearing a face mask and gloves held up his hand for us to stop. He pointed to a sign on the door in Chinese and English that read, "Novel coronavirus warning." He went to the reception desk and returned with a forehead thermom-eter and took everyone's temperature before he would sell Tom admission tickets.

"Hey, Gay," Jerry said, "you know why it's called the 'novel virus'?"

"Novel just means new."

Jerry laughed. "Nope, because it's a long story."

It took me a minute to get the pun, and by then, everyone was laughing before me. "Good one."

Tom signaled for us to gather around him. "Welcome to the 228 museum," he began. "Many of us consider February 28, 1947, the defining moment in Taiwan's modern history. On that date there was an anti-government uprising, which was put down violently. After that, we were placed under martial law for the next thirty-eight years." Tom's voice remained soft but it conveyed his suppressed anger.

All the walls were covered with photographs of men and women who disappeared and were never heard from again. "It has taken seventy years to bring the massacres of the White Terror to light—there were as many as twenty-eight thousand murders."

"Never knew any of this," I said to Tom as we headed back to his van.

"Now this is the other side of the coin," Tom said as he led us through the triple gate to the Chiang Kai-shek Memorial Hall, a massive 275-foot-high octagon-shaped white building topped by glistening blue tiles with red accents.

We were stopped at the entrance for yet another temperature check by a young woman wearing a face mask and gloves. "Phil, take a picture of that."

"Why?"

"It's an interesting shot."

Phil gestured for me to keep up with Tom as he led us around the museum that chronicled the president's life and career with pictures, awards, and documents, his uniforms, and even one of his state cars. One display, labeled "The Generalissimo Diet," showed

Mario having his temperature checked at Chiang Kai-shek Memorial Hall in Taipei on January 31.

plastic versions of Chiang's favorite foods. Everything, including the thirty-five-foot-high statue of the president seated in a Lincolnesque pose, was skewed to portray Chiang as a hero, but Tom had made certain we would view the exhibits through a shaded lens.

"I can see why you brought us here after the 228 museum," I said. "It puts all this"—I waved my hand indicating the memorial hall and the surrounding buildings—"in a different light."

After Tom took us to a simple lunch featuring the Taiwanese specialty *xiaolongbao*—a type of steamed bun floating in broth—he helped me and Vana negotiate with a tea seller to purchase the famous Alishan high mountain oolong tea.

"Do they usually take your temperature in public places?" Jerry asked on the way back to the port.

"Never seen it before this week."

"Are you worried about an epidemic in Taiwan?" Vana asked.

"No, because our vice-president, Chen Chien-jen, is a doctor with a specialty in infectious disease. He was the hero of the SARS epidemic, which is why we didn't have many cases here."

"What do you know about Taiwan's president?" Tom asked me since I was in the front seat.

"Sorry, I forgot her name."

"Tsai Ing-wen." He smiled. "Most Americans don't even know she's a woman." He went on to talk about her education in Taiwan, at Cornell Law School, and at the London School of Economics. "She's the first president who isn't married and is of indigenous descent—like my family." He continued to tell me about this progressive, fascinating woman. All day I'd been feeling hopelessly ignorant about the country's history and politics. Travel is supposed to be informative but Hong Kong, Vietnam, and now Taiwan left me with more questions than answers.

THE LAST PORT

Following the tides, riding the waves to the horizon,
How many travelers ever returned?
You may search in the city for wealth and power,
But remember always what happens to sand and waves.

—Po Chu-I (772–846)

Email from Terry, February 1, 2020

A man in New York City is suspected of having the corona-virus after returning from China, and a college student in Boston is in isolation after becoming the eighth confirmed U.S. case of the deadly disease. More countries including Russia barred trips to China and the Hong Kong govern-ment said it may tighten border controls after medical work-ers called a strike to demand more curbs on travel from the mainland.

—Bloomberg

Taiwan had tired us out. We were happy we'd be arriving in Naha, Okinawa, after lunch. It was the last port before the voyage would end in Yokohama three days later. I was already thinking about repacking for the next phase of the trip, which would involve connections between smaller rail lines and high-speed trains. We were going to send our large suitcases to our final hotel in Tokyo, using the highly reliable luggage forwarding service that guarantees delivery anywhere in Japan within twenty-four hours. You can even specify the time you want a package to arrive, not just the day. Our admiration for the country had not dimmed. We had no way of anticipating that a few days later, our most fervent wish would be to leave as quickly as possible.

That morning, though, I was out of sorts. Because we had forgotten to adjust our clocks to a time change after leaving Taiwan, we had woken up so late I couldn't both eat breakfast and go to trivia. I also had a headache.

"Maybe I'll skip breakfast," I said.

"You know that will make your migraine worse," Phil said. I knew he was right. He handed me a cup of steaming tea. My heart surged with gratitude. Phil always brings me morning tea in bed, which he calls "an investment in ensuring a good day for all."

As we entered the Horizon Court, one of the waitstaff smiled pleasantly and diverted the man ahead of me to one of two sinks. He tried to sidestep her, but she gracefully blocked him and he did wash his hands. Princess has sinks at every entrance to the buffet because people share the same serving implements to fill their plates.

I tossed my crumpled paper towel in the trash, but the man kept his in hand. Just as he picked up an empty plate, his head reared back. He caught his bellow of a sneeze in his towel. I stepped around him just in time to see him wipe his hands again with the snotty side of his towel. I froze. I wanted to send him back for another handwashing but figured he would not appreciate interference from a busybody.

I still rethink that moment, wondering whether I should have spoken up—or if it would have mattered. The scourge of cruising is how quickly communicable diseases like colds and flus multiply with so many thousands of people in so little square footage. Most everyone associates cruising with noroviruses—the group of highly contagious gastrointestinal diseases that spread to others mainly from contaminated foods and surfaces. Fever, muscle aches, vomiting, and diarrhea affect people twelve to forty-eight hours after contamination. People can be contagious without any symptoms, and even if someone feels better in a few days, the virus can "shed"—or replicate—in stool for several weeks. Noro, as it's called for short, sweeps through schools, nursing homes, offices, and other places people congregate in large numbers.

The main reason cruise ships are associated with noro is because the CDC tracks the virus on vessels worldwide in real time. When 3 percent of passengers and crew are sick, the ship is required to escalate its Vessel Sanitation Program. Phil and I have been on several ships with noro outbreaks. The crew intensifies routines for sanitizing surfaces like tabletops, handrails, counters, and handles. Salt and pepper shakers are removed from tables. Waiters wearing gloves serve all the food at the buffet, hand out silverware, and close down self-serve beverage stations. Public restroom doors are propped open and everyone is encouraged to use their stateroom bathrooms instead. Anyone who feels ill is supposed to contact the clinic and await instructions. The problem is that many people keep their illness secret, because if diagnosed, they may be restricted to their cabins for three days.

I once asked a ship's doctor why cruise lines had stopped requiring passengers to fill out health forms before boarding. "Because nobody admits to being sick, they're useless," she said.

"How can you prevent contagion if they lie?"

She laughed. "Spies." Apparently, cabin stewards are supposed to report if a guest has not left the room in more than a day. Room service staff will let them know if someone is ordering comfort foods like soup, tea, rice, or bananas, and if there are hints of illness in the bathroom.

When we arrived back at the cabin, there was a message from Jerry suggesting we all meet at noon in our dining room to discuss the new immigration instructions we'd received the night before, along with our disembarkation times.

"The ship's arriving in Okinawa at one-thirty," Jerry said after we were seated. "We've been given a departure time of four."

"We have three," Phil said.

"So is ours," Mario said.

"Our guide's meeting us at two-thirty," I said, since I was in charge of this tour.

"I talked to one of the officers," Jerry said. "The Japanese are insisting that everyone—even the crew—has to disembark and clear inside the terminal."

"Usually the immigration authorities do everything on board," Phil added.

Jerry spoke between clenched teeth. "Any way you look at it, it's going to be a fiasco."

Cathy touched her husband's wrist. "After we order, you guys should exchange the landing cards for the earliest possible slot. Since we're Elite, we're entitled to be in the first group, and you're all allowed to go with us."

"What a hassle," Vana said. "Is it even worth going ashore?"

"We have to go through customs in any case," I said. "I've already texted our guide and told her we might be late." I sipped my iced tea and buttered a warm roll. "I've always wanted to see the cherry blossoms—and today is the start of the cherry blossom festival in Okinawa."

"It's only the first of February. How is that possible?" Vana asked.

"This is the southernmost island, like the Florida of Japan, so their spring starts early too."

Vana, who has a beautifully landscaped yard and loves flowers, couldn't hide her delight. "I hope we can see them."

"What a pain in the butt," Phil said as he returned to his seat. "They said, 'The pace of the inspection is not in our control.'"

"They're canceling all the ship's tours," Jerry added. He held up "Group 1" cards. "They said we should line up at two and try to get as far front as possible. As soon as I finish eating, I'll hold a place at the front of the Elite line."

✦　✦　✦

A four-people-deep queue serpentined around the atrium. We squirmed our way forward, holding up our priority passes. Jerry, wearing his signature red jacket, was easy to spot close to the front.

"Everybody check your documents so nobody will be pulled aside." Jerry called out: "Cruise card, passport, Japanese arrival card—one for each person, not couple—and Japanese customs card, one per family."

A young Princess agent opened the gate strap to allow a group of more than twenty to pass in front of us. "Hey!" and "What the hell?" called a few people behind us.

I inched forward to stand next to Cathy. "How'd it go?" I asked because I knew she had arranged a call with her mother.

"Hard. My mother…she isn't talking. I just spoke 'at' her and I'm not sure she even heard me."

"She heard you," I replied and told her about the day before my father died. "Everybody said he was in a coma. But Robin, my much younger sister, who's a doctor, said that people who come out of comas report conversations they heard. Blake was on the phone telling him a story about a trip they took together when he was twelve to a city in far western China. He said, 'Grampy, remember when you saw a yurt and told the driver to stop the car. You went right up to them and asked if they would give me a camel ride. I can't remember where we were.' My father, who hadn't spoken a word in days, responded, 'Urumqi!'—which was the name of the place!"

Cathy brushed away a tear. "Thanks for that. I did feel like she heard me."

I touched her shoulder. "So hard, I know."

Jerry reached for his wife's hand as we all inched forward to the customs hall. Through the glass windows we saw a dozen agents standing around, but passengers were only being admitted two at a time.

"Look at this sign," I said to Phil. "They aren't kidding around." I snapped a picture because it seemed to be "shouting" in several languages, including English. There were all caps, underlines, highlights, and a map of China showing the location of Wuhan City and another of the province indicating the area of concern. It read: "Novel coronavirus pneumonia cases have occurred in WUHAN CITY, Hubei Province of China. If you arrived from WUHAN CITY with symptoms such as **cough** or **fever** or **are taking cough suppressants** and/or **antipyretics,** please contact a **quarantine officer.**"

When my turn came, an agent beamed an infrared thermometer at my forehead, checked the reading, and waved us on.

"Only one thermometer for thousands of people," Phil said. "That's ridiculous."

At the first counter, Phil handed in the pile of forms we had filled out, only to be given yet another—in Japanese—accompanied by a similar, but not exact, one in English, which we were to use as a guide. Then we each had to answer the same inquiries orally and have fingerprints taken. Once cleared to enter Japan, we were directed down a stairway, where our guide, a young woman named Masumi, was holding up a sign with my name on it. She looked calm, but we were over an hour late.

✦ ✦ ✦

By the time we made it to Masumi's van, we were all cranky. I turned to Mario and asked, "What's with all this temperature taking? I realize it's the first obvious sign of coronavirus, but can people be infectious before they spike a fever?"

"We don't know enough about it yet," he said, "but yes, many viruses are infectious before there are symptoms. That's why childhood diseases like chickenpox and measles spread rapidly in an unvaccinated population."

"Crowding everyone in lines for hours is the perfect way to infect more people," Vana added.

"Except that we've been fairly isolated from others over the past few weeks," Phil said.

"Come on!" Vana's voice sounded like a stretched rubber band. "We've been in how many cities and countries in the last week? All of them in Asia. In Vietnam, we were a stone's throw from the Chinese border."

"Don't worry," Masumi said in a sweet, lilting voice, "nobody's been sick in Okinawa yet."

"Do they usually do health inspections here?" I asked her.

"No, this may be the first time for the temperatures and I don't think they've ever requested that everyone get off the ship." She sighed. "I am so sorry you went through that. We Japanese take these infectious diseases very seriously. As a nation of many islands, we are naturally isolated from the rest of the world. That fact affects every aspect of our history and culture. In some ways, it has hindered our growth, but if we feel threatened by an enemy—even an illness—we can close air- and seaports and limit who comes or goes very swiftly."

There was no way of knowing that I would soon be analyzing what else I knew about the psyche of the Japanese and their approach to both isolationism and self-determination.

"This island was flattened during the war." I tuned back in to Masumi's history of Okinawa. "Half the population was killed." She pointed to a modern skyline that looked more like Miami than Japan. "Almost everything you see is postwar construction, although some of our historic sites have been restored."

Mario, who specializes in geriatrics, turned to Masumi. "Is it true that you have many people who live to over one hundred here?"

"Ah, you have heard about our Island of the Immortals. We have four times as many centenarians here as anywhere on earth. Even though we have many elderly, Alzheimer's is almost unknown. Supposedly, the secret is our diet—most everything is fresh and raw and mostly plant-based."

"What is a typical meal?" Vana asked.

"Tofu, bitter melon, seafood, and nori—seaweed. You must try our famous purple sweet potatoes—they make up more than sixty percent of our diet." She went on, "Another thing, we try not to overeat. Ushi Okushima, who lived to be one hundred and nine, often was asked her secret. She said, 'Eat until you are eight-tenths full.'"

"Did you hear that, Jerry?" Cathy called to her husband, sitting in the van's back row.

"Also, Okinawans like fresh air and relaxation. If we had more time, I would take you to Ogimi, which claims it is the longest-living village in Japan." She went on to tell us they have a monument that reads: "At eighty years old, I am still a child. When heaven calls for you at ninety say, 'Go away and come back when I am a hundred.' Let us keep going strong as we get older, and not depend too much on our children in old age."

"I like that very much," said Mario.

✦ ✦ ✦

We turned down a lane into the Shikinaen Royal Garden.

"It's unusual to see this parking lot this empty, especially when there's a ship in port," Masumi said as we passed between rows of ancient banyan trees each with their aerial roots creating a miniature mystical forest.

We strolled the classic circular garden, crossed over the arched bridge, and admired the hexagonal building in the middle of the pond. I lingered behind, noting the symmetry from almost every angle as an egret regarded his reflection in the silvery water. Swirls from a trickling stream looked like Japanese writing. This was a moment I wanted to memorize: the ancient garden was the essence of everything I loved about Japan. The Japanese have a philosophy called *ikigai,* which is difficult to define but revolves around an individual's reason for being—not unlike the French *raison d'etre.* Whether we like it or not, I thought, Phil and I are entering the last stage of life, which in terms of Erik Erikson's "Stages of Development" is defined as "Ego Integrity versus Despair." As we reflect on the arc of our lives, we can either feel a sense of satisfaction for our accomplishments or decide that we have failed to contribute to the world. At that moment, I had an overwhelming sense of peace because I had few regrets. I knew we would leave many legacies, including our very capable and contributing children, our hundreds of documentary and educational films—many illuminating social issues and offering solutions, some just to entertain. Both of us have written enough books to fill a short shelf. We have volunteered our time generously to foster and adoption issues. But as I gazed at a hibiscus bush, I sensed an incompleteness. I'm not done yet, I thought, and I felt pressure to complete whatever it was that I had not yet begun.

Maybe *ikigai* held the answer. I've seen diagrams of four intersecting circles that try to explain its sweet spot as the very center, not unlike the mysterious core of a flower. The petals are for attracting the pollinator but the business of seed creation is hidden deep inside the ovule. I was wondering what seeds I could still sow when Vana's voice broke my meditation.

"Cherry blossoms! Over here!"

There was one—one!—cherry tree in bloom, but the flowers looked much smaller than the traditional *sakura*. "This is a different species," Masumi said. "It does better in a warmer climate." Even so, we took selfies for the record, not realizing it would be our last free moment on land for more than a month.

GROUNDHOG DAY

*Once you have traveled, the voyage never ends, but is played
out over and over again in the quietest chambers. The mind
can never break off from the journey.*

— Pat Conroy

"Today's the day!" I announced when we joined our friends for
breakfast in the dining room the next morning, February 2. It was
our second-to-last sea day.

"You're in a great mood," Vana commented.

"What's not to like? Two final sea days and then a week of
pampering at the *ryokans*."

"What is this the day for?" Mario asked, getting back to my
declaration.

"Princess's famous James Beard French toast. Michael said you
could order it any day, but I've been putting it off because it's so
rich and sinful."

"I've tried to make it," Phil, who cooks breakfast every morning, said, "but it's tricky."

"Yours might need more nutmeg." I turned to Vana. "Crushed cornflakes are the secret ingredient. After dipping the bread in the milk-and-egg mixture, you press both sides into the cornflakes before frying them in butter. Then you sprinkle the toast with sugar and bake in the oven until the sugar melts."

Several others ordered it as well.

"Tonight is the best show of the cruise," Cathy said. "Have you seen *Bravo!* before?"

"My favorite too," I said, because the music—especially the operatic songs—was more to my taste. "They fly in singers just for this show. Tonight they're featuring Mia Flores, a Filipina soloist. Mario, you'll love it."

"I'm going to start packing," Cathy said.

"I refuse to think about it until tomorrow. Besides, my dance card is full," I said. I held up a list. "I've decided to do every single thing of interest. I'm going to milk this day for all it's worth."

Michael brought us tall glasses of fresh orange juice and passed an array of rolls and pastries. "Today is Groundhog Day," I said. "I'd be content just reliving this sea day over and over until it's perfect."

Jerry turned to Mario. "I don't understand why everyone is getting freaked out over this new virus. It's just a bad flu, right?"

"That's hard to say at this point," Mario said.

"I looked it up. Between nine and forty-five million illnesses are attributed to the flu each year with between twelve and sixty thousand deaths annually in the United States alone. So why they're getting all worked up over nineteen thousand cases and four hundred deaths in Wuhan—which sounds like a lot until you realize the province's population is over sixty million people?"

"Leave it to Jerry to have all the stats," I said.

"He's better than a calculator," his wife agreed.

Mario finally responded. "I'm worried about what we don't yet know. Does it require close contact with someone who is sick, or can it be transmitted on surfaces like railings and counters?"

"At least we've all been vaccinated against the flu," Vana said.

"But last year the vaccine was only forty or fifty percent effective," Jerry continued.

Michael served our breakfast platters.

"Carpe diem!" I cut my first piece of French toast. The center was just the right creamy consistency. "I definitely could do this again tomorrow!"

✦ ✦ ✦

Email from Terry, February 2, 2020

The Wuhan coronavirus spreading from China is now likely to become a pandemic that circles the globe, according to many of the world's leading infectious disease experts. The prospect is daunting. A pandemic—an ongoing epidemic on two or more continents—may well have global consequences, despite the extraordinary travel restrictions and quarantines now imposed by China and other countries, including the United States. Scientists do not yet know how lethal the new coronavirus is, however, so there is uncertainty about how much damage a pandemic might cause. But there is growing consensus that the pathogen is readily transmitted between humans. The Wuhan coronavirus is spreading more like influenza, which is highly transmissible, than like its slow-moving viral cousins, SARS and MERS, scientists have found.

—*New York Times*

Jerry, who was beginning to enjoy trivia, joined me for the first quiz in the morning, "I'm meeting Phil in the Horizon Court for make-it-yourself ramen," I said by way of an invitation on the way out.

"Sorry, but we're was going to try to connect with Cathy's mom for another video call."

"Good luck," I said, hoping her mother would rouse long enough to say a few words.

"What's next on your busy agenda?" Phil asked as we loudly slurped our soup to prove to the Japanese at the neighboring table that we knew the custom.

"The Lost in Translation quiz."

"Sounds amusing. Do you mind if I take some video?"

Karen, who usually came to afternoon trivia, waved me over as we walked into Club Fusion. "We have three Japanese but need two more English speakers." She looked hopefully at Phil.

"Not playing."

I saw a woman standing alone and looking around. "Want to join us?" I asked and she accepted gratefully, saying her name was Meg.

Karen passed around pieces of paper and we each wrote our names in English, as did the tallest Japanese woman. Karen gestured for the Japanese ladies to say their names and she wrote them in English on their sheets. It took a few minutes before we had mastered each other's names, which didn't bode well for us communicating during the game.

The six of us were gathered around a small cocktail table. Some of the questions were visual. A portrait flashed on a screen. If it was a Japanese celebrity, an international guest had to memorize the name, run up to the moderator, and pronounce it correctly, which was not as easy as it sounded. No matter, it was a lot of fun, especially when the questions escalated to tongue twisters. We had to teach our counterparts how to say "She sells seashells by the seashore." Karen scored with "*Nama-mugi nama-gome nama-tamago,*" meaning "raw wheat, raw rice, raw eggs."

"You did great," Phil said to Karen on the way out. "And I have the video to prove it."

Meg was walking beside me and I introduced her to Phil. "Are you going to the dance contest?" she asked us. "I promised our waiter we'd root for him. We heard he's an awesome dancer."

We decided to follow along. The atrium was standing room only on all three levels. "I'll try and shoot it from above," Phil said while I squeezed toward the front.

Six men and six women passengers who had volunteered were randomly selected and matched with partners from the crew and entertainment staff. Several were members of the Princess dance company. I was in awe of the professional women dancers who managed tricky routines in high heels on the high seas. Meg's Indonesian waiter was matched with a petite Japanese woman, who I had seen dancing in the atrium with her husband. They would have given Fred and Ginger some competition.

Everyone cheered the couples who had never met before, especially the burly woman security official and her much shorter partner. There were several elimination rounds until finally the tiny Japanese woman and the Indonesian waiter competed with one

The dance contest on February 2, our second-to-last sea day.

of the professional dancers and a tall, silver-haired passenger. The waiter had more nimble moves and his partner precisely nailed his rhythm and mood. Each round the music changed from fast to slow and from salsa to tango to waltz and they seamlessly came together and parted. At the finish, the audience stood and cheered as the waiter lifted her as easily as an Olympic pair-skating contestant, cradling her in his arms as the finale to a sensual tango. I wriggled through the throng to Natalie, the cruise director, and said, "That's the best performance I've ever seen on a ship."

"Just marvelous," she agreed.

✦ ✦ ✦

Captain Arma was giving his final cocktail party in the atrium. "We've missed every opportunity to meet him," I said to Phil as I saw a long line waiting to shake his hand.

"You're the one who asked everyone for an early dinner, so we shouldn't keep our friends waiting."

I glanced wistfully in the captain's direction and would have dearly loved a photo souvenir—he looked far more like a celebrity than a sailor—but I didn't want to be seen as a dotty old lady.

At dinner I just ordered two appetizers in order to leave early for the "All About Japan" quiz. "We have a chance to win this."

"I've never seen you so competitive," Vana said.

"Don't worry, I'll go back into my meek little writer shell tomorrow."

At that, everyone laughed. "I'll show you!" I said in jest as I left the table.

Karen and I, along with our frequent trivia buddies James and Debbie, were in top form. The two of us admitted to cramming on Japan facts. We high-fived and got down to business.

"Kurosawa's film *The Hidden Fortress* was the basis for what famous film?" Karen wrote *Star Wars* on our answer sheet.

"What Japanese word means Land of the Rising Sun?" I scrawled, "Nippon."

"True or false: Each Spring, the Japanese celebrate the Festival of the Steel Phallus?" Debbie marked a "T."

"What country has the largest Japanese population outside of Japan?" I knew it was Brazil.

We scored eighteen out of twenty, with the next team getting only twelve. The prize for the five of us was a solitary bottle of Champagne. "I have to meet Phil in the theater," I said. "You enjoy it."

"We're going too," James said. "Let's share it tomorrow at the last quiz."

When I reached the theater, Phil waved to me and I found the saved seat. It was standing room only for *Bravo!*

"I could have sold your seat," Phil said. "Did you win?" I nodded. "Then the entire trip has been a success!"

The lights dimmed. "Listen," I whispered to Phil.

"What?"

"Nobody's coughing! By this time on a cruise, half the place usually has the dreaded cough. I think we may have dodged a bullet, especially this time of year." The curtain parted. Phil gave me a thumb's up.

The soloists were excellent, even if the musical selections were sanitized classics like "Nessun Dorma" and "Con te partirò"—which is always the finale because it means "no time to say goodbye." Giulia always laughs about the lyrics: They don't make sense in Italian or any language because the characters are saying farewell to places they've never been and heading off on ships that no longer exist. Still, it hits all the right notes of loss and longing and leaves the audience ready to sign up for another cruise.

A standing ovation...a reprise of the song by the whole cast.... I chuckled as I thought: This could be the *Groundhog Day* theme song.

OH, MY GOD!

Life is shocking, but you must never appear to be shocked. For no matter how bad it is it could be worse and no matter how good it is it could be better.

— Maya Angelou

"Seriously, Gay, do you have to go to trivia this morning? I really want to sort out the gifts and souvenirs. They'll fill at least one suitcase. Then I'll pack another one with what we're not taking to the *ryokans*, but you might need in Tokyo."

"I promise I'll do it as soon as the game is over."

After the high of the night before, the match was anticlimactic. I kept my word and promptly returned to the cabin. The bed was heaped with purchases. "I had no idea—"

"Now you see the problem?"

"That's why we packed the folding duffel." I pulled out our "emergency" bag.

"Isn't there anything you can leave behind?"

"Like what? My shoes?"

"Seriously, Gay…"

I reached into a pocket of my largest suitcase and produced a paperback-sized nylon pouch. "It's a Wandf—and it's huge." I unzipped, unfolded, and demonstrated the voluminous capacity.

"You realize we're up to four large bags and two carry-ons?"

"Since we're flying first class, there won't be any extra charges."

After I gave Phil everything we didn't have to see again until we were home, I spent some time organizing all the paperwork for our ongoing trip and changing our pick-up time for the next morning because Phil worried we were cutting it too close to make our first train. We then met Katherine and Marlene in the main dining room for lunch to say goodbye and pick some tentative dates for our trip to Australia. After that, it was back to packing.

I emptied the desk of all the *Princess Patters* and port maps. "Why don't you dump all that?"

"I might use it as research for my next cruise mystery. *The Girl in the Box* took place on the Atlantic, so the next might be the Pacific. I even have the title: *The Man in the Lifeboat.*"

Phil looked dubious but he knew it was pointless to argue. I checked the time. I was almost late for the very last trivia.

"What is someone with ailurophobia afraid of?" The assistant cruise director had already asked the first question.

I pulled a nearby chair close to James, Debbie, and Karen. Karen had written down "cats" on the scratch paper.

"Yep," I said.

The tiny round cocktail table held our bottle of Champagne on ice and two cups of peanuts. Debbie had moved the glasses to the ledge behind her to make room for the answer sheet. Once the game was over, we were delighted to be tied for first place. The other team was closer on the tiebreaker: "What's the height of Mount Fuji?"

Who cares? James popped the cork and poured the too-sweet Champagne. No matter, I thought, I'll be having the Krug Grand

Cuveé on the flight home in a week. Karen said she wanted to order one of my books. I handed her a calling card. She was heading to northern California; the others were returning to Melbourne. I didn't know their last names or professions. Unless you really click, shipboard friendships are temporary and superficial. I declined a second glass of bubbly. "Phil wants our bags out in the hall before supper," I said.

James shot his wife a knowing glance. "Don't look at me," she said. "My bag is locked and loaded."

We hugged and said our farewells. James looked at Karen's glass. "You going to finish that?" She shook her head and he drank it down, a meaningless gesture at the time and yet it turned into a freeze-frame I would long remember.

I hightailed it back to the room just as Mario knocked on our balcony door carrying two beers. "I hope it's going better at your end," Phil said, indicating the piles of my clothes covering every surface of our cabin.

"I just wanted to thank you," Mario said. "It's been an amazing trip. Everything has worked out perfectly."

"I'm really glad." I felt relieved. "Seventy-five and still alive," I added. Mario and I were two of the three milestone birthday people.

Just then, we heard Captain Arma's mellifluous voice over the loudspeaker.

> Ladies and gentlemen, please be advised that we have been notified by the Hong Kong authorities that a Hong Kong resident who traveled for five days from Yokohama to Hong Kong, disembarking in Hong Kong on January twenty-five, tested positive for coronavirus on February first—five days after leaving the vessel. He did not report any illness or symptoms to the ship's medical center during the voyage and the fever was not detected during the screening on arrival in Hong

Kong. He is currently reported to be in a stable condition and his family traveling companions remain symptom free. We have proactively shared all relevant data for this voyage with the Japanese health authorities, and as is standard practice with all coronavirus cases, they have informed us they will conduct a review of the vessel upon arrival.

Vana rushed into the room, tying her bathrobe. "What? Someone has coronavirus on board!"

Mario held up his hand for her to be quiet. "…This will likely result in delays while they review health records and will likely conduct interviews along with additional medical screening. Hence, to facilitate the review, we will be arriving Yokohama earlier this evening [than planned] and I will keep you updated with the information on the evolution of the evolving situation."

"What does this mean?" Vana dropped on the couch beside Mario.

I hushed her as the captain continued. Even with my hearing aids I found it difficult to understand his accent. He was talking about "managing potential delays" and added, "Please be assured that the safety, security, and well-being of our guests and crew is our absolute priority."

"I don't like the sound of this at all," Phil said.

"….Monitoring people with cold and flu symptoms…"

"At least our plane doesn't leave until Wednesday," Mario said.

"We are also conducting an additional, intensive environmental disinfection…"

"We have a train at ten in the morning," I said.

"Shush," Phil said, pointing to the speaker in the ceiling.

"We have also made a delay in the embarkation of the next cruise by twenty-four hours to accommodate any potential delays," the captain added.

"What the hell?" Phil shouted.

"I thank you for your patience and understanding while we deal with this dynamic event and I'd like to assure you once again at present there are no reasons for concerns. Like I said, as the situation evolves and dictates, I will make a further broadcast in the course of the evening. Thank you."

"Wait, does that mean we're not getting off tomorrow?" Phil said, seething.

"That's not what he said," I replied. "They've delayed the *next sailing* by a day because those people would have started embarking around noon."

"That guy could have contaminated the whole ship!" Vana said, choking on her words.

"Not necessarily," said Mario, using the calm voice that soothes his patients. "He was only on board for five days."

She squeezed her husband's arm. "We could be sick already and not even know it."

"The chances are slim that we were anywhere near him," Mario countered.

"Remember we ended up departing Hong Kong late because they kept calling for passengers who hadn't returned?" Vana's voice became strident. "Maybe he was feeling sick then and decided he'd rather be in his own bed."

"If that's true," I asked, "why didn't he test positive for six more days?"

"We're all going to get this." Vana moaned.

I recalled our conversation before we'd even left Florida when she was talking about canceling. "I want to come up with a reason to disagree with you, Vana," I said, "but now I think you may have been right all along."

"This ship is huge," Phil said, rubbing his temples, "and we've mostly kept to ourselves. Even our dining room is small."

"Do you think the fact that we haven't been on any big bus tours or been in many crowded venues has been safer?" I asked Mario.

"I won't know until I find out whether the CDC has established an R naught number yet."

"What's that?" I asked.

"It's written like the letters R and 0 for zero." Mario wrote in the air. "It quantifies how transmissible it is. For instance, if R is less than one, each person who is infectious causes fewer than one other case—which is why the disease peters out. If someone infects one more person, the disease continues to spread, but it won't cause an epidemic."

"Most childhood illnesses are transmitted to many, many others," Vana said. "A single case of chickenpox can infect ten to twelve kids." She ran her fingers through her hair. "It makes me crazy when I hear of parents who have chickenpox parties so everybody will be sick simultaneously and they won't have to deal with it again."

"But there's a vaccine—"

She cut me off. "Don't get me started."

"This R naught," Phil asked Mario, "does it apply when most of the population has been vaccinated?"

"No, it's when nobody in a group has had the disease, nobody's immune because of a vaccine or a previous case, and there are no control measures in place."

"You mean a disease like Ebola?" Phil asked.

"That's a question for an infectious disease doctor."

"Or Google." Phil pointed to me. I was already looking it up.

"Actually…" I began, "Ebola's not that bad—at least not in terms of catchability—if that's a word—just a bit worse than the swine flu. Seasonal flu is only point nine to two point one. Yikes! Measles is twelve to eighteen."

"What's SARS?" Mario asked.

"Less than one to two point seventy-five. Why?"

"This one should be similar," Mario said, "which does make it more transmissible than the flu."

"That's theoretical," Vana said, "but if we were in the same buffet line or on the same elevator with that guy, then we're done for."

"Need some fresh air," Phil said, opening the balcony door. We followed him out.

I took a deep inhalation of Vitamin Sea. "Maybe he was planning to disembark Hong Kong anyway," I said.

"Then why were they calling someone named Mister Wu over the loudspeaker to return?" Vana asked.

"We don't know if Mister Wu is the man's name, do we?" I said.

"It's a mystery," Vana conceded.

"And right up Gay's alley," Phil quipped. He put his arm around my shoulder. "You should write your next novel about the Year of the Rat bringing a plague on board." Then he abruptly switched gears. "I can't wait to get off this ship." He turned to me. "Why don't we see if we can disembark later tonight and get a hotel near the train station?"

"We'll meet you downstairs," Mario said, steering his wife out so we could talk privately.

Phil and I were supposed to be met at eight the next morning by a driver who would take us to the train station in Yokohama so we could continue our vacation with the sojourn in the Japanese countryside. If we missed the first train, we wouldn't make the connection to the Izu peninsula.

"I already moved the pick-up time an hour earlier."

"You're right. I'm just jumpy."

"Me, too. I'm trying to be rational to keep everyone calm, but inside I'm freaking out. How long have they known that man was sick? And why are they telling us now? He might have been unwell even before he boarded the ship."

"He probably contracted it from someone who had been to China—or he could have visited China himself."

"And remember the crowds at the terminal for embarkation?" I continued. "There were lots of Chinese in line with us. And what about that clusterfuck of a line in Okinawa? James and Debbie told me that they were in it for five hours! The Japanese immigration authorities had to have some serious concerns."

Phil looked distressed. "Wouldn't it would be horrible if we infected Masumi or our driver? Plus, the town was crawling with other passengers."

"Supposedly older people are more vulnerable, right? We may have killed off the centenarians of Okinawa!"

Phil smoothed my hair. "You're letting your imagination run away with you."

"No, Phil. I've felt it for a few days now. I keep trying to bottle it up. Do you know how easy it is to get to anywhere in China from Hong Kong? For all we know this man was in Wuhan before he boarded the ship." I started to look at a map in my phone.

"We're going to be late for dinner."

"Just a sec. Okay, as of today, there are over twenty thousand cases of the coronavirus in twenty-four countries, according to the World Health Organization…four hundred and twenty-six deaths thus far, all except one in China."

Phil steered me to the door. "Keep that to yourself, okay?"

✦ ✦ ✦

Mario and Vana were waiting for us outside the dining room. I looked around and saw Jerry and Cathy exiting.

"Have you eaten already?" Phil asked.

"No, we decided to have a quiet dinner at Sabatini's," Jerry said. "It's Cathy's favorite. We just stopped by to leave our tips for the waitstaff and to say goodbye to you in case we miss you in the morning."

I understood why they wanted to be alone. Last we heard, Mary Lou Dowd was just hanging on. "Any news?" I asked Cathy.

"It's the middle of the night there. I told them to wake me if anything changes."

"I'm very sorry," Phil said to Cathy, then turned to Jerry. "What do you think is going on? I thought we cleared immigration the day before yesterday in Okinawa."

With so many cruises behind him, Jerry usually has a good handle on what's happening behind the scenes. "That was before they knew about the man from Hong Kong," Jerry said softly, out of Cathy's hearing. "What are the chances?"

"At least we weren't planning to fly out tomorrow," Vana said. The two couples were taking a shuttle to an airport hotel, where they'd stay before their flights home the following day. "A few hours' delay won't bother us."

"We're screwed if we miss our morning train," Phil said. He reached to shake Jerry's hand.

I hugged Cathy. "Text me, okay?"

Phil steered me to the dining room. Vana was wearing a pristine white jacket with large black buttons in a stylish cut that flattered her curves but would have made me look dumpy. Not only does she have an eye for fashion, the outfit had made it through our whole trip spotless. "That gorgeous jacket wouldn't last through the appetizer with me," I said.

"Did you put any bags out in the hall for pickup yet?" Mario asked.

"Are you kidding?" Phil looked at me tenderly, but his voice had an edge of impatience. "So…" He counted on his fingers.

"We're up to six pieces of luggage, two backpacks, and that travel purse she wears across her chest."

I smiled at Mario. "Don't worry, I have the medical pack in my rollaboard." It's a running joke that he and Vana have to ask me for medical supplies.

"Ours are ready to go," Vana said with a touch of smugness.

For obvious reasons, the last dinner on board is designed to be memorable. Phil and I ordered the escargot and lobster risotto. "The first time I ever had escargot was on the *Ile de France* in about 1956," I said. "It was my family's first cruise." I stabbed a snail without looking at it. Sure enough, I splashed some garlic butter on my Mandarin jacket, but it kept my secret.

Phil was facing the windows. "Look, the lights of Yokohama. They really did speed up. We weren't supposed to get in until early morning."

After dinner, I finished our packing as quickly as possible. When each bag was closed and tagged, Phil put it outside our cabin door. But before he had the last one out, Edwin knocked. "Not tonight," he said and slid the bags back into the cabin. He also handed Phil some paperwork.

"Apparently, we're not going anywhere," Phil said, dispirited.

"What about the two thousand people expecting to board the ship tomorrow?"

Phil looked at the forms.

"What are those?"

"Health questionnaires. We're supposed to let them know if we have a fever, cough—the usual."

"I thought everyone lies, which is why they don't bother."

"These are from the Japanese health department." Phil tossed them on the desk. "They're going to examine us and take our temperatures, going room to room all night."

"I'll send a message to the travel agency to see what alternatives there are. If we miss one night, it won't be the worst thing in the world." I opened the balcony door and beckoned to Phil. "Look, we're anchored in the harbor instead of being at the quay." I pointed to where a Coast Guard vessel was bobbing by an open door—the one usually used by the pilots who go to the bridge to guide ships in crowded harbors.

"Who's getting on the ship this time of night?" he asked.

"Maybe the health inspectors?"

A helicopter was circling the ship. "I feel like everything is closing in…"

Phil got into bed and started switching among the few English-language news channels: CNN, FOX, CNBC, BBC, and ABC Australia.

"Anything about our ship?"

"It wouldn't be on the news yet."

"That could have been a news helicopter. Just in case the kids hear about the ship, I'm going to tell them we're delayed."

"Coming to bed?"

Japanese health officials boarding the *Diamond Princess* in Yokohama Harbor.

"In a few minutes," I said, thinking I might as well stay up in case they came to take our temperature soon. Plus, my curiosity was aroused. Phil turned off the television. I pulled up the extra blanket we used on the couch and thought about our predicament.

At home I had a whole shelf of books about the history of medicine and various plagues, which I used to research my novels. In *River of Dreams* my heroine comes down with dengue fever; in *The Midwife* Hannah survives the 1918 influenza. Medical mysteries have always fascinated me, especially zoonotic diseases, those transmitted between animals and people like dengue, Ebola and SARS, swine and avian flu.

Here it was only a few days into February. At Christmas nobody had ever heard of this disease and now there were twenty thousand cases in more than twenty countries. It had been confined to China until mid-January, but every few days it popped up in another locale.

I checked my emails. There was a response from Inside Japan Tours with ideas about salvaging the trip. I wrote saying I would let them know as soon as we had more information. Then I sent a group email to the kids telling them about the delay in a lighthearted way so they wouldn't think we were in danger. But were we?

One man who was on our ship had the virus. Was he contagious before he had symptoms or only after? No matter, he had the potential to infect others. The *Diamond Princess* had more than thirty-seven hundred souls on board. If Mr. Hong Kong had infected two people a day for the five days he was on board, and they each infected two people…. I knew how that ended based on the tale about a sage who made a deal with a maharajah over a chess game. If the wealthy man lost, he would owe the sage only one grain of rice for the first square, two for the second, doubling until he reached the sixty-fourth square. But the debt could never be paid because by the twentieth square, the maharajah would have had to deliver a million grains of rice, and by the sixty-fourth, the amount was over two hundred and ten billion tons, enough to cover India with a meter-thick layer of rice. This was a classic example of exponential growth. No wonder the Chinese had locked down Wuhan! If they hadn't used draconian measures, this could turn into the worst pandemic in human history.

I climbed into bed and tried to relax, but doomsday scenarios kept agitating me. I went back to where my iPhone was charging. Somebody needs to know what's happening here…somebody who can investigate and…advocate…and get us the hell off this ship. Many years ago, a journalist at ABC News produced a story about my book *I Speak for this Child: True Stories of a Child Advocate*. Later, he took an interest in Ashley's story, then when Diane Sawyer was working on a special about juvenile justice, he asked me to consult on the project. Lately, we were Facebook friends. Maybe he would have some ideas.…

To: Jon M.

Subject: Guess where we are?

Thought you might be interested that we are in Yokohama harbor on the *Diamond Princess*. We were supposed to disembark tomorrow, but the news is that a passenger who disembarked in Hong Kong has tested positive. We were in Hong Kong Jan 25 just for the day. About 300 Chinese on board. Now we are waiting for Japanese authorities to do health checks. No word on what will happen next. Stay tuned. Will report if it gets interesting.

I hesitated briefly, then pressed "send." Finally, I went to bed but slept fitfully, anticipating the knock on the door for the temperature check. It never came.

✦ ✦ ✦

The next morning, the captain announced that thus far only half the passengers had been seen by the Japanese public health officers, so our departure definitely would be delayed for twenty-four hours and there was no chance of getting off the ship that day. "Please be advised that you may be required to undergo additional health screening by local health officials before you disembark the ship or exit the terminal," the captain concluded. We were free to roam the ship, he said, but we needed to return to our cabins when they announced that the inspectors were coming to our deck.

Jerry called everyone to meet for breakfast in the dining room.

"Guess you weren't expecting to see us again?" Phil said to Michael, who nodded perfunctorily. For an awkward moment we wondered if Michael had been displeased with our tips, which we thought had been generous.

Jerry leaned forward and whispered, "If we had stiffed them, we could never eat in the dining room again." Nobody laughed.

Cathy broke the edgy silence. "I guess it is Groundhog Day after all."

"This feels like a nightmare," Vana said. "Do you think we should move our flight home ahead one more day?"

"We canceled the airport hotel," Jerry said, "and will go directly to the airport tomorrow. We're still hoping Cathy can visit Mary Lou."

"We can move our reservations one more day, but that's the latest we can leave because Mario has to cover the practice Friday. What do you think we should do?" Vana asked.

"Why don't you play it safe if that will give you some peace of mind?" Phil said.

I shook my head. "I don't think we're going anywhere this afternoon or even tomorrow."

"Since when did you turn into Miss Gloom-and-Doom?" Phil said in a teasing voice.

"It's the vibes in this room. I think the crew knows more than we do."

Phil kicked me under the table—his signal to shut me up.

We all concentrated on our food after that, and as soon as he finished eating, Phil moved his chair back unexpectedly. "Let's go for a walk."

Once we were on the deck, he said, "Don't get involved in their arrangements. We don't know any more than they do."

"I'm worried about their change fees and points and—"

"We can't figure anything out until we have a better idea of when we can get the hell off this ship."

I looked down at my phone and saw a lot of new messages. "Oh, boy," I said.

"What?"

"Last night…well…" I told him about my email to Jon. "I need to go back to the room to answer these. The Wi-Fi signal here sucks."

A few minutes later, I counted more than fifteen emails from various people at ABC News. "I had no idea anyone would even care!" I scanned each one. "I guess Jon told them we do documentaries. They're asking for footage—and wait, more than that. *Good Morning America* wants you to film me on-camera to explain what's happening. They've attached an aerial shot of the ship."

"Must be from that helicopter."

"Should we do it?"

"I can't see any harm." He sighed. "I'm just sorry I didn't bring my new Canon RP with all the lenses and my laptop with Final Cut Pro. I expected to need it in Africa, but not on a cruise."

"I'm hoping we'll get off tomorrow without incident and the story will fizzle," I said as I unpacked my cosmetics bag. I made faces at myself in the mirror. I've never mastered all the creams, blushes, and eyeliners and I wished that Ashley, who is a magician with hair and makeup, were there. Then I remembered that a Japanese friend once admitted that women wear masks when they don't have time to do their makeup. I put on one of the ones I'd bought in Vietnam. "My new look," I said.

"What? I can't understand you with that thing on."

Phil shooed away the one I handed him. "Humor me," I said, "just until we're off this ship of fools."

✦   ✦   ✦

When we went out on deck again, I saw the ship more from the point of view of a producer thinking about what shots would be emblematic of the situation. Phil had replaced his iPhone with his pocket-sized camcorder. "Is that much better than your phone?" I asked jokingly.

Phil pointed the camera at me and emoted as though he was a spokesman for the manufacturer. "The powerful Sony FDR-AX33 gives me incomparable rock-steady hand-held shooting even at the longest focal length."

"Oh, baby, I love it when you talk like that," I said, pretending to swoon.

We passed the passenger service desk, where a long line of people was waiting with questions about their travel arrangements. "Get some shots of that."

"Why? Everyone looks frantic and pissed off."

"That's the point. What a difference a day makes."

Up on deck, I walked to a railing overlooking a giant movie screen. They were showing a classical music concert and a Strauss waltz was playing. "It's just like the *Titanic*. The orchestra doesn't miss a beat while the ship is sinking." I got in position for a standup in front of the screen. It took several takes—with and

Doing a stand-up for ABC February 4, when passengers were still allowed to roam the ship while waiting for health checks.

without the mask—to get what I was saying matched with the right piece of the music. "How about a shot of all those mah-jongg players. What if the gentleman from Hong Kong played mah-jongg? Everybody's touching the same tiles, drinking, eating, breathing close to each other."

I kept pointing out little scenes that suddenly had taken on a second meaning. Was that child sleeping in her grandmother's arms feverish? Was that Korean couple arguing about whether they had to submit to a Japanese health inspection? What about the group of fraternity boys with several pitchers of beer before lunch? Were they partying or drowning their sorrows?

The loudspeaker crackled. "Will the passengers on Dolphin Deck starboard side please return to your cabins for your health check."

"That's us," Phil said.

As we waited for the elevator, I started thinking about what my father once told me as we suffered through a long airline delay: "When you travel you're in a zone I call 'limbo' because you're trapped in a system you can't control. All you can do is relax and let it all happen around you until you arrive." He then crossed his arms, closed his eyes, and fell asleep in a straight-backed chair. While I've never mastered that skill, I knew this was a limbo moment. We had no choice but to submit to the authorities until we could regain the reins and make decisions about our next move.

Back in the room, I found a Coke in the fridge. "Want to share?" Phil nodded and I poured him a glass, then checked my emails. Nothing new from New York, where it was the middle of the night. "Hey, listen to this?" I said to Phil. "Here's an email from someone with the Beijing bureau of ABC News—they're on our time. He says we can send our video diary and photos to him and he'll make sure they get it in the morning."

"Isn't that convenient?" Phil said facetiously.

"C'mon. This is fun."

"Well, your mood has picked up."

"Making the best of it." I glanced at the rest of the message. "How sweet! He wants to know if I'm the author of *The Midwife* and *Code Ezra*."

My momentary high was interrupted by a double knock on the door. Two very young-looking men wearing masks and gloves took only a few steps inside. One touched the tip of an infrared thermometer to my ear and the other wrote down the reading. Without cleaning it, they did the same to Phil.

"Okay?" Phil asked expectantly. One of them bowed slightly. The other pulled a piece of paper from his clipboard and waved it at us.

"Oh, the health sheet." I looked on the desk but didn't see our filled-out questionnaires.

"I put them right there," Phil said tensely.

"Oh, here." They were under a *New Yorker*. I double-checked to see I had all the pages of both forms. The heading, which I hadn't noticed before, caught my eye. I pointed it out to Phil before I handed it to the temperature takers. The paperwork was from the "Quarantine Division."

"I thought they were going to give us more of an exam."

"They looked more afraid of us than we were of them," Phil said. "Now what do you want to do?"

"Unpack?" I meant to be funny, but Phil glared. "We should continue to get shots of what people are doing. Did you see this mini-*Patter*?" I held it up. "There's karaoke, a game show in the atrium, even trivia."

"You want to go to trivia?

"No. Karaoke would be more interesting to film."

"I'm not in the mood for a crowded bar," Phil said. "Besides, everyone looks infectious to me."

"That reminds me of a *Twilight Zone* episode. This kid would see people on a train with X's on their foreheads that nobody else saw. Then there was an explosion and the ones marked with the X were killed."

Phil touched his forehead. "Do you see an X?"

"No." I looked in the mirror over the desk. "Nor me—yet."

Phil turned on CNN and up popped a shot of our ship anchored off the coast of Yokohama. "...Eighty-year-old man from Hong Kong...had visited mainland China for only a few hours on January tenth..."

"So, Mister Hong Kong *had* been in China. Maybe he *is* the Mister Wu we kept hearing them paging."

"...flew into Tokyo...on January seventeenth with his two daughters and two days later said he began developing a cough.... On January twenty-fifth he got off in Hong Kong.... He sought medical attention on January thirtieth and was diagnosed with the virus shortly after. He is currently in stable condition."

I turned up the volume as the story continued. "It's also unclear how many passengers may have disembarked early. The Japanese health ministry said it is tracing people who may have disembarked in Okinawa, the cruise's second-to-last stop. The ministry is also investigating the infected patient's movements during his time in Japan but must rely on authorities in Hong Kong for information since the patient is there."

There were scenes of Japanese officials wearing masks, walking near an elevator bank on the ship. One of them was in full Hazmat regalia with a face shield and blue gloves. He was carrying an orange plastic bag of medical waste.

"When we get off," Phil said, "let's not tell people in Japan we were on this ship."

"You're right," I agreed but kept my next thought to myself: That is, *if* we get off...

✦ ✦ ✦

We were the last to dinner. For the first time, Faith wasn't smiling.

"Ah, the six amigos meet again," Jerry said with forced cheer.

"Have you heard anything new in the smoking room?" I asked Cathy.

"I think they're finally done with the tests," she replied. "One woman who's had a bad cough said they also swabbed her throat."

"Mario, I decided that we might waste too much time with the shuttle in the morning, so I've hired a taxi," Jerry said. "We can leave early enough for you to make your flight."

"I didn't even think of that," Vana said. "Thank you."

"Nobody's going anywhere first thing in the morning," I blurted.

"What do you know that we don't know?" Jerry asked belligerently.

"Sorry. That's just my spidey sense."

"Which is usually right." Vana's hand was trembling. "I feel the same, but I keep telling myself it's just my anxiety speaking."

"Why the hell haven't we even docked at the pier?" I said between clenched teeth. "Everyone coming from the shore is wearing Hazmat suits. They're treating us like lepers." Tears blurred my vision. All the tension I felt throughout the day was seeping through my pores. I felt blotchy patches break out on my face.

Mario's dark-chocolate eyes bored into me. "Tell me, Gay. What do you think is going on?"

"The men who took our temperature…they aren't health officers…they're quarantine officers. If they find anyone with this disease, they're going to take them to a locked facility—in fact, they could detain everyone on the ship for a few weeks—even months. There was this horrible place in New York harbor—they actually called it 'the Quarantine'—and a mob armed with hatchets and torches burned it down."

"When was this?" Vana asked.

"Ah, in the mid–eighteen eighties."

"Gay's wonderful imagination is running away with her," Phil said softly.

"But they don't really quarantine whole ships anymore, do they?" Vana was staring at me.

"Only in horror movies," Jerry said, trying to lighten the mood. "Can you imagine how many lawsuits they'd have if they tried to detain all of us?"

"At least not the way they did it in medieval times," I said in a frivolous way. "*Quarantena* means forty days in Italian, which is how long a ship had to stay offshore if they suspected bubonic plague was onboard. After two months, when everyone was infected—and dead—the plague ship was burnt."

To Phil's relief, Neville stopped by to describe the special pasta that Jorge, the headwaiter, was cooking at the tableside grill.

"That's what I had the first night," Jerry said.

"Ah, then you know our secret plan. Today we start the menu rotation over again, as if we were on a new cruise. We are just as happy to serve you, my dear friends, as we would be to welcome a new group." Neville raised his arms like a conductor. "For us, it is the same. Ten thousand meals a day!"

"May we dine here, just like usual?" Phil asked.

"Of course, as long as you are on board, this is your home."

I forced a smile. "Do you have crème brûleé tonight?"

"For you, every night, madam."

✦   ✦   ✦

Before we had left for dinner, Phil put our bags back out in the hall once again.

"Let's take our usual post-prandial stroll one last time," I said, my mood flipping to optimistic.

"What makes you sure it's the last time?"

"Well, in case it is, I want one more green-tea ice cream." It was my favorite shipboard snack.

Afterward, I said I wanted to walk through "the trough," Katherine's nickname for the buffet. When I grabbed a plate and filled it with Danish pastries, handed it to Phil, and reached for another clean one, he snapped. "What in the world are you doing?"

"I want some fruit for the cabin."

"But no food can leave the ship. We're going to have enough trouble getting all those bags through customs."

"Fine!" I said and slapped the empty plate on a nearby table.

Even though I half expected it, I winced at seeing the luggage crowding our room. Phil pushed the bags against the door to clear a path. I opened my overnight bag, fished out my nightgown and toiletries, and burrowed under the smooth sheets in record time. My lost sleep the night before caught up with me and I passed out before Phil made it out of the bathroom.

At 6:30 the morning of Wednesday, February 5, the speaker over the bed chimed to warn of an imminent announcement. "Good morning," the captain began, "the Ministry of Health has notified us that ten people have tested positive for the coronavirus." I slid out of bed and reached for my hearing aids. "All guests must return to their cabins and remain there for the time being."

"What the hell is going on?" I opened the drapes to the limpid dawn light. "We're still at anchor." I slid open the door. A bitter breeze ruffled the papers on the coffee table. I shut the door and crawled back into bed.

"Ten people!" Phil put his arm around me. "I thought it took a couple of days to get test results."

"Maybe they just had high temperatures" is what I said, all the while thinking that Mr. Wu, as I was now calling the departed passenger in my head, must have had enough contacts to give it to at least a few other passengers. I nestled close to Phil, pressed my feet to his calves to warm them, and fell back asleep.

"Good morning, ladies and gentlemen…"

"What time—" My travel clock read 8:12 a.m.

Phil hushed me as he sat up in bed. He pointed out the window. We were just coming back to the pier.

> …Princess Cruises can confirm that the first phase of health screening of all guests and crew onboard *Diamond Princess* by the Japanese Ministry of Health has been completed. We were notified that amongst the samples that have completed testing, ten people have tested positive for coronavirus. This includes two Australian guests, three Japanese guests, three guests from Hong Kong, and one guest from the U.S., in addition to one Filipino crewmember.
>
> These ten persons, who have been notified, have been taken ashore by Japanese Coast Guard watercraft and transported to local hospitals for care by shoreside Japanese

medical professionals. It has been confirmed that the ship will remain under quarantine in Yokohama. The length of the quarantine will be at least fourteen days as required by the Ministry of Health.

The ship plans to go out to sea today to perform normal marine operations, including, but not limited to, the production of fresh water and ballast operations before proceeding alongside in Yokohama where food, provisions, and other supplies will be brought onboard. Guests will continue to be provided complimentary internet and telephone to use in order to stay in contact with their family and loved ones, and the ship's crew is working to keep all guests comfortable. Princess Cruises will continue to fully cooperate with and follow the instructions of global medical authorities and the Japanese government. We will also be canceling the next two *Diamond Princess* cruises departing Yokohama on February fourth and twelfth and will begin notifying guests today.

"I don't understand…at least fourteen days…on the ship or do we have to stay in our cabin?"

"How would I know?" Phil got out of bed and opened the door to our balcony, which now overlooked the quay. "Oh, my God!"

"What?" I stumbled over my suitcase and went outside in my nightgown.

Ambulances and fire trucks were screaming down the road that led to the terminal. Military vehicles were lined up in rows. Everyone was wearing Hazmat suits in red, white, blue, and yellow. Workers were clumsily putting up blue plastic tarps to shield the gangways, at the bottom of which were ambulances positioned to take…to take what? People who were ill? People who had died? What the hell was going on?

All I knew is we were de facto prisoners of the Japanese authorities.

CRUISE TO NOWHERE

Between stimulus and response, there is a space. In that space is our power to choose our response. In our response lies our growth and our freedom.

— Viktor Emil Frankl

Email from Clare Hiler, February 5, 2020

Hi Gay, My name is Clare Hiler and I'm a booking producer for NBC News, I'm also copying my colleague Mohammed. Firstly—how are you feeling? I'm sure it's so stressful being on the ship right now, and I can't imagine what you're going through. Would you be open [to] speaking with us today about your experience? I'm available to chat any time.

We set our phones and my iPad to use our cellular service. "That's thirty dollars a day, but who's counting?" I said. So far, we had tried to avoid the cost of international calling. Besides, we like a break from feeling tied to devices. Any concern about economizing vanished the moment we realized we were confined to our stateroom for at least two weeks. Even though the captain said that both data and phone coverage were now free, everyone on board was whining to anyone who would listen—and straining the ship's capacity. Phil set up the Wi-Fi router we had rented in Tokyo. "It's working!" he announced, "And it's bypassing the ship's equipment."

The scene unfolding on the pier was both riveting and deeply disturbing, if only because so many uniformed figures were converging and peeling off like bacteria under a microscope. Those gathered around the ambulances wore blue outfits with matching jackets and gloves. Under white helmets with plastic shields, they wore surgical masks. A team of men in white Hazmat suits and white headgear were flanked on both sides of the ambulances to hold up blue tarps to prevent anyone from glimpsing the patient being loaded.

Another faction wore white pants, red shirts, and white vests, and had red crosses on armbands indicating they were on a medical team. At the perimeter, guys in bright green coveralls and matching gray face masks and helmets surrounded the fire trucks. We supposed the troops in camo were some branch of the military. Most officious were the personnel in navy blue slacks, matching overcoats, and peaked caps, wearing surgical aprons. They were the only ones easily identifiable because "Yokohama Customs" was emblazoned in English on the back of their coats. There were also a few men in suits and ties, some with and some without masks. A few younger salarymen seemed to be running messages back and forth to the terminal building, a good five hundred feet from the ship.

The controlled chaos and the ever-shifting battalion on duty were frightening. They were there either to keep us from leaving the plague ship or to transport us to a medical facility, which an early press report said was a "police hospital" in Yokohama. I assumed it was connected with a jail. I kept repeating to anyone who would listen: "I don't believe this is happening."

The door in the divider between our balcony and the Mendizabals was still open and we had no intention of locking it. We needed each other. Phil checked their Wi-Fi unit, but the battery was dead. He showed Mario how to charge it, then called Jerry to remind him as well. "I turned it in before we boarded," he said. "I didn't see the point of paying for it for another two weeks."

"Can you get on the ship's service?"

"No, that's hopeless. We're using the cellular, which works fine on the balcony."

Vana and I stood at the rail together. "Have you called your kids?" I asked.

"It's late there. We're sending emails to everyone and trying to sound like it's not a big deal. We're healthy and comfortable and—" She was trembling. I rubbed her shoulder, racking my mind for what I could say to soothe her. My penchant for saying "it could be worse" was pointless. We were perilously close to dire straits with no way to rewind the clock. There were only three possible paths: stay healthy and go home in a few weeks, get sick and be sent to a Japanese hospital and hopefully recover, or…or not. In Wuhan, the mortality rate was almost 5 percent, but among those who were hospitalized, it was 15 percent. Plus the risks were much higher if you were over seventy or had pre-existing conditions. Men were slightly more vulnerable than women. Most alarming was that the average time from the first symptom to death was fourteen days.

Mario came out and said, "Gay, about that Tamiflu, they're giving it to some of the Wuhan patients along with several HIV antivirals."

"Do you think we should take it prophylactically?"

"It can't hurt."

Vana touched her husband's arm. "There can be some unpleasant side effects."

"Like what?" I asked.

"Headaches, nightmares, some other psychological problems including insomnia."

"I already feel like I'm in the middle of a nightmare and can't wake up." I went inside, brought out the boxes, and handed Mario the package insert.

"The usual dose is two a day," he said, "but one for prevention."

"So if each couple shares a box, we'll all be covered," Vana said.

"What else should we be taking?" I asked Mario. "We have statins."

"Won't hurt to take an extra one per day."

"I also have a cold-prevention pack with zinc, echinacea, one thousand milligram vitamin C."

"Those are all good for immunities," Mario said.

I opened the Tamiflu packaging. We all had bottles of water on the outside table. "*L'chaim!*" I said as we popped the first pills.

✦   ✦   ✦

Phil and I were transfixed by the ever-evolving scene on the dock. We wore jackets, wool caps, and gloves as the wind buffeted the balconies on the starboard side. The press was squeezed behind a cordon a few hundred feet from the ship's bow. Through our binoculars, we could see the photographers had telephoto lenses. Some stood atop their satellite trucks and every hour or so a helicopter made a few circular passes around the waterfront arena.

"Phil, I know this sounds incredibly trite, but I just can't process what I'm seeing. It has to be a bad dream."

"To me it's a poorly directed B-movie."

"Then it's past time for a superhero to leap on this balcony and scoop me up and—"

"What about me?"

"Superwoman is more your type."

Our banter seems amusing now, but our voices were shrill and seething with misplaced anger.

"You okay?" Vana said, coming out of her cabin. She probably had never heard us say a cross word to each other except in jest.

"I can't even explain how helpless I feel." My voice choked. Crying would have been a relief, but tears don't come easily—and when they do, they're always unexpected.

"I keep saying to myself that it's only two weeks. We'll be warm and fed and—"

"Speaking of food, I'm starving. What time is it?"

"Almost noon," Phil replied. "Did you get breakfast yet?"

"We made instant coffee and I ate some chocolates leftover from the hotel."

"The hotel in Tokyo?" I said. "Doesn't that seem like years ago?"

"Mario wanted to ask you about insurance. Didn't we get the travel policies from the same place?"

"I didn't even think about that. We actually have two policies—the one we got from the SquareMouth site and the annual membership policy I told you about—the one that evacuates you to the hospital of your choice in a medical emergency. You weren't interested in it for this trip, but I was worried about Africa."

"We were wondering if the one we both bought covers this situation. It's going to cost us a fortune to fly home if we can't use our points."

"This is a trip interruption and I think we both have up to a hundred and fifty percent of the total insured amount."

Vana buttoned her sweater. "I'm freezing out here. Do you want some coffee?"

"I want James Beard French toast."

"In your dreams," Vana muttered, closing the balcony door behind her.

I also went inside. Phil was on the desk phone. "I'm holding for room service. Maybe we were supposed to order breakfast."

I glanced to the counter over the mini-fridge and saw the pastries from last night wrapped in a linen napkin. "I knew these would come in handy." I offered Phil first choice from the plate.

"Thanks." He picked the cheese Danish. "Would be better with some fruit."

I started to scowl but cracked up. What rabbit hole had we fallen down and when would we reach the bottom?

✦   ✦   ✦

Phil had forgotten that at 9:45 a.m., the captain had made a brief announcement saying we eventually would be getting meals in our rooms but we needed to be patient since this was a unique situation for the crew.

"Breakfast" arrived just after one in the afternoon, consisting of two tiny fruit cups and two small plain yogurts. There were no drinks. We had the electric kettle—a special amenity on this ship because the Asian clientele demanded tea-making facilities—but my tea bags were packed in the suitcase we didn't expect to open again until we were home. I went to the bathroom and filled a glass with tap water, telling myself it was time to start roughing it.

"Where's our trip notebook?"

"In my backpack," Phil said. "Why?"

"I'm going to read the insurance policies."

A few minutes later, I carried the loose-leaf notebook across to the Mendizabal's room. "There are some benefits that may apply," I said cheerfully.

Vana waved for me to come sit beside her. "Do you think it's illegal to be in each other's cabins?" she asked.

"We're a family traveling together. Right, sister?" I started to do a high-five and changed it to a fist bump. "Can't be too careful."

"You're in a better mood."

"Nothing like a little yogurt to cheer me up." I looked at her tray. "You didn't eat yours."

"I'm too nauseous. You want it?"

I did, but said, "Save it. You might get hungry later."

I showed her the pertinent clauses in the insurance policy. "We should call them to start a claim."

"What time is it in Florida?"

I had trouble calculating the difference between Japan and Eastern Standard time, which was fourteen hours behind Japan. "Right now, it's 1:30 p.m. here…that means it's…ah…11:30 p.m. yesterday in Florida."

"That means I can't call them until…when?"

"Ah…if you call them at eleven tonight, it will be nine in the morning at home."

"What day will it be there?"

The other tricky part was figuring out when it was the same day here, but still a day earlier at home. "Wednesday, same as today."

There was a knock on the door. I ducked back to our balcony so they wouldn't see me "illegally" in the wrong room. Phil had just received another tray. "Lunch!" he said. "I guess dinner will be served in another hour."

Compared to breakfast, this meal looked sumptuous. The dry chicken sandwich came with a macaroni salad, a soft roll, chips, and chocolate mousse. Still no beverages. The phone rang.

"What did you get for lunch?" Jerry asked. "We got a chicken sandwich—exactly like the one we had for breakfast."

"Hey, we didn't get a sandwich for breakfast! What about drinks?"

"We had some in the fridge, but I ordered more from room service. Don't hang up. It can take an hour to get through. You know Cathy has to have her Cokes!"

While eating, I dialed room service. Only fifteen minutes later, I ordered Sapporo beer, Pinot Noir, Pellegrino—and Earl Grey tea bags. A few hours later, we received a few Cokes and ginger ales and, to our surprise, a couple of surgical masks.

"Desperate times call for desperate measures," I announced. I opened the "Florida only" suitcase, rummaged through Phil's masterfully packed bags and found my stash of tea. I also unpacked a thermos cup, a small funnel, a Brita water bottle, personalized chopsticks, reusable plastic straws, an extra nightgown, make-up used on formal nights, and self-grip hair rollers. I had tossed the bulky rollers into a pocket on the suitcase's exterior at the last minute. I'm hopeless at blow-drying and my thin hair loses volume quickly. If I don't have time to wash my hair, I can improvise with a damp brush and rollers and I'll be presentable for a few hours. I'd only used them once on the trip, but if ABC asked me to do anything on-camera again, I would be ready. Within a few days, though, the rollers became an essential.

I then riffled through my backpack to find my emergency snacks. Whenever I change time zones, I find it easier to adjust to a new sleeping schedule than convince myself it's not time to eat. With a day-for-night transition, I'm often hungry in the middle of the night so I keep a supply of mixed nuts and dried fruit, protein bars, crackers, and cookies. Phil prefers pretzels and chips in airline-sized portions. I managed to excavate enough goodies to fill the empty ice bucket, which I doubted would be refilled.

"Do you think Edwin will still clean our cabins?" I asked.

"Not a chance. They handed off lunch as fast as possible as if we were contagious zombies."

"I guess I can forget about four washcloths." How quickly the tables turn, I thought. "I bet Edwin is thinking: Screw the rich bitch! See how she likes having none."

Phil looked at the unmade bed. "Not even clean towels or sheets?"

"Or access to all the restaurants, bars, shops."

"What about all the passengers who planned to fly home this week? They'll be running out of medications and I doubt the pharmacy can cover routine prescriptions for thousands of people!"

"We have almost enough," I said, because we expected to be in Japan another week and I always carry extra "in case of volcanoes." Everyone I mention this to—including our current travel mates—thinks that's ridiculous even though when the ash cloud from the eruptions of Iceland's Eyjafjallajökull volcano caused disruption to air travel across Europe in 2010, more than ten million passengers were stranded.

Just then the phone rang. "What are you doing about meds?" Jerry asked. I said we were okay. "Cathy needs refills on all of hers," he said, "so I called the front desk. They'll be passing out forms tonight, but they took down what we needed right away."

"Wouldn't you usually call the clinic about that?"

"Can't get through! Every hypochondriac on board is trying to get tested."

"Or maybe they really are sick. Have you looked outside lately? There must be twenty ambulances parked and they've been loading people all morning."

"I timed one," Jerry said. "Took almost an hour for one person. Have you seen the process? There are twenty guys with clipboards and now they have uniformed soldiers holding up more plastic privacy sheets so all the windows are covered."

"Lots of people die on ships," I said. "A few years ago, some guy stroked out in our dining room. Maybe some of them are corpses."

"Just watching the lack of leadership is enough to give me a heart attack," Jerry said without a hint of sarcasm.

"All decisions in Japan are done by consensus. Everybody has to buy into the plan."

"While that might work at the Toyota factory, it's not the way to run a disaster site."

"Maybe that's how they screwed up the Fukushima nuclear accident."

"Well, that gives me even more confidence," he said and hung up.

"Phil?" I turned around and saw him lying on the bed, eyes closed.

"What?"

"We've got to get the hell off this ship!" No response. "I'm not kidding!" No response. I went over and sat beside him. "People are dying."

He sat up slightly. "Nobody said anything about dying."

"Of course not! They don't want to start a panic. Yet, every time you hear a statistic about this epidemic, they rattle off 'a thousand more cases and fifty more deaths.' The numbers in China are going up exponentially and the mortality rate seems to remain around the same percentage—and that's just the official figures. I'd bet they're minimizing them."

"Okay," Phil said with a sigh of resignation. "Ten people are sick or at least have symptoms. They probably haven't had the official test results yet. But let's presume they have the virus. Mister Wuflu was on the ship for five days, and in that time, how many people could he have been in contact with? Six or eight at his table in the dining room, forty or fifty on a bus tour, those within sneezing distance in the theater, three or four more in a hot tub? What if he played mah-jongg or cards? Did he play bingo or use slot machines? Eat pizza by the pool…"

"Or green tea ice cream?"

"Not a problem. There are no tables or chairs there. Everyone walks around with their cones."

"Well, that's a relief!" I said with a mock sigh. "Wait, though, you've come up with over sixty contacts and if one or two people caught it they could have another ten or twenty contacts and—"

"The point is that there are going to be more cases, but that doesn't mean any of them had anything to do with us."

"How many times a day are we in elevators or in narrow hallways? We don't know how contagious this damn crap is, do we? What did Mario call it—the R-naughty."

Phil threw his head back and laughed. "That's funny."

"What?"

"You said 'naughty' instead of 'naught.'"

"Nothing about this is amusing! I'm telling you, we're in danger and we need to get outta here!"

Phil put his arm around my shoulders and pulled me toward him on the bed. "I'm going where you're going, darling. If anyone can figure it out, it's you."

"One more thing…" Phil kicked off his shoes and pulled his sweatshirt over his head. "Did you ever cancel the rest of our trip in Japan?"

"Of course!"

"What about our flights home?"

"Honey, I've canceled the rest of our life."

✦ ✦ ✦

I curled beside Phil but couldn't find a comfortable position. I slipped away so he could rest. I turned off the overhead lights and sat on the couch, my brain spinning with ideas like making parachutes out of bedsheets and leaping off the balcony in the middle of the night and taking a train to a secret *ryokan* where we could soak in mineral baths until…. Then the refrains, "It's a bird, it's a plane, it's Superman!" and "Go down, Moses…Let my people go!" reverberated in my head. My psyche had sensed a problem before I could articulate it: We were in prison. Our food would be provided and we would have no choice about when or what to eat. If we left this room, perhaps worse would happen. And then again, if we left this room, it would only be to be taken to a facility where we would have the distinct possibility of dying. Since we could not see who was getting into the ambulances, we had no idea if the healthy spouse could accompany the sick one. Given the virulent nature of the disease, that was unlikely. Phil and I had never been apart during a crisis—no, not true—we *had* been separated for a couple of days during the infamous "No Name" storm of 1993 that brought four feet of water into our downstairs. That was just a massive loss of property. This could mean loss of one—or both—of our lives.

I heard the rotors of yet another helicopter circling about the *Prison Princess*. We'd been on several ships where helicopters had evacuated people in medical emergencies. I'd even written just such a scene in *The Girl in the Box*. Now all we needed was a pilot and—

An idea clicked. I opened my notebook to our annual membership in CrisisFlite, which I'd renewed in anticipation of our Africa trip. We had also signed up for their Ex911 plan, which claimed to respond to terrorism, hijacking, and national disasters. I turned to the list of the fourteen membership benefits and gasped when I read: Response to Pandemics.

"We're covered!" I shouted, waking Phil. "Listen to this: Our CrisisFlite plan includes 'Any sudden outbreak of one or more causative organisms belonging to the same genus or species that is infectious or contagious to which the member is exposed outside his or her permanent country of residence, threatens life or long-term health of the member, and becomes widespread affecting a whole region, continent or the world. The infectious or contagious disease hereunder includes, but is not limited to, those defined by the relevant Ministry of Health, Labor and Welfare and/or the World Health Organization (WHO).'"

"Are you saying that they'll evacuate us from the ship?"

"It says they offer advice and 'possible deployment of crisis consultants, security personnel, and transportation assets to assist a member directly impacted by a pandemic...' I'm going to call their hotline right now!"

"What time is it there?"

"Who knows? They could be anywhere: New York, Nairobi, or Timbuktu."

I called CrisisFlite and they said they'd forward the situation to Ex911 and I should expect a call from one of their crisis coordinators.

"Gay," Phil said, looking up from his phone. "Ah...have you checked your email lately?"

"Who's it from?"

"Let's see...several more producers at ABC News, the *New York Times* Tokyo bureau...the *Sydney Morning Herald* responding to an Instagram that Ashley posted."

"Ashley?"

"Yes, the kids seem to know more than we do."

"And NBC out of their London bureau."

"What do they all want?"

"Interviews with us."

"Is that a good idea?"

"It's too late for that question. It's splashed all over the internet. Ashley's getting a huge response on social media and she has thousands of followers. Apparently, people are extremely interested in cruise passengers stranded on a ship with a highly contagious disease."

"I couldn't get away with such a plot in a novel," I said. "It's too melodramatic." I stood up and opened the balcony door. It was getting dark and long shadows draped the pier in funereal tones. Spotlights lit up the gangway as an ambulance backed up and drove away. At the western end of the pier, there were only two satellite trucks left. A vermillion sunset backlit the phalanx of cameramen still on duty despite the plummeting temperatures.

I could hear the captain's voice and hurried inside. "What did he say?"

"We're going to sea so they can run the equipment for making fresh water and other tasks and we'll return to port tomorrow for supplies."

"I thought I heard a mention of refills."

"Oh, right. Tonight we'll get forms to fill out if we need medication and there will be no charge for refills."

"Did he happen to mention dinner?" I asked. The sandwich had long since worn off.

About 7:30 p.m. there was another knock on the door. I already was having a Pavlovian response to the stimulus. We were handed heavy plates with a steamed chicken breast and a succotash-like mélange of veggies. There was a potato and a separate serving of zucchini. Plus, a nice square of cheesecake. More college steam table than nicely plated cruise fare, but a step up from the earlier offerings. There were also two cans of soda and two bottles of water.

Before we ate, Phil opened the door to the balcony and stepped out. I followed him but stayed just inside the cabin. "It feels creepy to be at sea without any destination, making lazy circles, a cruise to nowhere."

"The truth is that nobody gives a damn about us. They'd rather torpedo the ship than let us land and possibly infect one of their precious citizens."

"But, there are lots of Japanese on board."

"Who they seem willing to sacrifice!"

"Gay, where's your cheerful we-shall-overcome attitude?" he said as he returned inside. Then: "Have you see the latest emails from NBC and the Australian newspaper?"

"I haven't had a chance."

"Let's talk to everyone—anyone who will listen. We have to humanize this. We're parents, grandparents. We want to go home and see our family. We want to be treated by American doctors if we get sick, but more importantly, we want to travel home long before we come down with anything."

"Let's see what CrisisFlite says first."

"Do you know how much it will cost to send a plane to bring us halfway around the world in a private aircraft? They'll do anything they can to weasel out of it."

"You might be right about that," I said slowly as my idea deflated like a cooling Yorkshire pudding. "But don't you think it will be a lot harder to ignore us if we tell the media that they should be coming for us any minute?"

Phil held up his hands to concede defeat. "Normally I would suggest we wait a few days…but what if we don't have a few days?"

I was surprised by his earnestness. Usually I'm trying to sell him on an over-the-top idea. "You're right! Even if we're okay, many of the passengers are fragile: the elderly, babies, people like Marlene with compromised immune systems. Not to mention the crew in cramped quarters who are being forced to serve us. Have you noticed that there are double the ambulances they suppos-edly need parked on the dock? It looks like they're embarking on a

military operation. And the enemy is us! We can either retreat or…
or…start our own campaign."

"Okay, as long as it's not just about you and me. I hate saying
it, but it's never been truer: We're all in the same boat."

BOOTS ON THE GROUND

If many remedies are prescribed for an illness, you may be certain that the illness has no cure.

—Anton Chekhov, *The Cherry Orchard*

Email from Blake Courter, February 6, 2020
To: usgshipcontact@state.gov

Dear State Department Official,

I received your email address from American Citizen Services in Tokyo, who I contacted about my parents' situation on the *Diamond Princess* off Yokohama. I am advocating for Phil and Gay Courter (copied) who are under quarantine but do not appear infected.

The recirculating air on the ship is likely spreading the coronavirus infection, which is why the infection rates are doubling daily. Hospitals use ventilation with negative pressure to prevent infection from spreading, but these passengers are being continuously exposed to increasingly concentrated contamination.

We request an immediate evacuation of our parents, under appropriate quarantine, to US facilities where then can be cared for as you have done for other Americans. We do not believe that the Japanese government is acting responsibly and without your intervention they and many other souls are at severe risk. A failure to act will cause loss of life.

Even before Captain Arma made his announcement the morning of February 6, we knew the latest number of positive tests because Ju-min Park from Reuters had emailed: "Ten more infected with the virus, among some seventy-three results. The Japanese health minister is speaking in a few minutes, so will give you more details afterward."

"Phil, that was Ju-min—we're doing an interview with her later today. She said there are ten more cases."

"That's from yesterday."

"She wrote *more*. That makes twenty-one so far."

The ship was moving, so we went out to the balcony. The moment the pier came into view, we could see more ambulances lined up as if ready for formal inspection. Two fire trucks moved into place to block the gangway from the long line of photographers, their tripods looking like wading birds in the pools of morning sunshine.

"Ding! Ding!" blasted from the ceiling speaker. We hurried back inside.

Good morning, ladies and gentlemen. This is the captain speaking from the bridge. We have been notified that among the second set of samples that have completed testing, ten additional people have tested positive for the coronavirus. Local health authorities will begin disembarking those guests for transport to local hospitals immediately. We acknowledge that yesterday there were some challenges with your room service deliveries…. Trusting you understand that this is a new operation for our team and the logistical challenges in delivering room service to over fifteen hundred staterooms can take approximately three hours. We aim to improve our service and thank everyone for their patience and hope you understand that everyone is working very hard for you.

After his announcement, I said, "They must be giving the actual coronavirus test to people with symptoms. I wish they'd test us before we get deathly ill."

"What's the point?" Phil asked. "There is no treatment and also you could pass the test today and become ill tomorrow."

"What do you think about Blake's concern about the ventilation system?"

"That would be the simplest explanation of how people are still getting sick without leaving their cabins."

"Do you think the virus can circulate through the ducts?"

"That's one logical explanation."

"That would mean we're breathing contaminated air."

The knocks on the door were a welcome sign that breakfast had arrived. There were two hard-boiled eggs, a croissant and a muffin, fruit salad with granola, and a yogurt. "This is a feast compared to yesterday," I said. "Do you realize we have no control over when or what we eat?"

"Like a lot of people in this world."

We both were silent and knew what the other was thinking. We'd made films about hunger and food insecurity and were supporters of our local food bank. "Another lesson in what not to take for granted."

"The point is that we don't know anything about this virus, how it can be transmitted, or how long the incubation period is."

"We need some facts—and fast!" I started with Ken Rand—the infectious disease specialist at the University of Florida who had helped during my flu episode in 2016 and would be traveling to Africa with us in a few weeks—and copied my sister, Robin Madden. She and her husband, Josh, are both pediatricians in Maryland and might know experts in the D.C. area.

Phil was peeling his hard-boiled egg. "Did you see any salt?"

"There are no condiments, not even butter." I held up my finger as an indication of a bright idea. I went into the bathroom and rummaged through the pouch where I kept my dental supplies. "Here you go!" I handed him a tiny plastic salt shaker.

"Where'd you find this?"

"Sometimes I use it for a gargle."

"You never cease to astonish me!"

"Let's go over the media requests," I said between bites of dry muffin. "There's a list of questions from the *Globe and Mail*, that's a Canadian paper, which I can answer by email, so that's easy. Also from Canada, the CBC wants an on-camera interview at nine-forty tonight Japan time for their morning show tomorrow. I mean, our yesterday, their tomorrow…"

Phil reached for a pad of yellow sticky notes. "I'll start putting each one on a separate sticky and then put them in order over the desk. That's the easiest way to see if there are conflicts."

"Okay. Then there's South Korean JTBC TV—just a request—Elmi at the Tokyo bureau of the *New York Times*, someone from Poland (most of this message is in Polish), a guy from the Netherlands, and—I'm not kidding—Anastasia from Russia. Somehow she knows Ashley. Then there's Louise Connelly from CNBC and also some from MSNBC." I blew out my breath. "I don't know how to schedule Russia and the Netherlands! What crazy time zones are they in?"

"Looks like you have all twenty-four hours of the day covered."

"How did this happen so fast?"

I looked down at my phone. "They're coming faster than I can read them. Matthew from the Australian newspaper is checking up on us, as are ABC News and Jon. And there must be dozens from worried friends and family." I checked my watch. "But we haven't heard back from CrisisFlite."

"Prioritize," Phil said logically. "Are the Koreans or the Dutch going to get us out of here? Start with the American television networks and the *New York Times* and…Reuters."

"What about Anastasia? Maybe she can get to Putin and he can call Donny and—"

"You're right about one thing. It's all political. Why haven't the Japanese let us quarantine on shore? Because of the 2020 Olympics. If we were in a hotel and tested positive, we'd be counted as a Japanese statistic."

A new thought formed. "Every time one of these media people check back with us, we have to engage with them. They're looking for personalities to follow—people their viewers might care about. We know both sides of that drill."

"Do you think other passengers are communicating with the media?"

"Probably, but maybe because Ashley has very active accounts on Instagram, Facebook, and Twitter, we're easier to find."

"It doesn't matter. We need as many people as possible to tell the world what's happening here," Phil said. "We want our quarantine to stay in the headlines."

"I doubt that's possible."

"Maybe not, but we can try. Nobody does it better than the president. If he says something outlandish or sensational, that's fine."

"What are you suggesting? A geriatric strip show on the balcony?"

"We'll save that for when their attention lags," Phil chortled. "The point is that the best communicators control the information for their sole benefit. Right now, they want the scoop on what's happening on this ship. What do *we* want?"

"To get evacuated out of here!"

"The only way that will happen is if both governments think it's in *their* best interests."

"Right now, I don't think their prime minister or our president cares a hoot about us."

"Maybe not yet. But this could make or break someone else."

"Who's that?"

"Buzz from CrisisFlite. His company has the most to gain—or lose—at least at this moment in time."

✦ ✦ ✦

Our immediate family has a private text message feed, sharing the latest gap-tooth smile, finger-paint masterpiece, or home-grown cabbage. After three weeks of photos and superlatives from our Asian peregrinations, we tried to make light of our sudden "extended vacation." "Don't worry," Phil wrote, "I'm able to order Pinot Noir."

After Giulia captured our first appearance on ABC and posted it to the feed, I decided to be proactive with the news and texted about the ten new cases. Ashley responded in minutes. "That's what a reporter just told me. I was hoping that was old news." Not long after, Josh chimed in: "That's scary shit."

I wrote back: "Okay, kids. There's only so much we can do from here. Listen up and take charge."

"Tell us what you need us to do," Ashley zipped back.

I replied: "We have a membership with CrisisFlite. It's a type of travel insurance that extracts people from situations like riots and pandemics. They're our best hope of getting off this ship before we get this crud. I called them, but I haven't heard anything yet. One of you needs to be our contact person with them. We told Blake about it before we left home."

Blake, our eldest, is perhaps the most independent and—on the surface at least—the most cerebral and unemotional of our children, so it was surprising that on our last call before we left for Japan, he said, "I'm really concerned about you traveling right now, especially going to Hong Kong." He was worried about the demonstrations, but I assured him our guide would watch out for us. "What about that Chinese virus?" I wondered if he also was receiving Terry's worrywart emails. On a recent trip home, Blake had invited Terry for lunch to hear his take on various political issues. Even though he isn't as involved in high-level Republican politics as he once was, Terry remains in frequent contact with Newt Gingrich and some friends in the State Department. We wouldn't have been surprised if our mild-mannered neighbor was invited to a prayer breakfast in Congress or tea in the Rose Garden.

"Would you feel more comfortable if we were in London?" I'd asked Blake. "Think how many terrorist attacks *they* have."

"Mom, I'm specifically concerned about Hong Kong. The protestors have daily clashes with police."

"Would it help you to know we have coverage for terrorism, kidnapping, or other disasters? If there's a problem, they'll arrange medical care and fly us to the hospital of our choice to recuperate."

"Send me their info along with your itinerary," Blake said, which I had done.

Ashley messaged Blake for the information on CrisisFlite. "Blake's slammed with work, so I'm on it." An hour later, she messaged that she had finally reached Buzz somewhere in California, who would be in touch soon. "He sounds incredible. Are you in the CIA and never told us?"

An hour later, Buzz called me. "Don't worry, ma'am," he said in a clipped military style, "we've got boots on the ground in Yokohama."

"How soon can we get off the ship?"

"Everything's going to be fine. You're safest where you are for now."

"What's your plan?"

"We're working on that. We got several families out of Wuhan, so we know the drill."

"You evacuated them?"

"Yes."

I pumped the air with my fist. Phil looked over quizzically. I held my hand up for him to wait until I was through. "Listen, Buzz, we once arranged a medical evacuation for someone."

"That was the U.S. This is Japan. They do things differently here."

"Buzz, we're watching them take people off under the strictest protocols. Our friend had what they thought could have been a virulent, contagious disease. Her husband had just died from it and she was evacuated in Hazmat conditions. Even if we're not sick, we're willing to follow every protocol. Isn't it better to transport us while we're still healthy?"

"That's assuming you'll be allowed to enter the country. There are only ten or twelve cases in the U.S. so far."

"We get that. We're perfectly willing to quarantine at home or in a hospital if we can find one that will accept us." Phil was signaling me that it was almost time for a live interview.

"Listen, our kids are taking over the communications with you. It's just too hard with the time difference and when we go out to sea, we lose connectivity."

"I would like to assure you that you will be completely satisfied with our services," Buzz said, "but you will have to be patient."

I muttered a quick thanks as my phone whirred with a FaceTime request from ABC. "Phil, remind me to tell Ash that I spoke to Buzz and ask her to contact Ken in Gainesville and

Summer—you know, Josh's old friend who's a doc—about their quarantine beds." I handed the phone to Phil so he could hold it while I sat by the window, where the light was more flattering.

"How do you feel about the new cases?" the newscaster asked.

"We're very worried," I said. "We don't feel safe here."

✦   ✦   ✦

Lunch had arrived, but I had been too occupied to eat more than a few bites of the toast and pâté until after the interview. The goulash-like stew and rice were cold. "Wish we had a microwave," I said but kept spooning it in. "There's more sauce than meat."

"Beggars can't be choosers."

"You are so right! Last week we were paying patrons, now we're…prisoners they're obliged to feed."

The activity on the quay was continuous. "We should have been counting ambulances," Phil said, "because it looks like they're processing more than ten people."

He was right. That evening Captain Arma announced, "I have been notified by the Japanese Ministry of Health that an additional forty-one people from the target samples have tested positive for coronavirus."

I was stunned. "How many is that altogether?"

"Forty-one, plus the twenty from before. So that's sixty-one people on the ship—so far."

"It's sixty-two if you count Mister Wu from Hong Kong, but who's counting?" The last few words, usually said in jest, came out as a snarl. "I guess because he didn't come back to Japan, they're leaving him out." I combed my fingers through my hair, using my nails as rakes as if it would help integrate the facts with the implications. "What the hell are 'target samples'? Shouldn't they be testing every single person on this ship, especially the crew?"

"Absolutely. If there are sixty-one sick out of fewer than two hundred tested…" Phil paused to calculate. "That's about thirty percent! Thirty percent of the whole ship is more than a thousand potential cases. And based on the Chinese stats, some of them are going to die."

"You mean some of *us* are going to die."

✦   ✦   ✦

As I told Buzz, we had been through a medical evacuation. What had then been a lifesaving mission now seemed like a dress rehearsal for the task at hand.

Twenty-three years earlier, Josh and a friend from Hampshire College joined Annette and Gérard Pesty, close friends of ours who lived on a trimaran in the Caribbean, on a voyage to Haiti to produce a documentary about an island community without any modern infrastructure. Afterward, they sailed to the Turks and Caicos so the boys could return to school and the Pestys could meet their next charter group. Three days later, we received a 7 p.m. call from a mutual friend saying Gérard had "flu-like symptoms," then collapsed suddenly and died. Annette seemed to be following the same course. Phil and I sprang into action. We called several doctors, including my sister and Dr. Rand in Gainesville, who arranged for her to be admitted to the university hospital. But first, we had to convince U.S. Customs and Immigration to drive from Jacksonville to Gainesville because the clock was ticking. "Life or death situation!" we repeated to anyone who tried to stonewall us. The public health officer in Miami said they would have to examine Annette before allowing her to enter the country. "No time!" I insisted. Miraculously, every bureaucrat, every doctor, and every official responded to the urgency—leading with their hearts rather than the rulebook—and Annette was flown to the hospital in Gainesville.

When we arrived, she was just being wheeled into an exam room. The staff was gowned in yellow-hooded jumpsuits, blue gloves, face masks, and shields—outfits that we would not see again until the *Diamond Princess* was quarantined. I ran toward Annette but was shoved away. "You can't come in here!"

"Listen to me! Do a malaria test, stat!" The room quieted. Then I blurted, "Our son was with them…he just told us that he met people with malaria…but he's fine because we insisted he take the pills. Annette and her husband skipped them because of the side effects." I left out the irony that Gérard was a pharmacist.

In a few minutes, the rapid test revealed that Annette's level of red blood cell destruction was over the usually fatal limit. Aggressive blood transfusions and anti-malarial medication saved her life. In the following days, we contacted every official who had broken protocol to help. Each one was a hero. Heroes break rules. The end justified the means.

So how would we convince Buzz and his buddies to do the same for us? That's why we needed Blake.

✦   ✦   ✦

Blake lives with his wife, Amber, and toddler daughter, Xanthia, outside Boston. His company headquarters is in Manhattan, but mostly he works from home, which means he works all the time. A high-tech company founder, he is considered an engineering software and 3D printing visionary. He's usually far too busy to be concerned with family matters, but we knew he could analyze the situation pragmatically. Some of Ashley's impassioned pleas on social media had backfired with hate mail. One jerk (who turned out to be a fellow passenger named Bruce) started a petition to send her to Japan so she could die with the geezers. More than a few others also suggested we should be sacrificed rather than infect healthy Americans.

"How many new victims?" Blake asked dispassionately when we called him. I told him there were forty-one.

"Is that cumulative?"

"No, Blake, just today. If you count the man from Hong Kong that's a total of sixty-two—and that's only from the two hundred they tested."

"Wow." There was a long pause. "I haven't taken this as seriously as Ashley and Josh. I tried to cheer them up by saying you were probably researching your next cruise." His voice cracked. "I'm sorry I let you down."

"Not at all. Ashley said you've called the State Department and we got a copy of the great letter you sent."

"Maybe the sixty cases will get their attention. Logically, though, that could be the tip of the iceberg—sorry for that metaphor—but the numbers in China are increasing almost exponentially. I assume they'll be testing everyone on the ship, right?"

"We have no idea. All we know is what we hear from the captain or in the media. So far, we're fine and so are the Mendizabals and our friends from Texas. The State Department just echoes the Japanese line that we're safest sheltering in place, but we don't feel safe at all!"

Blake asked how he could best assist us. I made it clear that we were frightened by the news, felt in danger, and wanted to escape as soon as possible. "Josh and Ashley are getting the runaround from CrisisFlite. They might respond better to your more—ah—assertive approach."

"On it!" He waited a few beats. "Are you still getting blitzed with media requests?"

"That's the other problem. We can't keep up. There are new ones daily and the old ones want to continue to follow our progress and we can't prioritize."

"Who are the big players?"

"The *New York Times*, *Washington Post*, BBC radio and TV, Sky News UK, many Canadian press and TV, ditto Australia, CNN, ABC, NBC, Fox—both national and local stations, especially all the Tampa Bay area outlets. Then there's the Asian press and TV—everything from China to Korea to Japan. Plus lots and lots of Europeans."

"Whoa, Mom! Stop! Tell me you're not exaggerating."

"I forgot to add the *Wall Street Journal* and—"

"Forward every current request to me. I'll make up a spreadsheet with time zones and rank them by the most influential. Then I'll do a schedule that makes sense and still lets you get some sleep. You need to concentrate on your talking points and sending a consistent message. Then I need to make CrisisFlite's management aware of the scope of publicity you're generating. They'd have to be idiots if they didn't see this as a once-in-a-lifetime marketing boon."

"You're amazing!"

"How's Dad handling this?"

I told him Phil was keeping busy filming from the balcony. "That's another problem. All the networks are clamoring for his stills and footage and he's even recording the captain's announcements because each one is another bombshell of bad news. However, it takes forever to upload everything for each request. One more issue: We have to go out to sea to keep this ship running properly and once we're out of range of cell towers or our private internet receiver, we're on the ship's satellite system competing with thousands of others for bandwidth."

"Mom, calm down. I handle big problems all the time. This is what I do! May I have permission to act as your rep on this?"

"Of course!"

"Then I'll do a media repository on Google Docs. Have Dad send me all his files. I'll sort it out."

Some of the many scenes unfolding just below our balcony on Daikoku Pier during quarantine.

"What about your job?"

"Let's worry about you—not me. I'll circle back in a few hours."

"Don't forget we're on Japan time."

"Yes, Mom, I was just there last year—in Yokohama, remember?"

"You know I get up a few times at night. I'll check the emails somewhere between two and three in case you have any questions."

"Perfect. I'll have everything scheduled before I go to sleep."

"This will really help."

"Mom! This is what I do!"

Once again, I had underestimated my children. When I was pregnant with Blake in 1973, we visited Montessori educators who had five remarkably independent children. Even the

Photographers and TV satellite trucks restricted to one end of Daikoku Pier.

eighteen-month-old baby ate her meals with a fork and drank out of a glass without making a mess. "Every child is far more capable than we ever believe," the mom told me. "The secret is teaching them a skill, and then they have it forever." This became our child-raising motto. Now we were putting our fate in their capable hands.

We forwarded all our media requests to Blake. To each one he replied with his phone number, email address, Twitter handle, and this message from us:

> Because of spotty communication and some overlapping calls, all coordinating, scheduling, and news updates will be handled by our son Blake Courter, who is in the eastern US. He will also put you on our update list to facilitate communication.

Dinner arrived just as I was about to do another on-camera interview. I munched on a freshly baked roll while Phil framed the shot. Instead of holding the iPhone and trying to keep it steady, Phil—my personal cinematographer—had rigged a "tripod" by balancing it between the handles of my rollaboard. He set a chair by the window and put a pillow against the back, which forced me to sit slightly forward and straighter. During the day, he adjusted the curtains over the sliding door because the sunlight was more complimentary. At night, though, the ceiling lights created harsh shadows, so he created a soft fill light by aiming the lamps at the wall.

Vana popped in. "What's going on?"

"We're setting up for an interview with Korean television and then CNN after that."

"I wonder if all this publicity is a good idea."

"Why?"

"Wouldn't it be better to just wait out the fourteen days and go home quietly?"

"That presumes that we don't get sick *and* that they will let us leave in two weeks."

"That's what they told us."

"Anything can happen. The Japanese government might want us to quarantine for another week on land or force the ship to go to another port. The airlines might not accept us. And the U.S. might close its borders."

"Not to citizens!"

"Sure they can, especially if they think we could be contagious."

"Well, we're not."

"That's the message we need to get out. They need to see us as regular people, not plague-ridden freaks."

"What if you get punished for complaining?"

"What can they do to us? We're telling the truth about what's happening. People are falling like flies. Who's next? Will it be another forty tomorrow? Nobody's ever seen anything like this on a cruise ship."

"I hope you're right." Vana sighed. "Anyway, I came to tell you that Mary Lou—Cathy's mother—passed away this afternoon."

"Oh, no! So soon?"

"The tragedy is that if we hadn't been quarantined, Cathy might have been at her bedside."

"I'm so sorry. Do you think I should call her?"

"Wait till tomorrow. I think she was up all night talking to her family and she may be sleeping. A bigger problem is that she hasn't gotten all her medications. Mario's been helping because she's having trouble coming up with a prescription. They haven't been able to get one of the ones she needs the most."

"What does she need?"

"It's confidential."

"I have a fully stocked pharmacy, remember?"

"Okay. But keep it private." Vana explained the issue.

"Got it!"

"I don't believe it!"

I went into the closet, opened my medical kit, and found what Cathy needed.

Still stunned, Vana said, "Now I have to figure out how to get it to her." The Giambalvos' cabin was only ten doors away but the hall monitors wouldn't let us get very far.

Phil pointed to his bottles of red wine. "Use my method. I put out a note with a five-dollar bill and the wine came in ten minutes!"

My phone buzzed. "Showtime!" I fluffed my hair, took off my glasses, and accepted the FaceTime call.

✦   ✦   ✦

CNN February 7, 2020 - 06:30 ET

Will Ripley, CNN Correspondent: We've been speaking for a couple of days now with passengers on board the *Diamond Princess*. We've been asking them to take videos and send them to us, which we've showed you. And once the news broke that the number of cases tripled overnight from 20 to 61, well, the whole mood changed. People are very concerned, saying that this ship behind them, which now has the highest concentration of coronavirus patients anywhere in the world outside of mainland China, is starting to feel like a floating prison.

Gay Courter, Florida Passenger: We're in a contaminated prison, possibly.

Ripley: Florida passengers Gay and Philip Courter are among the lucky few with a balcony. Many of the 2,600 plus passengers are in cramped cabins, no windows, breathing air circulated throughout the ship.

Courter: This is not a safe environment. And we don't think anybody, let alone the Japanese government, wants to be responsible for making a bad decision about quarantining us in an unsafe place.

Ripley: The Courters are in their mid-70s. They know the vast majority of coronavirus deaths are people older than 60. And she says the *Diamond Princess* is packed with retirees.

Courter: We want off this ship and we want to go in health and not in dire medical circumstances.

Ripley: She even has private insurance that covers crisis extraction. But the Japanese government says they can only be extracted after the 14-day quarantine period.

WE'RE NOT SAFE!

Everything can be taken from a man but one thing: the last of the human freedoms—to choose one's attitude in any given set of circumstances, to choose one's own way.

—Hector Garcia Puigcerver, *Ikigai: The Japanese Secret to a Long and Happy Life*

As the number of people coming down with the coronavirus increased, the food sent to our rooms became more delicious and abundant. The chefs had previously catered to the Asian guests but now they were adding enough choices to satisfy as many as possible. Breakfasts of scrambled eggs, sausages, yogurt, fruit, croissants, and muffins were more than enough and we started to fill the mini-fridge with snacks. Lunch was usually rice-based, with chicken or beef on top, a cabbage or other veggie, the ubiquitous round—and always freshly baked—roll, plus an appetizer like lunch meat with a dollop of fruit and salad. They must have had tons of frozen shrimp on board because that became a common main dish. The highlight of the first week came when we received menus with three choices for lunch and dinner.

Even more impressive was the new delivery system they must have developed on the fly. At mealtime, we'd answer the door knock with our masks on. Someone with a clipboard would call out our room number and then a color, which matched each of the three selections on tray trolleys. "Two reds" or "one black and one green" would signify which dishes we had ordered. After the main dishes were served, the second waiter pushed his cart forward with the appetizer plates, followed by the dessert. Last came the drinks wagon. Since the door was set to spring back, I had to keep my foot against it while twisting toward the corridor to grab the plates, before handing them to Phil, who set them on the table. There was an urgency for the crew to avoid prolonged contact with our "contaminated" presence, so any attempt at polite conversation was cut off. Before closing the door, I always called out, "Stay healthy!"

"Our biggest risk may be 'death by chocolate,'" I told Phil, since the pastry chefs were sending us sublime creations, with chocolate the most prominent ingredient. I gave up worrying about my waistline and my migraines—both swelled with chocolate—for the dopamine high.

✦ ✦ ✦

Email from Blake Courter, February 8, 2020

Outreach:
    Blake: CrisisFlite
    Robin: Centers for Disease Control and Medical Team
    Josh: Oregon congressmen
    Ash: State Department
    Gay and Phil: Media

Strategy: Use media influence to draw attention to the *Diamond Princess* and our folks. Stay on point!

Talking point: The virus is fomenting on the boat and the Japanese government response is inadequate and putting everyone's life at risk. The situation is deteriorating, with the infection rate doubling daily. US government action is needed to save American lives. **We demand an immediate evacuation to American quarantine as has happened with at least seven other concentrations of American expats.**

Talking point: The Japanese government is creating a humanitarian crisis by putting healthy passengers in an unsafe quarantine due to improper ventilation on the ship....

Talking point: Mom and Dad are in nonstop communication with U.S. and international press. Local ABC and CNN crews are standing by to cover the evacuation.

Medical opinions from Robin and her contacts:

1. Mom and Dad are safer in American quarantine than boat. Removal from boat is our top priority.

2. Meds: Do not take any steroids which may make it worse (unless given in hospital). Consider Tamiflu if you start to experience symptoms.

As promised, Blake was on the case. From the time we woke up until we collapsed into bed, he had us going nonstop. Besides being the technician, Phil was joining me in many of the interviews. "Everyone's asking how I keep from going stir crazy," I said while munching on a salad long after I had eaten the dessert. "How can I explain that I've never worked harder in my life?"

We knew that most everyone else was trying to overcome boredom. Cruisers expect round-the-clock entertainment, which Princess understood, and they invented a new playbook to keep everyone as content as possible. Nobody was angry at the staff or management, especially once they announced we would be reimbursed for what we had spent on the cruise, which included not only the cost of our cabin but almost everything we had charged to our onboard accounts: alcoholic beverages, sodas, specialty restaurant

横浜消防

OUTBREAK **QUARANTINED AT SEA**
PASSENGERS SPEAK OUT

CNBC

Getting our message out was a full-time project; this is a clip from one of the many interviews we gave while quarantined aboard the *Diamond Princess.*

meals, excursions, tips, taxes, and even some shop purchases. Also, anything we needed would be provided—if available—for free, including beverages, medications, and personal grooming items. Requests could be made by calling the front desk or room service, but the wait times would have frustrated a Tendai monk—until we started implementing the note-and-cash-tip system.

Vana and Mario were delighted when Princess doubled the number of commercial TV channels and the library of movies expanded. Natalie and Mikiko, the two cruise directors, came up with creative diversions broadcast on the dedicated Princess channel. Princess has a mascot, Stanley, a human in a fuzzy bear suit who wears various cruise-related costumes, and Natalie and Mikiko took turns reading him bedtime stories in both Japanese and English. Every cabin was supplied with a fresh pack of playing cards so passengers could learn tricks from Sunny Chen, the Taiwanese magician, who had not been able to Houdini his way off the ship. Neville the maître d' offered napkin-folding lessons. The fitness instructors had several levels of workouts doable in small spaces. Various members of the entertainment staff gave dance lessons. Eventually, they added a trivia show—which I glanced at only once while blow-drying my hair. When I checked in with a family we had met in our dining room to see how five-year-old Abigail was coping, her mother said she was receiving a new toy daily.

We had no time for viewing or exercising because our personal dance card was filled. Requests came via email, Facebook and their messaging link, my phone's texting app, and all the same on Phil's phone. Also, all our children—especially Ashley—were forwarding queries from around the globe. After I sent each request to Blake, he took over the scheduling, but I still had to respond to the initial query, approve the schedule, answer questions, and make sure the writer received a personal thank you.

While we are better informed about world politics than the average American, we had to do some Wiki-cramming. Both China and South Korea have negative feelings about Japan and are only too happy to embarrass them publicly. During the 1937–1945 Second Sino-Japanese War, China suffered between seven and sixteen million *civilian* deaths, with many atrocities, including the Nanking Massacre. Both Korean and Chinese women were forced into brothels as "comfort women," and some Manchurians were used in biological warfare experiments, which is why reporters from China and Korea pressed us to criticize Japan.

This was tricky because while we blamed Japan for our predicament, we needed Prime Minister Shinzo Abe to cooperate with President Trump to send us home. We suspected that if the United States repatriated their citizens, the other governments would be shamed into following suit. As far as we were concerned, the *Diamond* was being held hostage by Katsunobu Kato, the Japanese minister of health, labor, and welfare, and his agency's misguided decisions. Every expert we—and our family—talked to said the

Japanese were breaking the first rule of quarantine by locking the healthy with the sick.

Other passengers had made contact with the media, especially in their own countries, but there was a vast difference in technical quality. Almost all nonprofessionals make the mistake of shooting vertical videos, which then requires masking both sides of the screen and creates a narrow image. They don't hold the camera steady; rather, they move endlessly to try to "capture the scene," but that results in nauseating images. Phil's professionalism shined through.

Every time there was an announcement of more coronavirus cases, the news ricocheted around the world. The press kept coming back to us for comments on the latest developments. If we had been on the *Today Show* that morning, NBC News followed up later in the day. Once we had been on JTBC in South Korea, *Spotlight,* their investigative program, asked for a more in-depth interview. Soon we realized that we were having a mutually beneficial relationship: They were getting their story; we were being heard.

✦　✦　✦

February 9, 2020. U.S. Embassy Tokyo
MESSAGE TO U.S. CITIZEN DIAMOND PRINCESS PASSENGERS

The U.S. Embassy and the Department of State continue to closely monitor the situation and to coordinate with the Government of Japan, as well as representatives from the cruise line, to ensure the well-being and safety of passengers. We have no higher priority than the welfare and safety of U.S. citizens abroad. Current guidance from the U.S. Centers for Disease Control (CDC) states that the safest and most reliable way to prevent further spread of viral infections on cruise ships is for passengers to <u>shelter in place</u>, as passengers on the Diamond Princess are doing. Per current information from CDC and the Government of Japan, after passengers finish their 14-day quarantine period they will be permitted to depart Japan on commercial flights, which are readily available, and will not be subject to additional quarantine upon return to the United States.

Jerry called shortly after this email arrived. "I've been on hold with ANA," he said. "What day are you making your reservations for?"

"I just can't wrap my head around that yet," I said, since he didn't know about CrisisFlite.

"Well, since our quarantine officially started on the fifth, it should end on the nineteenth—so I'm going to try for the twentieth."

"Let me know when you get seats."

"Jerry's making reservations home," I told Phil. He seems to think that at the fourteen days, we'll be able to walk off the ship and fly home."

"That's what the State Department notice says."

"It also says that we won't be subject to an additional quarantine in the U.S. but I don't believe it. Everyone from China has had to spend two more weeks at a military base."

By Monday, February 10, any semblance of calm evaporated with the news that sixty-five more people had been diagnosed. Once again, I had a cognitive lag. Sixty-five meant only one more than the previous day, right? But no. The total had doubled overnight so there were 135. If that numerical progression persisted, every soul on the ship would test positive in five more days.

"This is the chessboard of doom!" I wailed melodramatically, then, "Seriously, Phil, how are so many getting sick so fast?"

We were hardly the only ones asking the same question. The "Red Dawn" chain of emails between top epidemiologists and infectious disease experts, released in April, shows they were pondering this simultaneously.

Email From: Dr. Eva K. Lee (Georgia Tech) sent to James Lawler, MD (University of Nebraska) February 10, 2020

Strategic testing is a must....*Diamond Princess*...offers the biggest opportunity to study in multiple levels and I am afraid it has become a quarantine nightmare with missing opportunities and missteps. And it shows why strategic testing is a must.... The cruise ship is a tiny community...and it shows we have no ability to test even just that. [There are] 136 confirmed cases out of 336 tested thus far. Japan still maintains they are going to test those with symptoms and the elderly. They should and must test all, and truly use that opportunity to get a good sense of symptoms vs. no-symptoms.

Phil called me out to the balcony, where he was filming anything that moved: ambulances, fire trucks, helicopters, various clusters of men huddling and disbanding. "Bring the binoculars!" He pointed to what looked like a Japanese family of eight, including an elderly person in a wheelchair. "That's the third group today that seem to have golden tickets out of here."

"I wonder who they are?"

"Either they're famous, rich, or politically connected. For all we know, they could be members of the government."

"Lucky ducks," I replied. "I don't even resent their privilege. When Buzz shows up, I'm not looking back."

"What has he done for us so far?"

"Besides his 'boots' in Japan? He said he's contacted our local congressman. Oh, and I asked whether the Mendizabals can come with us because Mario's our doctor. He said they 'might be able to accommodate them,' whatever that means."

"Honey, let's be realistic. As I said before, a medical jet from here to Florida would cost a fortune. They will use every excuse for why they can't evacuate us."

"But Buzz said they did it from Wuhan and that's even farther away."

"See that limo pulling up near the ship?"

We watched a woman in a long fur coat stop at the end of the gangway and wave back. A chauffeur opened the door and she slid into the back seat before I had a good bead on her with the binoculars. "I think that was the opera singer from *Bravo!*" I touched Phil's shoulder. "Did you get a close-up?"

"No, I was focused somewhere else."

"Damn! It would be great ammunition for Buzz because they wouldn't be making an exception just for us and we've agreed to leave in full protective gear."

"That's what I love about you. You're relentless."

"The question is, how can we convince the Japanese in a way that allows them to 'save face'?"

"Tell the press about these 'most favorite people'?"

"No, that would be humiliating."

"Forgetting about just us for a minute," Phil said, "why don't we start asking for everyone on the ship—including the crew—to move on land where we could be better isolated from each other and the crew wouldn't have to serve us."

"What hotel or facility could take all of us?"

"Their brand spanking new Olympic Village can hold twice that and they even have a section for the Paralympians—so that would mean facilities for the walker-and-wheelchair contingent."

"The Japanese won't risk any publicity about us contaminating the Olympics." My phone rang. "It's Motoko Rich from the *New York Times*."

"You just talked to her yesterday."

"I'm keeping her up to date and vice versa."

"Don't forget you have CNN in thirty."

After a brief hello, I told Motoko, the paper's Tokyo bureau chief, about the exodus we'd seen from the ship. "They know the quarantine is not working, and these people are getting a free pass."

"Do you have any theories?"

"Obviously, 'sheltering in place' isn't working because more and more people are getting infected. Some bugs like Legionnaire's disease can be spread through air-conditioning ducts, so that's one possibility. I'm mostly worried about room service to thousands of people at the same time. Just because the cooks and waiters are wearing rubber gloves doesn't mean they can't be spreading it. They hand us napkins, cutlery, fruit, bread, and drinks and then do the same again at the next door. If the person just before us has the virus on her hands, it could transfer to the waiter and then to us in a few seconds."

"Do you think you might have met the eighty-year-old man from Hong Kong, the one they're calling Patient Zero?"

"We have no idea although we could have ridden in an elevator or sat next to him in the theater. We did share a table in the buffet with a young couple who lived in Hong Kong. Now that I think about it, I think they were getting off there too. They'd been on board since the first segment from Singapore."

"So that could have been a scheduled stop for the man?"

"If he only embarked five days earlier in Yokohama, that seems unlikely. There were no five-day segments." I added that we had received thermometers and were supposed to check our temperatures twice daily.

"Who do you report the results to?"

"Nobody. It's voluntary." I considered my next words carefully. "Princess used to require us to fill in a health form as part of the boarding process, but they recently eliminated it. Nobody would admit to having respiratory or gastrointestinal symptoms because they'd be turned away. So, everyone lied." I waited a beat. "The same has been true with noro. People avoid calling the clinic because they don't want to be quarantined for three days." I laughed. Three days now seemed like nothing. "Room service and cabin stewards would let the medical staff know who was ordering soup and not leaving their cabin. Now, with no interaction, there's no way to know—except by testing."

"Have you been swabbed?"

"No, and we want to be. Otherwise, how will we know we're okay when this is over? And the sooner the people who are positive are removed from the ship, the safer everyone will be."

"Are they testing the crew at least?"

"Motoko, we only know what the captain tells us."

"What's happening with your private evacuation?"

"Phil thinks they're stonewalling. I'm hoping that the publicity they'll get will help offset the costs."

I promised to text her if there was any news on board. Likewise, she would get back to me if she got wind of any information early.

Sandi Sidhu, a producer for CNN in their Hong Kong office, contacted us shortly after she arrived in Yokohama to cover the story with Will Ripley and Matt Rivers, and we seemed to connect beyond the journalist-source relationship. One afternoon she called to check on us and asked, "What do you hear from the CrisisFlite people?"

"They said they had an appointment at the American consulate to discuss paperwork issues."

"Gay, I think you may need to think about what you would do if you never had that plan."

"What do you mean?"

"It's just a thought. Will's going to interview you later. Tell him—and the world—what you want to happen."

I felt as if Sandi must have information I didn't, but she couldn't say it aloud. I dialed Buzz's emergency line without caring what the hell time it was wherever he was—and where the hell was he? Tokyo? California? A sleepy voice answered. "Buzz, Gay Courter. Who exactly is your 'boots on the ground' in Japan?"

"That's privileged. We're all retired from various security forces and all Americans."

"Yeah, I looked you up. Seems like you were in the Secret Service, right?"

"I cannot confirm or deny—"

"That's not why I'm calling…" I had to be circumspect. "Tell me, when you evacuated—or as you say 'extracted'—your members from Wuhan, did they fly home in one of your jets?"

"I never said that."

"That's the impression you gave me." I was seething. "What exactly did CrisisFlite do for them?"

"Actually, I work for Ex911." He waited a beat for me to react, but I just let him stew. "We helped them with the exit paperwork and arranged transportation to the airfield. We are in touch with them daily and when they are released from quarantine in California, we'll assist them with transportation home."

"In one of your jets?" He was silent. "So, you essentially provided nothing that they couldn't have arranged on their own, right?"

"They appreciated our help because Wuhan was in lockdown and we cut some red tape."

"Is that what you're doing for us?"

"Yes, ma'am, and we're staying in touch with your sons and your daughter. Just yesterday, we advised the sheriff's department in your county that your house needed more security because you're getting so much publicity that bad actors may know your house is empty."

"We have elaborate security on our house, employees checking it several times a day, watchful neighbors, and we're in a very low crime area."

"Just taking every precaution, ma'am."

"Listen, Buzz, you sold us pandemic insurance and CrisisFlite is all about rescue flights. Perhaps you've heard me on television promoting your company and telling the world that you're coming to save our asses because we were smart enough to buy insurance that includes pandemics. If you actually do what your literature implies, you'll sell a million policies this year."

"Mrs. Courter, you know very well that we are not an insurance company and we are not regulated like one either. We are a members-only organization. Further, we cannot violate either the Japanese or American government's immigration rules."

"Your promotional literature specifically says you don't depend on hard triggers like government-issued mandates to protect your travelers."

"That's true in the case of natural disasters but—"

"Have you explained to the Japanese and American authorities that we will leave under Hazmat conditions from ship to ambulance to airplane and airplane to ambulance to U.S. hospital without even setting a foot on the ground?"

"That possibility has not been up for discussion."

"Because of the cost?" I couldn't keep my voice from splintering. "Is your company all bullshit? Because, if it is, we have the ears of the world media. You know those emails you've been sending to 'the family'? Our family lawyer—a former judge—is following along. She already knows you have an office in Florida. Did you know I am also a travel writer? Go to my web page and read my article on trip insurance. My syndicate goes out to over two thousand publications with around forty million readers. I think it might be time for an update on how deceptive your—"

"I understand that you are very upset, but just let us do our job, and in the end, we believe you will be happy with our service."

"Do tell me what that 'service' actually includes."

"When you are released from the ship, we'll have a limo to take you—and your doctor—to the airport and we'll provide business-class tickets to Florida, with another limo from the airport to your home."

If I had been wearing a blood-pressure cuff, it would have exploded. Instead, I burst out laughing. "We already have first-class tickets and paid-for private transportation through the people who were handling the last part of our tour. Plus, we have arrangements for someone to meet us at the airport and drive us home. So, we won't be requiring any of your incredible services." I disconnected.

"Are you really going to go to war with them?" Phil asked.

"Hell, yes!"

"How about we get home first?"

✦ ✦ ✦

That was the moment I settled in for the long haul. Phil had always been dubious about a *deus ex machina*. There wasn't going to be a helicopter, private jet, superhero, or Greek god descending to whisk us to either Mount Olympus or Fuji. We were either going to leave on gurneys or walk off at the end of the quarantine. Vana and Mario had long since resigned themselves to waiting it out. Cathy was in mourning and I could tell she was suffering. We talked a few times a day. It's impossible to know what to say, but a grief counselor once suggested: "I can't imagine how you are feeling…" as an opening line. To that I added, "…being away from family and friends. I would be angry to have missed being at my mother's bedside because of the quarantine." I told her that the night of my mother's funeral, Tropical Storm Florence flooded our house with several feet of water. "I was furious at my mother because the least she could have done is to stop it." Cathy laughed a bit, so I added, "When a clergyman friend made a condolence call, I told him how I felt. He said, 'It's not her fault. She was still in orientation.'"

"At least I got to tell her I loved her," Cathy said, "if she heard me."

"Of course she heard you," I said emphatically because I was sure it was true.

That conversation reminded me how close the emotions of rage and sorrow are and how I find it easier to be furious than miserable. That night when I found it hard to settle into sleep, I admitted that the battle to get everyone off the ship was partially fueled by the very primal fear that either of us could become feverish in the night and be dead in a few days. No amount of verbiage or campaigning would confer immunity.

"Maybe the archaic miasmatic theory of disease wasn't so crazy after all," I said to Phil, who didn't have any context for my comment. "I first read about it when I was researching *The Midwife*. For centuries people believed that epidemics like cholera, venereal diseases, and bubonic plague were caused by a noxious form of air, or miasma. In fact, some who believed that bad air was responsible for many common ailments posited that obesity was the result of inhaling a food's odor."

"That's definitely true about chocolate."

I laughingly agreed with him. "It took until the end of the nineteenth century before scientists proved that specific germs cause diseases."

"Your point being...."

"That somehow this coronavirus is wafting around through the air vents, seeping under the doors, or swirling around the food carts. Nobody is going out. Nobody is mingling. So how are we getting sick?"

"Actually, *we're fine*. We wash our hands every time we accept food or anything from the corridor. We keep wiping down the door handles and cleaning our room. We're wearing masks around anyone else—even the Mendizabals. So, how about we look at the upside for a change?" Phil said. "Don't laugh. I just thought we could try a role reversal."

"I'll look at the upside when the number of new cases on board starts to diminish. I used to love to hear the captain's charming voice, now I dread it."

The next time I had an interview, I said we were worried about the virus being circulated by the air conditioning system. In the captain's very next message, he assured everyone that they were only pumping fresh air to all the cabins. Blake had written about his air-handling concerns to the State Department; the next email from the American consul included: "Some passengers have expressed concern about the possibility of the novel coronavirus spreading through air vents on board the ship. Carnival Cruises assured us today that no cabins on the ship are using any recycled air." In our next several interviews, I was asked how we felt about the denial and replied, "Until a scientist checks whether there are virus droplets in the air-handling systems, nobody knows whether it enables transmission of this disease or not." In fact, the latest studies validate our claim that air conditioning disseminates the virus.

There was a steady stream of ambulances from daybreak to late into the evening. We wondered if all the patients had the virus or whether the stress had precipitated other problems like heart attacks or strokes. In several interviews, we expressed concerns over the most elderly and frail passengers we'd seen during the cruise. "There's at least one stroke victim in a wheelchair," I said, "and many have portable oxygen units. A respiratory illness could be fatal if someone already is battling a lung disease."

The next day there was an announcement that the Japanese health officials were planning a disembarkation of the most medically vulnerable guests, including older adults with pre-existing conditions. Ventilation issues had not been mentioned in the press until we brought it up and then the concern even appeared in the *New York Times*. Was it possible that our home-grown media campaign was influencing policy? Blake insisted we were, but we didn't quite believe him until I did an interview with Neil Augenstein at WTOP—one of Washington, D.C.'s most popular news radio stations. He asked me if the meals had changed. "Before the quarantine, we were eating filet mignon, lobster tails, and crème brûlée. So, they went from gourmet to ghastly overnight."

After dinner the next day, there was a knock at the door and a guy in a chef's toque handed me two crème brûlées. "I guess the powers that be at Princess are listening in."

"Maybe that's what everyone is getting."

I called Jerry, Katherine, and Vana. "Nope. They all had strawberry cheesecake."

HERE THERE BE MONSTERS

I felt despair… It's maybe close to what people call dread or angst. But it's not these things, quite. It's more like wanting to die in order to escape the unbearable feeling of becoming aware that I'm small and weak and selfish and going without any doubt at all to die. It's wanting to jump overboard.

— David Foster Wallace

Updates from Passengers Phil and Gay Courter on the *Diamond Princess* **Quarantine**

Yokohama 10 Feb 2020

65 new cases were announced today, more than doubling the total to 135. 273 "close contacts" from patient zero were tested, so 61 positives from 273. Now there are 74 more positives from outside that group.

Phil and Gay Courter are in their fifth day of quarantine aboard the *Diamond Princess* and are continuing to request removal of all passengers to appropriate facilities or allow medical evacuation. The *Diamond Princess* is the site of the largest outbreak of the novel coronavirus outside of China….

The U.S. Embassy Tokyo has responded to public outcry of the passengers, crew, and their advocates: "Some passengers have expressed concern about the possibility of the novel coronavirus spreading through air vents on board the ship. Carnival Cruises assured us today that no cabins on the ship are using any recycled air." We welcome such continued public conversation.

We seek to learn more about the ship's ventilation system, as we are concerned with the rapid increase of new sick individuals. Does the ventilation system create a negative pressure in rooms? Does Japan have enough negative pressure hospital rooms to receive and care for all those being removed from the ship? If not, would it be possible to reduce risk by separating those on the ship into safer facilities?

Meanwhile, the fate of the Courters remains difficult to determine. Will the authorities extend the quarantine if the infection rate continues to increase? At what point does the world realize that the containment experiment has failed?

"Mom," Blake said with some urgency, "I've spent the last three days on this nonstop, but I can't keep up with the volume of requests either. I'm up half the night with the baby, and in between, I'm dealing with the Asian emails and then segue into Europe and then the East Coast."

"That's not sustainable," Phil said, since the call was on speaker. "You also have a demanding job."

"I have that sorted for another day or so, but we need twenty-four-hour coverage." I started to speak. "Wait till I finish. We need to bring in a pro. We already have the top media in the world knocking at the door, and now we have to prioritize and manage the message so we can dominate the news cycle."

I rolled my eyes at Phil, who indicated agreement that Blake was losing it. "You really do need to get some sleep," Phil told him.

"Terry told me how, in the nineties, some of his friends in Congress used C-SPAN's continuous coverage to promote their platforms. He said, 'Not only should you be telling the story, you must articulate the outcome you want.'" He paused for a breath. "Are you willing to spend some money to get everyone off that ship?"

"Since Buzz turned out to be full of it, what's Plan B?"

"We need professional help." Blake said we should partner with a PR pro and recommended one he knew, Bobbie Carlton.

"Use your best judgment," Phil said. "We trust you completely."

He copied us on an email to Bobbie, admitting he was "in over his head" in terms of expertise and time.

Thirty minutes later, Bobbie called Blake. "I checked out your parents in the media. What you've already accomplished is incredible. Your father's a machine! There's a ton of videos, stills, even audio recordings. And I could put your mother in front of anyone."

"Am I crazy for thinking we could dominate the news cycle?" Blake asked.

Bobbie laughed. "There is no bigger story in the world! And our mission is to get everyone off that damn ship."

"That's what I thought, but my parents are worried that I'm losing it."

Indeed, Phil and I were spending so much time talking to the press that we had no idea of the extent of our impact. We didn't see or hear any of the television or radio and only glanced at a few articles. Apparently, if you're occupied making the news, you're not only too busy to see the result but you can't judge the effect you're having. Nor did we understand that we were becoming characters in a drama and that almost everybody we had ever known was watching—and would soon be in touch.

Bobbie called us Monday morning in Japan. "First, let me say that what Blake has done is nothing short of miraculous. However, this is just too huge for any one person to handle. Also, the reason the same reporters keep coming back to you is that you give both context and detail—not just 'yes' or 'no' answers. You're quirky—and they love it."

"Quirky granny" is not how I would define myself, but if it was working…

"What we all need to do—that includes you two and Blake—is stay on message and not lose the focus that everybody needs to get off that ship. Keep it simple; keep it direct. You have some good sound bites, but pare them down so the core nugget doesn't get cut."

I told her I'd been through media training before a book tour and knew the drill. "I learned that you don't have to answer the question, you can just respond with your takeaway message."

"Blake said you were a pro," Bobbie replied.

"I would take one of the boys out of school to be my assistant on tours, so he's seen the sausage being made."

"Don't forget you're a bestselling author. Mention that."

"You mean 'was.' I'm more of a has-been these days."

Bobbie ignored that comment, saying only that she'd be back to us with the schedule. She also added our concerned friends and family to the list to receive the daily press releases, which helped lighten our email load.

From then on, we just forwarded every message to Blake, who replied: "In order to more effectively manage this situation, we've contacted Bobbie Carlton of Carlton PR & Marketing in Boston. Please reach out to her directly with interview requests and other inquiries."

The telltale ping! Phil grabbed his cell phone, turned it on to record, placed it on top of his bald spot, and stood directly under the ceiling speaker because he was now recording all the captain's messages. He forwarded every photograph, sound recording, and video to Blake, who put them in a public folder accessible to the press. As a result, Phil's credit pops up on many of the photos used worldwide.

"The Japanese Ministry of Health has informed us of thirty-five more positive cases." A wave of dizziness made the room spin in that stomach-churning way you feel just before you pass out. I lowered my head and waited for the black veil to lift.

Phil scratched the new number on our tally sheet. "That's the highest spike so far, bringing the total to a hundred seventy-four. I wonder how many are crew."

"Hopefully they're fighting it off because they're younger," I said, heading outside to see how many ambulances were on the pier. I called to Phil. "It looks like a battlefield. If it still takes an hour to load one person in one ambulance, it's going to take a couple of days around-the-clock to clear the backlog, not counting any new cases."

We texted Blake—and some of the media—the numbers. Now that Bobbie was juggling our interview schedule, Blake worked on an action plan. He stayed in touch with Terry, who was reaching out to his contacts in the State Department, and Robin, who serves on the board of a Maryland hospital alongside Dr. Eric Schoomaker, a former Surgeon General of the United States Army. At that moment, very little was known about the novel coronavirus, how to prevent contagion, and what to do if we had symptoms. Dr. Schoomaker got back to Robin with information from Dr. Anthony Fauci's team at the National Institute of Allergy and Infectious Diseases, saying that most people recovered and with some suggestions about self-care in the meantime, which was kind, but not reassuring.

Blake made certain that Karen Gievers, a long-time friend and our family's attorney, was copied on CrisisFlite emails. She contacted Jack Hickey, a maritime attorney in Miami, about

quarantine law and passengers' rights. He stated that the cruise
line had a responsibility to get both sick and healthy passengers
"off that ship ASAP and to a place the sick can be quarantined
and well-treated. Everyone else needs to be tested and provided
transport back home."

+   +   +

Monday night we once again untethered from Daikoku Pier and
chugged offshore to make lazy figure eights during essential marine
operations, including dealing with fresh and wastewater issues as
well as ballasting—the process by which seawater is pumped in
or out of tanks to balance weight for the best performance. The
captain informed us that a helicopter would be bringing medications while we were at sea. Phil was looking forward to filming it,
but the drop was canceled because it was too windy. This turned
out to be our last "cruise" because, with the number of positive
cases climbing, we had to stay in port so those infected could get
prompt medical care.

The next morning Phil and I dressed warmly to be on the balcony while the *Diamond Princess* headed back to port. Even from
a distance, we could see the fresh brigade of ambulances. Then,
when the ship rotated, backing into her berth, our view changed
from the activities on the wharf to the more scenic Yokohama
harbor, the bridge, and Mount Fuji in the background.

"Do you think they turned to ship around to spite us?" I asked,
knowing that Phil's coverage of the military-like maneuvers was
circling the globe. The "assignment" alleviated his sense of being
an impotent bystander who could be the next victim. Even though
he was frustrated not to have his best camera or a tripod, he had a
far better angle than the media relegated to the farthest end of the
wharf. Now there was nothing to cover.

"That's a bit grandiose," Phil said with a hearty laugh, "even for you."

I was suddenly overwhelmed with a rising panic. A tinnitus-like buzz made me forget what I wanted to say. "But we need to see what's happening!"

"Sorry, I didn't bring my drone," he said as a joke, but I knew he continued to be upset about his lack of equipment. "Call our friends in port cabins," Phil suggested. "They can snap some pictures and email them to us."

A few minutes later, Sandi from CNN emailed me with the latest casualty numbers, which we already knew. I wrote back: "This is obviously not going well. They're not containing the outbreak. They've turned the boat around so we no longer have a view of activities at the port. It's time for all people on board to be tested, perhaps in order of age. I'm scared."

She responded: "Please keep your spirits up, Gay. I hate to see you go downhill emotionally like this. It must be so horrible. You have no symptoms and we should hold on to that."

Phil answered his phone. "Hi, Blake." He listened, then turned to me. "Don't be alarmed when you see the email from CrisisFlite."

I immediately checked my Inbox.

> We have received a call from Deputy Sheriff Prentice from the Citrus County Sheriff's office. The deputy reported that they have been conducting additional patrols of your property knowing your situation in Japan. This morning they found a door open on the bottom floor. There were no signs of forced entry. There were no apparent signs of burglary. However, they can hear music playing on the second floor.

I looked up at Phil and silently mouthed: WTF? He made the okay sign with his fingers and continued listening. He kept shaking his head and laughing. "Keystone Kops!" he said as he handed me his phone.

"Hi, Mom. Dad will fill you in. Everything's handled. No worries. Bobbie's been busting her tail but she still doesn't have today's schedule. Lots of interviews are being rearranged to accommodate the big guns."

"Like?"

"Anderson Cooper wanted you, but you're already booked with Erin Burnett and they can't let him hijack her story."

"She told Anderson Cooper to take a hike?"

"Something like that." He was chortling.

"You are enjoying this!"

"Come on, admit it, Mom, you are too."

"It's better than rewriting my own obituary."

"That's a joke, right?"

"Well, not exactly. I wrote one a few years ago and it's in our will folder so—"

He cut me off. "Anyway, Bobbie's prioritizing. The next one for Japanese TV is very political."

"What does that mean?"

"They are anti the current regime, so they want you to be critical."

"Is that wise?"

Phil piped in. "Gay can use an 'I' statement…for instance 'I'm or we're frightened of getting the virus and want the government to agree to let us off this ship.'"

"Exactly!" Blake said. "Also, Bobbie put Swedish National Radio on hold until she gets SkyTV, the BBC, and Squawk Box lined up."

"What's Squawk Box? And hooray for the Beeb."

He ignored me, which was a well-honed how-to-get-along-with-your-mother reflex. "Bobbie will brief you. She told me that in the thirty-five years she's been doing PR, she's never seen such a global media frenzy around a story."

"That's hard to believe." I looked around at all the sticky notes on the mirror and lined up on the suitcase-tripod, our makeshift studio.

"Anyway," Blake added perfunctorily, "our FUD strategy is working."

"What's that?"

"Fear, uncertainty, and doubt. It's a disinformation ploy used in PR and politics to sway perception by disseminating negative information—because if people are *afraid*, they pay more attention. Why do you think the nightly news always leads with a scary story?"

"We're not making anything up; the numbers on this ship *are* terrifying. And I don't just mean the positive cases. Eighty percent of the passengers are over sixty, another two hundred are in their eighties, and about a dozen are in their nineties. Most of the very elderly are part of Japanese multigenerational family groups."

"I know, Mom, and we're all worried. The good news is that there's pressure from the Japanese side too. I saw an article about how people with chronic illnesses could decline rapidly just from the stress of being confined in their cabins. A lot of them don't even have windows."

"Maybe this will be the tipping point and we'll see some action from Washington."

"Right, because next we're going to analyze how much impact we're really having. You're going to lead every interview with one word: *triage*, then repeat it as many times as possible. Today's message is 'This is a *failed quarantine* and now they are *triaging* who gets to leave the ship first.' We're going to track it and see how fast it populates on the internet."

"Blake missed his career as an influencer or whatever they call it," Phil said after we hung up.

"Now tell me about the email from CrisisFlite."

"A comedy of errors," Phil said. "Nobody was inside except some deputies. Buzz felt it was his duty to secure our home, so he asked our sheriff to keep an eye on it. The night shift went in through the pool enclosure and found one of the downstairs sliding doors open, but they failed to notice the hose leading from the hot tub into the pool."

"Michelle," I said, referring to our part-time housekeeper, "was planning to clean the hot tub. She must have left it to drain overnight."

"Right, but the funniest part is that the deputies got spooked by the 'weird' music coming from upstairs."

I hooted. "Alexa! I told Michelle to have the device play Mozart because that would surely freak out any of the local 'criminals.'"

✦ ✦ ✦

From: Blake Courter
To: Courter Media List
Subject: Triage, Triage, Triage! *Diamond Princess* Corona-virus update

Quarantine policy pivots from shelter-in-place to triage.

Between the lines, the authorities have admitted that it is not possible to preserve safe quarantine on the *Diamond Princess*. Their strategy has now shifted from containment to rescue. This pivot is both a welcome change and a gut-wrenching admission.

We are pleased about the suggestion that more and more passengers will be removed from harm's way. The authorities have started with those with the highest risk of mortality and appear to be reaching out to the next most vulnerable....

Triage protocols demonstrate that everyone on board is at risk of infection. If there was a provable negligible risk of infection, why release anyone in a special category? Did new information cause the authorities to change their mind, or did they know it was a bad idea all along?...

Note: My parents only received proper N95 face masks for the first time yesterday.

Something in me stirred from simmering desperation to anticipation. Was this the turning point? Several journalists wanted Blake to comment on the press release. He was quoted in the *Asia Times:* "The Courter family supports the triage approach and removing anyone possible from the boat, especially crew, as diluting the concentration of illness makes everyone on board safer." The last time we faced the pier, Phil had filmed as approximately eighty passengers, and possibly some crew, walked off the ship and filled two buses and several vans. There was no official explanation. All the captain said was "Thank you for your continued perseverance and patience as we navigate this unique event together."

One of the next day's headlines read: "Authorities Adopt Triage Approach Following Passengers' Complaints That Cooping Them Up on Ship Is Dangerous." "Triage!" kept popping up on various newscasts, where the *Diamond Princess* was still a lead story. A few desperate passengers had hung homemade banners over their balconies saying they needed medicine. Any scrap of communication from the imprisoned to the press immediately received attention.

When we docked the day after our last "cruise to nowhere," forty-five doctors, fifty-five nurses, and forty-five pharmacists had come on board to assist. I called to check up on my medication order and mentioned that I was running out of insulin. In my case, it probably wouldn't be life-threatening, but I didn't want any complications, even with my doctor in the next room. Phil received some of his pills, but he had to take half of one tablet and two of another to equal the American version. Josh's friend Summer had asked me in a private Facebook message if I had enough medication and she followed up daily. Summer had met Josh in middle school and they had been best buddies until they graduated from high school. Once a highly competitive swimmer, Summer now directs a 3D anatomical modeling and printing division at a major teaching hospital's department of radiology. Coincidentally, because Blake has innovated in medical 3D printing, they've been in touch professionally. From the start, Summer had railed against the quarantine because they were keeping the healthy with those who might be infected. For some reason, this very busy woman took it upon herself to first get us our meds and then get us off that ship. As we found out, Summer—who still gives her all until the race is won—is a woman to be reckoned with.

✦   ✦   ✦

I regretted blurting out to Sandi, the CNN producer, that I was frightened. I did not like people knowing how vulnerable I felt. Privately, I admitted that the frenzy of our media campaign was a smoke screen hiding the beasts lurking just beyond the horizon, like the uncharted seas depicted on ancient maps with fanciful dragons, sea creatures, and other nameless monsters lying in wait to devour unwary explorers. I tried to convince myself that knowledge would mitigate my morbid thoughts of a "miasma"— an invisible undercurrent waiting in ambush. Even if I confessed my dread, who was going to comfort me by saying, "Oh, don't be silly" or "That's not going to happen" when nobody could utter those words with sincerity?

Vana had assumed the worst from the beginning and never wavered. Once the ship was turned around, our balconies were bathed in sun most of the day. Instead of shivering in the chilly air and worrying about the passengers being carted off to some distant hospital, Vana was drawn to the railing. "How far down is it?" she asked Phil.

He guessed it was fifty feet. "If you do a big scissors leap, you should land in the water. Feet first would be safest. If any other part of your body hits the water, it's going to hurt like hell, but it could be survivable."

Vana turned to Mario. "Do you think I could swim to those bridge piers?"

"One of those guys would pick you up." He pointed to several small boats with signs indicating they were from Japanese TV and giving their phone numbers. They wanted to interview passengers.

"They'll fight over you," Phil said, "to get an exclusive."

"Let's not and say we did," I added. "A Japanese prison won't have fresh rolls or chocolate decadence. And, ah…did you see the notice about mental health counseling?" I slipped in nonchalantly.

"I sure hope the hold time for the suicide line isn't anything like the one for room service," Phil said sarcastically.

The next time we were out on the balcony, Mario approached me. "Any bad headaches?" he asked, since he prescribed for my chronic migraines. "Not so far," I said, "but I'm slightly dizzy all the time, which is odd because I never get seasick. It's more of a visual problem."

"We're going to have to watch that." He lowered his voice to almost inaudible. "There's no way you're going on a safari in April."

I wanted to protest, but I knew he was right. The virus aside, there would be no time to get the required vaccines or start taking anti-malaria pills.

"Is everyone sleeping okay?" Mario asked.

Phil admitted he was having trouble falling back to sleep in the middle of the night.

"Are you taking anything?" Mario had prescribed sedatives.

"Only on the plane and the first few nights in Tokyo."

"Try a half for anxiety and a whole one at bedtime," Mario suggested.

"I needed one yesterday," Vana admitted. "Everything keeps changing. I need to know what's going to happen and when."

"Have you seen this?" Phil showed her a new bulletin called "Voluntary Guest Disembarkation Plan" that had come with the *Japan Times* and a book of crossword puzzles. "They're going to allow what they're calling the medically most vulnerable guests off first, to be followed by older adults with pre-existing conditions."

"I don't think it would work for us," I said, pointing out that the Japanese-run housing they would take us to was a college campus. "We'd have to stay in our rooms and there's no medical facility."

"I'm tempted," Phil said, "if only to get away from whatever pestilence is seeping through these walls."

"I feel better knowing Princess is taking care of us," Vana said.

"You just like all the new movies," I teased. "We haven't had time to watch a single one."

"You might still get a chance," Mario added. "The fourteen days could be extended."

"Really?"

"They might want fourteen with no new cases."

"That doesn't make any sense," Phil said, "or we'd be here forever."

"If we aren't able to go home on the nineteenth, I'm going to freak out," Vana admitted.

"Nothing about this makes any sense," Mario agreed.

✦　✦　✦

That same day, February 11, the World Health Organization named the *disease* COVID-19. The *virus*, Severe Acute Respiratory Syndrome coronavirus-2, or SARS-CoV-2, had already been designated by the International Committee on Taxonomy of Viruses—the virologists who develop the tests, vaccines, and medications and reference the genetic structure. Six weeks earlier, it was virtually unknown and nonexistent. At that moment, there were only thirteen cases in the United States, forty-two in Hong Kong, eight in the U.K., and 44,730 reported in China, including 1,114 deaths. So far there had only been one death reported outside China.

Later in the day, the captain's voice sounded weary as he gave us the latest: thirty-nine more were leaving for hospitals. He did not differentiate between passengers and crew.

"At this rate…" Phil said, "we're following the same progression as China." Normally, I'd look for a contrary statement to mollify him, but this time I couldn't quiet my internal alarm bells.

There was a knock at the door long after dinner had been delivered—and it was one knock, not two. A man in a uniform different from any worn on the ship was carrying a large package with delivery instructions written on all sides. "It's here!" I shouted in surprise.

"Just in case…" seems to be my special brand, so when Summer offered to help with our prescriptions, I already had copies of the originals in my phone. Summer's pharmacist, who had seen us on the local news, expedited everything so the insulin would get to us before my supply ran out. "It was like the *Amazing Race*," she told us. "When I got to Publix, there was a long line. The pharmacist waved me forward saying, 'This is for the people on the ship in Japan.' Every single person moved aside and when I left, they shouted, 'Go get 'em!'" Summer said, "I couldn't believe it, but everyone knew who you were."

Summer described her maddeningly slow rush-hour trip to FedEx at the airport. "They were ready to close, but after I explained the situation, the guy said he'd seen you on TV and asked them to hold the plane!" She then tracked the package to Tokyo, where it arrived in twenty-six-hours but never moved from the customs office. That's when we learned that the *Diamond Princess*'s certificate of landing had been canceled in Okinawa and the ship was technically in quarantine status, which meant it had not been accepted into Japan legally. Summer then played her best card: Someone close to her family worked in the White House. This connection led to the package being forwarded as far as the port, but there still was no way to deliver it to the ship. Undaunted, Summer somehow located a State Department official on the wharf who carried the package to the ship, where it was handed to us with much bowing and smiling. We snapped a picture and texted it back. Summer wrote: "Tears of relief here!" Then, without telling us, she thanked everyone in Washington who had helped and said, "Now, let's get them home!"

✦ ✦ ✦

Whenever we travel, I buy a pocket-sized notebook and record staccato-like memos that bring instant recall of each day. A typical cruise jotting would be meaningless to anyone else, but I can visualize every minute of "Tai Chi…25 min…B'fast Horizon… Carole like Joan Didion…sushi, eel bento…shuddering ship…." Every page in this cruise's little book is filled until February 3. It begins: "B'fast in dining room, morning trivia…" And that's it for the rest of the trip. Considering everything that happened in the next month, nobody is more shocked than me that I didn't write a single word. What this tells me is that I had moved from any normal habits into another space. As plush as the cabin was, I felt trapped, held against my will, and I used every atom of energy to keep functioning while simultaneously looking for a way to escape—taking everyone with us, most especially the loyal crew.

Since the room stewards were not allowed to service our cabins, I'd leave notes outside requesting clean towels, a washcloth or two, toilet paper, or soap. Then Edwin would knock on the door, supply the items, and hurry away. One day I held my hand up and asked, "Please, can you tell me, are you okay?" He backed against the far wall of the corridor, looked anxiously to his left and right, and said, "We are all worried." His eyes registered an expression closer to panic. I turned to Facebook and asked if one of our friends could help start a GoFundMe account on behalf of the crew. I'd swear that Princess was also monitoring my social media because a few hours later the company announced that, in addition to paying the crew their wages, it would cover the tips they would have received on a regular cruise.

Somewhere buried in the barrage of emails about interviews, queries from worried friends and relatives, and payment due notices, we found one from the U.S. consulate. Excitedly, I called Jerry and Cathy.

"Remember Kagoshima?" I said. "The guy from Hong Kong took the ship's tour there—the one you were thinking of doing instead of going with our Goodwill Guide. At least two others on that tour have come down with coronavirus. They're testing thirty-six more who were in close contact with him."

"We dodged that bullet," Jerry exclaimed with a long whoosh. "That would have been a high price to pay for a free glass of sake."

I tried not to consider what would have happened if Jerry and Cathy had gone on that tour. They probably would have been exposed and considering how much time we spent together, especially at meals, we all could have been infected. So far, nobody we knew was stricken. We only had the last names and cabins numbers of a few shipmate acquaintances. Eventually, we found a Facebook group limited to passengers and we learned about a British couple who tested positive at the same time and were sent to a hospital together. Phil and I were pet-rified that if one of us turned positive, we would be separated. Robin, who checked on us daily, reminded us that most people just have mild cold or flu-like symptoms and recover with no lasting problems, but I didn't believe her. Every time I lay in bed, I tried to imagine being intubated and unable to commu-nicate. Then I read that the majority of those my age with my pre-existing conditions didn't survive ventilation, so it was best to say your farewells before you went under sedation. That gave me another dilemma: Along with a "do not resuscitate" order, should I also refuse ventilation?

✦   ✦   ✦

I had no way to unpack my unruly emotions. I wondered if my vertiginous sensations were caused by a spike in my cortisol levels due to anxiety or even a coincidental brain tumor. I did feel steadier when I was busy because purpose puts fear on the back burner. Maybe exercise outdoors would help. At first, only those guests in windowless cabins were allowed on deck. The privilege was then extended to people in cabins with sealed win-dows. In the last few days, we had a printed schedule that cov-ered everyone on the ship. Our forty-five-minute period came only every other day, so when I heard the officer of the watch—the deck officer on duty who reports to the captain—announce it was time for anyone on Dolphin Deck starboard to exercise, I was eager to take our turn.

This was our first experience with "social distancing"—though that exact term was not used. We were told to remain six feet apart from others and had to wear our masks at all times. The elevators were reserved for people with disabilities, which was fine since walking two flights down to the Promenade Deck felt like a jailbreak.

Practicing social distancing, though the term wasn't used yet, one of the few times we took the opportunity to walk on deck during quarantine.

"Now I understand why they turned the ship around," Phil exclaimed when we walked to the side facing the pier. He pointed to several trucks pumping sewage from the ship into large tanks. "This is how they're disposing of the liquid waste and why they're pumping fresh water from the barge on our side of the ship."

We also noticed the continuous ambulance service. "I don't think they'll ever catch up with the backlog of people who need medical care onshore."

As we walked up and down the deck, everyone was avoiding each other like—well, like the plague. We were each alone in our own private circle of hell. Many of the passengers looked older than we were. There were a half dozen wheelchairs. A man with one leg made slow progress with crutches. A few teenagers behaved like horses at the starting gate who can't wait to break into a gallop.

It could be worse, I thought. We could have been stuck in a windowless room with petulant adolescents.

✦   ✦   ✦

One morning, watching the harbor scene from the balcony, Phil's face lit up. "Remember when we were in Okinawa? Our guide said that our base there has wonderful medical care and that Japanese residents are welcome. What about American citizens? This ship could take us back to Okinawa. In fact, American planes could land on the base and take us home without anyone putting a foot on Japanese territory."

"What a brilliant idea!" I exclaimed. Excitedly, I went inside and called Abigail's mom. Their family lives on another American base near Yokohama, where Abigail's dad works for a military contractor. "Phil, Abigail's mom says they were wondering the same thing. Their base is so close we can see its lights from our balcony." I pointed in the approximate direction. "That means there's a place for the ship to dock just a few kilometers from here."

"Don't you think our government would have thought of that already?"

"Ah…not necessarily…"

I pondered, then discarded, various ways to bring up the idea with the media. I didn't want to sound foolish because I knew so little about the treaties that allowed the U.S. military to be so present in Japan. I finally decided to mention it more as a question: Would it be possible…? or Have you considered…?

One direct effect of our outreach was that people did try to cheer us up. We received good wishes from acquaintances we remembered—and some we didn't—from all parts of the globe. The staff at Inside Japan Tours—the agency that had meticulously arranged the aborted last part of our trip—stayed in touch in case we needed anything. Even though our payment was nonrefundable, as a goodwill gesture, they reimbursed us. One of their executives in Japan emailed us a picture of a fearsome warrior with a note saying, "This is Shoki the Demon Killer. Legend has it that he protects people from disease. Here he is scaring away two germ demons. In the past people would hang his picture to ward off the plague, so I am sending this to you in the hope that even an electronic version will have the same effect."

I showed it to Phil who said, "I wish we could print it out and post it outside our door."

For me, though, professional interest in my writing brought me the most moments of joy, especially when my literary agent, Joëlle Delbourgo, wrote that someone was interested in a film option on *Flowers in the Blood*. I love imagining the movie that might be produced from one of my novels. Most of my books have had film options; none have made it to the screen. Still, it was a nice diversion from the latest virus statistic.

The next day an editor at *The Atlantic*, one of my favorite periodicals, asked if I would write "about your experiences…and that in doing so you might relieve some of the boredom and fear of the situation, as well as communicate the nature of what you're going through to the wider world." Since I'd much rather write than talk, ideas about how to describe the byzantine assortment of feelings about losing our freedom and our free access to food, of being captives of a foreign government—all while being stalked by a deadly virus—darted through my mind. Just when I had a lede in mind, another thought would seem more essential to explain or I would be interrupted by an interview, or I just plain lost the thought. It also didn't help that our situation—and my moods—changed so often that I couldn't get an emotional bead that made sense. Now I understand that traumatic stress compromises the ability to think clearly and concentrate, which is why I couldn't explain my feelings when I hardly had time to feel them.

Yes, I had the fear the editor mentioned, but not a trace of boredom. What did she imagine I was doing: rereading Jane Austen with fresh insight? Did *The Atlantic's* readers want to hear that we were doing nonstop media? The cabin was more like a jury-rigged film set and operations center than a haven for geriatric cruisers. Phil had used our "emergency" roll of duct tape to make a steadier cell phone holder and to secure the angle of the lamps we used as auxiliary lighting. Once I was in position in front of the iPhone set-up at my "battle station," I stayed put. Usually, a producer would call in ahead of a live interview to make sure we had a good sound and picture. Once it was established, it was best to leave it on. Connectivity—on both sides—was a continuous struggle. So I didn't confuse the Dutch with the Danish, Phil would give me a sticky with the names of the producer and presenter, approximate pronunciation, and Bobbie's notes. I also needed the day's schedule, so I wouldn't stay on a call too long, and a précis of the talking points of the day. And also, something to drink and a part of whatever meal was last served. Maybe they'd be more interested in the disintegration of politeness between Phil and me. I rejected that idea as far too personal, but I have profusely apologized to Phil for my curt demands and general rudeness to get this and do that.

A few days later, Bobbie called. "I am thrilled to tell you the *Washington Post* wants you to write an op-ed."

"You're thrilled? I'm over the moon!" I'm always writing op-eds that never get published, except in our hometown newspaper. I told Bobbie I was struggling with the piece for *The Atlantic* because my ideas kept evolving—and without a proper keyboard, I had resorted to dictating into my iPhone, but it wasn't the same as typing. She offered to help. "You can dictate to me, I'll send it to you to correct, and after a few passes, it'll be done. For now, just decide what you really need people to know." I realized it would be hard to garner sympathy for being forced to remain in a luxury cruise ship cabin for free, but the stakes became crystal clear when the captain became the caller in the bingo game from hell. February 12 added twenty-eight new victims, February 13 was "only" seventeen, bringing the total to 218. Then the announcements stopped abruptly.

I called Katherine, who was on the port side. "There are as many ambulances as ever," she said.

"You're a nurse," I said. "Do you think they should be testing everyone on board?"

"As I understand it, the Japanese have a limited supply of test kits."

"What if we test positive even before we're symptomatic? Wouldn't it be better to be somewhere where we could get treated early?"

Katherine doubted there was any way to pressure the minister of health, who I had decided was personally to blame for the rampant infections. My thoughts focused. I knew what to write for the *Washington Post*:

> …The Japanese government must protect its citizens while also treating all on board this ship ethically…If healthy tourists risk exposure through forced quarantines, what might that mean for, say, the Tokyo Olympics this summer? Who will risk sitting in a crowded stadium in Japan, or sending their athletes to compete?

Peering out at the lights of Yokohama, I imagine that some of the twinkling comes from the U.S. military base, with its dock and hospital. Isn't that considered U.S. soil? A few people have been allowed to leave this ship. Those still stuck here are desperate for everyone on board to be tested so that those who are healthy today will not be infected tomorrow.

✦ ✦ ✦

I wasn't the only one acting out of character. Phil's personality also underwent a sea change. He became a clean freak, like Felix to my Oscar in the *Odd Couple*. My "life-saving" hair curlers filled the sink. I left makeup for touch-ups on the counter. Wet towels, no longer automatically replaced daily, were draped on the tub. Most annoying for him were the half-eaten plates of food I wanted to save for noshing on breaks.

"I don't know why so many clothes are on the bed," he complained when he tried to straighten it, "when you keep wearing the same shirt on camera." Because Blake had suggested we leave the sliding door open to dilute any toxic air coming through the vents, there were only two well-fitting tops that kept me warm enough—but I would change to a sweatshirt off-camera. I also learned another fact a few months ahead of the Zoom curve: Nobody sees you from the waist down.

"Were we getting on each other's nerves?" a few commentators asked, and when I mentioned the Felix and Oscar routine, they laughed.

Not really. Mostly, we were very companionable because we gave each other wide latitude for the circumstances. At home, I'm generally very organized and tidy. Now my free moments were prioritized: bathroom, beverage, "beauty," bites of food, catching up on messages, and hand washing the laundry.

The day we went into quarantine, the captain announced that all "services" would be free—including laundry and dry cleaning. When Vana saw my clothesline, clips, and wet clothes draped on the balcony, she wondered why I wasn't sending everything out. "We could get off this ship at any moment," I said, at that time still believing CrisisFlite would whisk us away. Even after I accepted that defeat, I expected we'd be chugging off to an American base where red-white-and-blue striped planes would arrive and there might not be time to retrieve our laundry.

One of my greatest fears has been imprisonment. When I was a guardian ad litem, I visited incarcerated fathers and mothers, sometimes bringing their children for visits. What reverberates most is the sound of the doors locking behind me. I supposed they coped the way we did: We developed routines. Phil dealt with the food and dishes; I put out the trash and brought the cans back inside. We put on smiley faces when we opened the door and thanked everyone for their help. Meals soon came at expected intervals and were plentiful and delicious. All my just-in-case items were coming in handy. If we had not been afraid of the coronavirus, we might have even said we were content. In fact, Phil and I had everything we needed—the most important being each other. We had done something quite unexpected: We had adjusted.

There's a fine line between laughter and tears and sometimes it didn't take much to provoke a laughing jag. One afternoon, somewhere in the limbo between lunch and dinner, we heard the squeaky wheels of a solitary food trolley. I anticipated the door knock. The cart was loaded with Styrofoam cylinders of CUP-NOODLES. I accepted an armful in a variety of flavors. Now we could rehydrate them with water from our kettle and have a meal anytime we wanted. What a concept!

"Phil," I called out. "Guess what? We didn't go to the CUP-NOODLES factory, so it came to us." Then I started to laugh. "I bet they donated it to us poor, starving passengers." Just thinking about going from privileged passengers to pathetic displaced persons cracked me up.

"You sure do amuse easy," Phil said as he tried to juggle the containers.

Expecting a potentially fatal disease to strike at any minute made us into hypochondriacs. Was this just a dry throat or the first sign of respiratory failure? Was the soreness in our bones the normal aches and pains owing to our age and inactivity, or were the white cells trying to fight off the infection causing inflammation in muscle tissue? One morning I started limping. Both my feet were killing me as I assumed my position in front of the camera and waited while the tech guy from a Tampa TV station made a few adjustments. I looked down at my painful feet.

"How are you feeling?" came the cheery voice of the on-camera talent.

"Actually," I said, "I thought I was holding up awfully well under the circumstances, except...it seems I'm having problems with my feet."

"Oh, no!" she said sympathetically.

"That was until I realized I was wearing two different shoes—both left feet!"

✦ ✦ ✦

We didn't know it at the time, but our children were far more worried than they let on. Ashley had started the campaign on social media. Journalists searching for "Courter" found her first and she dealt with the earliest media requests. Blake offered to take over the mainstream effort, so she could rally some of her thousands of followers on Instagram and Twitter to contact their representatives and ask for the Americans on board to be repatriated—as with our citizens in Wuhan, China.

In Oregon, Josh participated in the early planning and had been the Pacific time zone coordinator. He had the idea to reach out to congressional representatives and was the original contact with Summer. If Ashley is the heart and Blake is the brain, Josh is the soul in our family. We used to say that the three of them together had what it would take to deal with any tough situation. And indeed, that's what happened. Josh didn't so much listen to what we said in our interviews as see the weariness, the strain, and insincere laughs. He called Blake and told him we were exhausted. "If they don't get more rest, they'll be more prone to infection. Don't work them so hard."

"Mom told Bobbie they'll do anything that will motivate the powers-that-be to bring the Americans home."

"What's that saying about killing the messenger?"

After Josh suggested making sure we had a good night's rest, Bobbie announced that there would be no interviews before seven in the morning or after nine at night. (Exceptions were frequently made, but only with our approval.) Bobbie also decided to limit second appearances to media that could influence U.S. officials. Her list included Molly Hunter at NBC and Will Ripley at CNN, who joined the merry band of press at the far end of the wharf. Both had promised to help get us home. We also kept in touch with Motoko Rich at the *New York Times* and several other journalists and commentators. We summarized every shipboard announcement and forwarded pictures of notices we found in our mailbox.

At one point, Will Ripley asked me what we thought needed to happen. I said, "We would like to make a plea directly to President Abe and President Trump to work out a way to repatriate all the Americans on board, including some very elderly passengers and small children. This will lead the way for other governments to get involved. There are quite a number of Australians, Chinese, Koreans, folks from Singapore, a large Russian contingent, and more than four hundred Americans." I noted that Will looked over to where Sandi, the producer, was sitting and rolled his eyes. She made a gesture to let it go. I had said something wrong. When we were off the air, I realized my faux pas. Mr. Abe is the *prime minister*—not the president! And the polite way to refer to him is "Prime Minister Shinzo Abe," including his first name. I wrote that large on another sticky note and put it front and center.

So much was happening, appointments were always in flux. Sometimes I was talking to someone with an Asian name in Canada or an American in Hong Kong. Trying to keep track of multiple time zones was bad enough. I lost track of the day of the month, let alone the day of the week. Time was delineated by awake, asleep, and meals. I don't know what I would have done without my cue cards and scribbled notes strewn around the cabin.

✦ ✦ ✦

Summer kept in touch. Just in case CrisisFlite came through, she had met with the clinical directors of the local CDC and health department. They explained that because we were considered "potentially exposed individuals," they no longer had jurisdiction of the matter. Although this was disappointing, we knew that the private evacuation "ship had sailed" and our next best hope would be government-sponsored repatriation. I usually think of "repatriation" as the euphemism for returning a citizen's body home for burial, but it also refers to bringing someone back to their country of origin.

Summer reiterated that a close friend of her family works in a senior position in the West Wing. "He's the one who put me in touch with task force people who helped get your medications package onto the ship." She said that "they"—whoever they were—were "very aware of your situation" and to tell you that the CDC, Department of Defense, and the National Institutes of Health—and other agencies—are working on a solution." She added that we should keep speaking out publicly. "I know it's working. And I promise to do everything I can from here until we get you all home. Please stay safe. Get out in the sun and use that balcony for fresh air as much as you can."

CABIN FEVER

How did I escape? With difficulty. How did I plan this moment? With pleasure.

—Alexandre Dumas, *The Count of Monte Cristo*

Updates from Phil and Gay Courter on the *Diamond Princess* Quarantine

Yokohama 14 Feb 2020

Yesterday, we were trying to understand why we heard two numbers of infections reported: 38 vs 39. We now understand that there were 39 new infections, and one was not a passenger. He was a government quarantine officer. If one of Japan's experts in quarantine self-contaminated with presumably sick patients, how do you think the crew is doing with dirty dishes and trash?…

"Do you think we're going to die from this?"

"What brought that up?" Phil asked, his voice raspy from sleep.

We were lying on the unmade bed, heads propped up by two fat Princess pillows and three of our own boudoir-sized ones, waiting for breakfast to arrive. It was Valentine's Day, which Bobbie had declared a day of rest. I was worried that we'd lose our slots with NPR, the BBC, and MSNBC. "They were happy to move it to the fifteenth," she reassured us.

Now, instead of sticking to a publicity agenda, it was time to talk about what we would find at the bottom of the rabbit hole.

"We're on the wrong side of the equation," I said to Phil. "Forty-eight percent of cases over age seventy-five die from this coronavirus."

"And over sixty percent are male. I might as well cash in my chips."

"Sorry, the casino on the ship is closed." I swallowed hard. "Really, we should talk about this. For instance, if one of us goes to a hospital here, should the other head back to Florida?"

"I couldn't do that," he said.

"Me either." I closed my eyes.

He reached for my hand. "Do we *have* to do this now?"

"It would help me to have a plan."

"Okay." He sighed. "Plan away."

"Remember the Intercontinental, the hotel where we stayed last time we were in Tokyo?"

"Best breakfast buffet!"

"It's close to the American embassy, which would be helpful because the consulate provides services if a citizen is hospitalized in a foreign country, like when my father was in that plane crash in Ecuador. So, if one of us is taken away, the one left behind will go to that hotel and wait until the other is released."

"One way or the other." I pretended I hadn't heard that. "A week or two there would cost a fortune."

"Think of all the credit card points we'd earn."

Knock! Knock! The signal for the first breakfast trolley. There was so much more I wanted to talk about—where our wills were filed, the master passwords for my accounts, what the Japanese did about DNR requests...

"Look at this!" Phil, quick to change the subject, held up a red-glazed croissant. "The chefs are pulling out all the stops." There was also a muffin, two boiled eggs, sausages and sautéed mushrooms, plus yogurt, a banana, and a box of apple juice.

"And don't forget the *Yakult*." I'd looked it up online. The Japanese believed the yogurt-like product helped fight upper respiratory diseases. It was tart but tasty, and why pass up anything that might boost our immunity, even if it did sound a bit like snake oil?

Two more knocks. Edwin handed Phil cleaning supplies: large antiseptic wipes, several types of dust rags, a spray solution, a plastic apron, and pink rubber gloves. "Be my Valentine?" Phil said with mock-sweetness and handed me the package. "Ah, my dear! We need some cleaning-the-cabin footage," he added, in the voice a villain planning revenge might use. Phil pointed the camcorder at me like a weapon. "First, let's get you cleaning the bathroom... starting with the toilet."

I kidded around with the toilet brush, but once I got started, I was determined to thoroughly scour every crevice where the virus might lurk.

Later research indicates that COVID-19 does cling to surfaces for many hours—possibly days—so Phil's instinct to constantly clean our cabin, with me pitching in more than he'd like to admit, may have offered some degree of protection.

✦   ✦   ✦

We didn't understand why the Japanese only tested passengers who displayed symptoms. When questioned by the media, Katsunobu Kato, the health minister, claimed they were saving tests in case they were needed later in Japan. "After fourteen days, if people have no symptoms, logically we can say these people are not infected by this virus," Gaku Hashimoto, his vice minister, said in a television interview. In retrospect, he probably didn't know that someone can be completely asymptomatic but also infectious.

Because the Japanese position seemed both illogical and self-serving, we decided to use our media pulpit to demand testing of everyone on the ship—especially the crew—and instead of testing by deck, they should concentrate on the oldest and frailest first. One reporter asked me, "What sort of health care have you received?" I replied, "None. After the temperature check the first day, nobody has checked on us in person, by phone, or by email." I went on to say, "While we mark our temperature chart twice a day, we assume that some people aren't bothering because they don't want to be taken away unless they're desperately ill."

Afterward Phil asked, "Why are you pushing so hard to be tested?"

"If we get treated early, there's probably a better chance of survival."

"You're missing the point, Gay. Let's say we're tested today and the results are negative. Great. But we could still be infected tomorrow, so what does it prove?"

Knock! Knock! Another delivery. This time it was our former headwaiter, Jorge, with a bundle of Valentine gifts. He handed me a long-stemmed red rose and said, "Compliments of Captain Arma," which—silly me—almost made me believe I had been singled out. There was a huge fan of dark chocolate; six packages of another confection; a box of Milky, a children's candy; a book of sudoku; a lip balm; and two masks to beautify the face rather than cover your nose and mouth. "I think that's their idea of a joke," I said with a mocking "Ha, ha."

"The chocolate is for you," I told Phil, "because Japanese women give the finest chocolates they can afford to the man they love. Then, on March fourteenth, the man is expected to return the favor and the woman hopes her gift will be even more extravagant."

"That sounds very mercenary to me," Phil said, then switched to a "Shakespearean" voice. "However, there be but one rose, which is for you, my darling!"

I lifted an empty wine bottle from the trash, filled it with water, and set it in the middle of our coffee/dining table. "Princess must have ordered two thousand roses."

"Don't people give flowers when they feel guilty?"

"Is that why you rarely give me flowers?"

Phil's face glowed as he came toward me with arms wide for a hug.

✦   ✦   ✦

An Australian couple stuck on board a cruise ship in Japan have had two cases of wine delivered by drone....
—*Daily Mail,* U.K.

While waiting for lunch, I scanned Facebook. Ashley's timeline was filled with news about our predicament and replies to her included prayers and good wishes from around the world. A few days earlier, she had posted an article about some Australians receiving wine by drone, but this was the first I'd seen it. "Can't be true!" I said to Phil, who uses a drone for aerial photography.

"I checked Japan's laws and was surprised to find them exceptionally lenient. Apparently, the prime minister is a drone fan."

"It would have been great to have one for taking shots from above and outside the ship."

"Too much to carry."

"Still, how could a drone lift two cases of wine—even one at a time?"

"If that's what it says, there's something fishy about the story."

Another "Knock! Knock!" interrupted us and we never returned to speculating. Eventually, we would learn how widely the drone tidbit was distributed and discovered that it would bring us an unexpected—and perhaps lifesaving—benefit.

Phil was giddy as he opened the lunch boxes. "Fish and chips and mushy peas!" During the first week of quarantine, the food had been served on china. Now everything arrived in disposable containers, less elegant but more sanitary. "How did they know this is my favorite lunch?"

"Whoever sent us the crème brûlées checked our 'dossier' and discovered that's what your usual order at Wheelhouse Bar."

Phil did a double take before he realized I was teasing.

After lunch, I turned on the television, determined to watch at least one first-run movie. Very few interested me until I saw *The Goldfinch*. "You'll like this," I said. "The book was superb."

Phil fell asleep during the first ten minutes, so I dimmed the lights and clicked off the TV. The balcony door was open, as usual. I snuggled under the covers, turned on my heating pad, and clicked back to Facebook. There were some unread notes in Messenger. The first was from Summer, written twelve hours earlier. I gasped. "Phil!"

"Wha?"

"Summer.... Oh, my God!... Listen to this. She says: 'Please hold on for just a little while longer. I can't tell you how I know this and you must keep this completely confidential, but you are coming home.'"

Phil reached for my iPad to read it for himself, then spoke sternly. "Gay, I know you can't wait to dash over to see Vana, but you can't tell her—or anyone. Don't blow this trust."

"I promise, I won't," I said. I'm ashamed to admit what most everyone in our family knows: I can't keep a secret, or at least that's

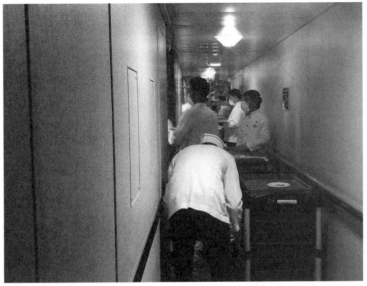

Gay briefly stuck her iPhone out the cabin door to capture this scene of the hard-working crew delivering meals. *Credit: Gay Courter*

Valentine's Day lunch: one of Phil's favorites, fish and chips and mushy peas.

my reputation. The problem is that nobody realizes how many secrets I *have* kept.

"But what does she mean?" I asked. "Did they finally get permission for CrisisFlite?"

"Maybe they're going to do a Wuhan-style—what do they call it?—extraction."

"I hope we won't have to go to a military base and quarantine for two weeks like they did." I felt my head beginning to pound. "Technically, we've already done a quarantine."

"That's true, but we've been telling the whole damn world that this a *failed* quarantine."

"Where would they put us? In barracks?"

"Drill sergeants, KP duty, the works!" Phil swung his feet over the side of the bed. "At least if we got sick we'd be in an American hospital."

I laughed. "Maybe the plus side of this whole thing is that we've undergone a role reversal. I'm the one who usually begins sentences with 'at least'!"

✦   ✦   ✦

Phil turned over and tried to fall back asleep. Knock! Knock! Phil groaned at the interruption. He put on his mask and came back with an iPhone box and an instruction sheet.

"What's it for?"

"We can use it to inquire about medication, talk to a mental health counselor, or contact a doctor about medical concerns."

"Sounds better than being on hold forever."

Phil's phone rang. "Blake," he said to me and looked at his watch. "Hey, buddy, it's the middle of your night. Is everything okay?" He switched to speaker.

"Just up with the baby—she's teething. Thought I'd check in before going back to bed. Hope you're having a nice Valentine's Day."

I moved closer to the phone. "Princess gave us lots of gifts—even a long-stemmed rose."

"And all your money back too, I hope."

"Actually, they're giving us a generous compensation package."

"Hope you're enjoying your day off. You can thank Josh and Giulia for insisting on it."

"Without talking points, Phil and I have nothing to stay to each other."

He laughed. "Bobbie's playing bad cop. Several of the reporters pretended to be understanding, then wanted her to make an exception. Your fans miss you."

"That's ridiculous." I shook my head in disbelief and whispered to Phil. "Tell Blake about—"

Phil put his finger up to his mouth. "Not that," I whispered, "about the new phone."

"Hey, Blake," Phil said, a touch of relief in his voice. "The Ministry of Health just provided an iPhone loaded with communication apps."

"Don't turn it on!" Blake blasted. "It's probably packed with spyware that can report all your movements to a central-command computer. That's how the Chinese know so much about everyone—the Koreans too. In Japan, everyone has an app so they can be located in case there's another earthquake."

"But they know precisely where to find us."

"They can listen to your conversations and see you with the camera. That bit with the crème brûlée was proof enough that they want to know what you're up to."

"They can turn on CNN for that," Phil said. "We haven't activated it yet, so we'll take your advice."

"If you don't have to return the phone, bring it home. I know people who would pay to jailbreak it."

"I'm sure we can't keep it."

"One more thing, Dad, your photos are populating all over the 'net. Bobbie's getting requests for some fresh shots of what's happening on the pier."

"We're still facing the bridge and we haven't heard any new numbers. In this case, no news is probably very bad news."

"I don't like where this is going." He took a long pause before asking, "How's Mom taking it?"

"You know her, she gets all worked up if someone stubs a toe, but in a real crisis she turns into a battalion commander." Phil reached for me and began rubbing my arm. "When this is all over, she's going to melt into a puddle."

"Don't worry about me," I chimed in. "I'm into megavitamins and *Yakult*."

"What's that?"

"Look it up. Love you."

"Okay, love you, too. But Dad, one more thing. Terry and I have been talking. He's so modest, but he's one of the smartest men I've ever met. He said to tell you to keep up with the interviews because it's helping sway public opinion."

"I'm glad he approves."

"*Way* more than that. What he's really saying is that it's changing the attitude of some high-level government officials about getting you off that ship. I don't want to discuss it any more right now, but he has some—let's just say *interesting*—friends in high places."

Phil was grinning. "Good to know."

"How's your Valentine's Day going so far, Blake?" I asked.

"It's just early the morning of the fourteenth here. Don't worry, I've taken care of it."

"Just don't give Amber a trash can," I said, referring to the time Phil gave me one with a big heart on it.

"See you soon," Phil said. This time I gave him a cockeyed stare.

He shrugged. "It's just an expression!"

✦ ✦ ✦

I turned on the second TV opposite the sofa and found our place in *The Goldfinch*. "So, catch me up here. We have a little boy and his mother dies in the first scene. Is it just one barrel of laughs after another?" Phil asked.

"Partly, but it's really interesting."

"How about a comedy?"

I handed him the remote and he landed on one of the Princess channels that broadcasts eternal reruns of *The Love Boat*, which not only features the Princess brand but supposedly was responsible for popularizing cruising. I started laughing at the absurdity, jumped up, put on my mask, and began dancing in front of the screen while singing—off-key—"It's the Looooove Boat!"

Phil lifted his camcorder off the shelf. "Do that again for posterity!"

More knocks. Three this time, louder and more insistent.

"This had better be Captain Arma in a gondolier's outfit singing 'O Sole Mio.'"

It was even better. Two Japanese medics—in yellow surgical garb, with face masks and shields—bowed. "Would you like to be tested for COVID-19?"

"Of course!" I indicated they could enter our cabin.

The woman pointed for me to stand on the threshold instead. "Mrs. Gay Courter?" I nodded. "Your permission please?"

"Yes."

The man wrote a note on his clipboard. The woman showed me how to tilt my head back and open my mouth wide. I followed her instructions and she reached past the tonsils I no longer had and swabbed before I gagged. "It's not too bad," I said, coughing.

After Phil's turn, he asked, "When do we get the results?"

"Three to five days…or sooner," the woman said.

"Sooner if it's positive?" I asked.

She gave a tentative nod.

I closed the door and went to scrub my hands while Phil took a disinfectant wipe to the doorknob.

I looked at a paper the health worker had handed me. "So, they *are* testing people by age!" I said, since we had suggested it. Of course, that was the most logical way to proceed.

"I heard that more than half the passengers are over sixty," Phil said, "and that's over a thousand people right there. I bet the number of positives is going to explode."

Knock! Knock! "Happy Valentine's Day!" the diminutive woman at the door cried to Phil.

"Hi, Faith!" he said. The hostess's beautiful smile was back.

"You are fine?" she asked.

"So far! You?"

She nodded. "Stay healthy!" Phil said as he passed the dinner containers to me.

While Phil set up our meal on the coffee table with the rose in the center, I went to the bathroom and brought back two battery-operated tea lights that served as nightlights.

There was a shrimp-and-avocado salad and coq au vin plus a heart-shaped chocolate mousse and a small cake decorated with strawberry cream. Phil poured himself a glass of Sauvignon blanc and Pellegrino in the second wine glass. "Home?" he said as a question as we toasted each other.

"I'll believe it when I see the whites of Willoughby's eyes." I couldn't wait to snuggle our "puppy"—a four-year-old Cavalier King Charles spaniel.

DEUS EX MACHINA

What we call the beginning is often the end. And to make an
end is to make a beginning. The end is where we start from.

—T.S. Eliot

"Today is the worst day yet," Vana said as we watched a Japanese
military boat pull alongside a runabout with television reporters
trying to solicit phone calls from passengers. "What if they extend
it for a few more weeks either on the ship or on land?"

"Then we'll muddle through day by day just like we have till
now."

"Why didn't the captain tell us how many more cases there
were yesterday?"

I shrugged. "Maybe he didn't want to ruin Valentine's Day."

Vana pointed to the highway on the bridge. "I keep imagining we're on one of those buses heading to the airport." I almost
blurted what I knew but swallowed that thought when Vana asked,
"Did you get your flights home squared away?"

"Not yet."

"But you always have a plan plus a couple of contingencies."

"There's too much up in the air."

"Worst-case scenario, we get off on the nineteenth." Vana's voice was high-pitched. "Unless one of our tests comes back positive."

"We might be immune. Remember that 'cold' we both had— yours started after Hong Kong? Could that have been a mild case of this virus?" As a helicopter approached the ship, I waved frantically. "Take me! Take me!"

"It doesn't say CrisisFlite."

Ouch! I knew that if Buzz evacuated us without Vana and Mario, our friendship might unravel; and because the stakes were so high, I wouldn't have blamed Vana for being resentful. "I'm still fantasizing about some sort of rescue by *deus ex machina*."

"A what?"

"It's a Greek theatrical term meaning literally 'a god from the machine' or a cheap solution to a complicated drama."

"You mean someone swoops in and saves the day?"

"Exactly."

"Anyway, I need the reassurance of reservations, which is why I moved our flight to the twenty-first."

I bit my lower lip to prevent myself from divulging anything. Did Summer really have inside information or was she just trying to give us hope?

"CNN in five," Phil called out and I went back to my battle station.

✦   ✦   ✦

We were delighted with the evening lineup: BBC radio, NPR's Weekend Edition, and MSNBC. "Has Rachel Maddow called?" I asked Bobbie when she checked in.

"Not yet, but do you want me to pitch it to her?"

"Sorry, I'm getting a little big for my britches."

Bobbie laughed. "No, just stir crazy, I'm sure. I'd be losing my mind."

I glanced at Phil shaking his head as if to say, "You can't tell anyone, not even Bobbie."

I did feel she deserved to know our situation might be changing, even though we had no clue what—if anything—was coming down, but I followed his advice.

I opened my breakfast box with scrambled eggs, sausage, and what looked like a Bird's Eye mix of peas, pearl onions, and corn. "The chef must be cleaning out the freezer."

As Phil handed me one of the cardboard tubes of mystery-flavored orangish drink, I asked, "What do *you* think Summer's message meant?"

"Probably an airlift similar to what they did for the Americans stuck in Wuhan."

"I'm picturing the helicopters hoisting people off the roof of the American embassy during the last days of the Vietnam War."

"More dramatic, but less plausible."

Phil clicked on the television. "Want to see more of *The Goldfinch*?" I nodded. "Does this story have a happy ending at least?"

"Do books that win Pulitzers ever have one?" I answered in a snippy tone. "Sorry, that was rhetorical. I liked the way the book ended, but it might be different in the film."

Another knock on the door startled me. Jorge the headwaiter handed me a little dustpan/broom combo, a box of instant coffee, and some Swiss chocolates with a pop-up lid that revealed a 3D chalet.

"For a second, I thought that might be the news that one of us tested positive," Phil said, back to his normal gloom-and-doom mode.

"Let's hope it's both of us so we can share a hospital room. They probably put miso soup in the I.V.s."

Both phones buzzed with a message from Bobbie's associate Crystal, who was trading shifts with her. She apologetically asked if we would both do CNBC at 11 p.m. I answered with my usual "Sure." She then asked for a media check for a Toronto TV station at 8:35 p.m. as prep for a 10:30 p.m. slot. "Ditto," I replied, then said to Phil, "But I'm not sitting in that damn chair for two hours." My mood continued to sour.

Phil knew it was best to leave me alone. He disappeared into the bathroom with the latest edition of the *Japan Times,* another Princess purgatorial perk.

✦   ✦   ✦

Faith and Jorge delivered a St. Patrick's Day feast—albeit a month early—for lunch. I opened the box with a flourish. "Corned beef and cabbage!"

Afterward, as I helped Phil seal the boxes, I said, "It was good to see familiar faces and to know they aren't sick." He stacked the remains of lunch in the corridor, careful so no bits of food fell on the carpet. I felt sorry for the crew who had to bend and lift everything. With every single passenger eating in their room, there had to be miles of piles. "Let's see, if the ship is nine hundred fifty feet long, and there's the starboard and port hallways, then…"

Phil held up his hand. The captain was back on the loudspeaker. "Ladies and gentlemen, I'm sorry to interrupt your afternoon but I'd like your attention to a serious matter. The media is reporting that the U.S. government is considering a plan to evacuate American citizens and permanent residents from the *Diamond Princess…*" I held up my fist in a power salute. "…We continue to see this is a very dynamic situation…there will be further announcements within the next few hours and I'll be back as soon as I have news to share."

A few minutes later, there was a knock on our balcony door. Phil waved the Mendizabals in. "What did he mean by media reports?" Vana asked.

"Somebody already wrote 'Welcome home!' on my Facebook page," Phil said, holding up his phone.

"Hold on!" I waited for a story to open on my iPad. "Here's a headline saying 'The U.S. State Department will evacuate all Americans from *Diamond Princess* cruise ship quarantined in Japan.'"

Any details?" Vana asked impatiently.

I scrolled down. "'The aircraft is set to arrive in Japan on the evening of February 16 and will land in the U.S. at Travis Air Force Base in California.'"

Phil waved for them to take a seat on the couch. "Want a drink?"

"Got any scotch?" Vana asked.

He shook his head. "Plenty of wine, though. I guess we'd better use it up!"

Vana gave me a piercing stare. "Is that why you didn't make reservations to fly home?" I nodded. "How long have you known?"

Phil jumped in to rescue me. "We only knew *something* was going to happen, not *what*. And we were sworn to secrecy. I had to superglue Gay's mouth shut."

"Wouldn't it be better just to wait a few more days on the ship, walk off, and then take our scheduled flights home?" Mario asked.

"Wait, here's more information from Bloomberg," I called out. "Japanese Health Minster Katsunobu Kato just announced an additional sixty-seven cases and called the ship 'the largest infection cluster outside China.' It goes on to say that 'Some passengers will then continue onward to Lackland Air Force Base in Texas and all passengers will be quarantined in the U.S. for a further 14 days. Those symptomatic passengers unable to board the flight will receive the required care in Japan...'" My voice became more facetious. "And—get this—the State Department is expressing its gratitude to Japan for its 'extraordinary care and hospitality and assistance.'"

An email notice popped up from Motoko Rich, who also had just heard about the sixty-seven cases. We had been bantering back and forth almost daily and had a long talk two nights earlier, which Phil said sounded more like a therapeutic session than a news interview. Afterward, I had written that I appreciated being "temporary friends in this strange situation" and had asked her whether she'd heard about new cases on board saying, "Instead of giving me hope, I am feeling they are withholding the number from us because it will be so terrible."

Now it seemed my guess was correct. Vana, Mario, and Phil were debating the pros and cons of staying on board or taking the evacuation flight. All I heard was a buzzing in my head that canceled out their questions. Finally, a cogent thought pierced the noise. "Phil, tell them the story of the helicopters in the flood—and what happened to us in Miami."

Phil nodded that he understood where I was going with it. "When the boys were about seven and nine, we were flying from Miami via Suriname to meet the Pestys in South America. The flight kept getting delayed. Finally, a distinguished-looking man came up to me and asked to speak privately. He said I shouldn't take my wife and kids on the flight because there was going to be a military coup in Paramaribo and there would be no power or water. He also hinted darkly of executions."

Mario added, "That was a very unstable time."

"When I told Gay the trip to South America was off, she tried to argue with me. I reminded her of the story of a guy who wanted to stay in his house during a flood. He sent the first boat away, saying 'Thanks, but God will protect me.' He did the same for two more boats. Finally, he was on the roof and a helicopter lowered a rope. Once again, he said, 'God will protect me.' Then he died. When he got to heaven, he said, 'God, I trusted you to save me! Why did you abandon me?' God reminded him, 'I sent you three boats and a helicopter.'"

I looked up from the torrent of emails in my Inbox. "The point is that we think this charter flight is the damn helicopter."

"Two weeks more of quarantine? I can't stand it!" Vana said.

"At least we'll be off this ship where more and more people are getting sick daily. It's only a matter of time before people start dying. I want to be in an American ICU if it comes to that," Phil said.

"Still, I'd rather be home in a few days instead of two more weeks," Vana said.

Mario was shaking his head. "What if we have to quarantine in Japan once we get off the ship?"

"Nobody has suggested that yet," Vana said.

"There are a lot of unknowns," Phil began. "If we take the evacuation flight, we'll have to quarantine for two weeks in the States. If we stay on the ship, there's a chance we can fly home, or the Japanese and/or the U.S. can require a quarantine before we can go anywhere else."

"For two weeks or just a few days?" Vana asked.

Phil shook his head. "Who knows?"

"I can imagine having to quarantine for two weeks in Japan," I added, "and then the U.S. might insist on another fourteen days on one of the military bases."

Phil had a faraway look. "At some point the United States could close the borders."

"Oh, c'mon! They can't keep citizens out," Vana said.

"They can do whatever they want,' I insisted, "and so can the Japanese."

"There are a million ways they can screw us," Phil admitted, "but this is the evacuation we've been asking for, so we're going to take it." He looked at me to see if I was going to object, but I knew this was not the time for a metaphorical temperature-taking of feelings. I was—uncharacteristically—silent.

✦   ✦   ✦

Updates from Phil and Gay Courter on the *Diamond Princess* Quarantine
Yokohama 15 Feb 2020

Today, the CDC announced that two State Department–organized planes will carry up to 380 Americans from the *Diamond Princess* to bases in the United States. "We are relieved and honored that the American government is mobilizing its considerable power and resources to repatriate American citizens aboard the *Diamond Princess*," said Gay Courter.

"So far, we have remained healthy, and although yesterday we were tested, we do not expect to know the results for a few days. Regardless of the result, we believe we will be in the safest medical hands in the U.S.…We'd like to thank the White House, the State Department, and the CDC for working with *Diamond Princess* and the local authorities to make this transfer possible."

…At the same time, Gay and Phil have deep concern about their multinational fellow passengers and how they will be repatriated. They continue to be mindful of the crew, who have fewer resources and agency. We expect that Princess will be able to provide a more restful and healthy way for them to complete their quarantine and help them return to their homes, the security of their loved ones, and more familiar services.

For the next couple of days, Motoko Rich was my most reliable—and informative—pen pal.

February 15, 2020

Motoko: You must be frantic with trying to get news of the American evacuation. Neither State Department nor CDC has confirmed but has anyone reached out to you so you can get ready? I am on my way to Yokohama so maybe you will be able to wave at me. With binoculars, since I am sure I can't get close. Fingers crossed for you.

Gay: I'm breaking protocol with my team writing this, but there has been no announcement on board or information from the ship or the American Consul. News indicates we will be split into two groups, and we are confused [as to what this means]. It is our assumption that we will be moving from Japanese government control to American govern-ment control and will have to follow whatever rules are in place to keep the American public from freaking out about us pariahs.... We are very thankful that our government has come through.... We know that there are many boots on the ground already....

[We are] deeply concerned about the crew as well as our fellow passengers. For the safety of the crew, they should... not have to work or live in crowded conditions. Plus, other countries must find a way to repatriate their countrymen.... We are looking at all this as a scary adventure...but one we will certainly work through in the best spirit possible.... The bottom line is staying healthy. In life, there is no life without health.

Phil made me a cup of tea, poured himself a half glass of wine, and sat down beside me to read that day's edition of the *Japan Times*. Without looking up, he said, "Wow, this a disturbing report." He read some of the worrisome snippets aloud, includ-ing: "The whole situation is like 'a game with no end in sight,' said Koji Wada, a professor of public health." Then he said, "He suspects that secondary infections are occurring on the ship, which is why the fourteen days might prove meaningless. Then he says, 'the cruise ship is almost completely infested'!"

"Which is what we've been claiming all along!" I said, seething.

"They are confirming the Bloomberg numbers. Now the total is two hundred and eighteen, plus one of the Japanese quarantine officers." "And…. Yikes!" Phil exclaimed. "Some new expert insists that quarantine periods are typically reset every time an additional case is reported. He says, 'Keeping the passengers in a place with such high risk of infection is questionable, not only from a virus prevention standpoint but ethically as well.'"

The phone rang and I waved for Phil to take it. It was Jerry. "As of now we're going on the government flight," Phil told him. "Sure, we'd rather be in first class too, but let me know if you still feel that way after reading the front-page story in today's *Japan Times*."

A few minutes later, Motoko asked if we had gotten an email from the consulate yet. I scrolled around until I found it and forwarded it to her.

URGENT MESSAGE TO U.S. CITIZEN DIAMOND PRINCESS PASSENGERS AND CREW

The attached letter contains important information about special charter flights that will allow you to return to the United States. If you intend to travel on the charter flights, please [reply to this email] NO LATER THAN 10:00 AM February 16.

"The email from the consulate is here!" I called to Phil, who was out on the balcony filming a gorgeous sunset behind Mount Fuji. "Check to see whether you have one too."

Phil came inside and reached for his mobile just as the desk phone rang again. "Yes, Gay just got it. You don't have it yet? Gay, can you forward it to Jerry?"

"I'm not sure if we should. It looks as though it might be coded to us."

"Sure, Jerry, just give me a chance to read it." Phil pulled the phone away from his ear. I could hear Jerry yelling "Right now."

"He hung up on me."

"What's his problem?"

"He seems to think we're withholding information."

I showed him the email. "This is just to me. Did you get one in your name?"

Phil scrolled to the one he'd just received. "Yes, but there's nothing personalized in the body of the message. Jerry can just take my name off and put in his own." He looked at me for confirmation. I shrugged. "Then I'll forward mine to him now, if that's okay with you."

"If you don't see any problems, sure." I felt a wave of nausea. "I'm sorry I said anything to piss him off."

"I've never heard him so furious."

"We've all been under a lot of pressure…"

"He just needed to blow off steam."

"My fault. I'll take care of it," I said. "I'm going to see if Vana got hers." I went across to the Mendizabals' cabin. The lights were dark except for the glow of the television. They were in bed with the covers pulled up to their chins. The door was open to circulate fresh air, so I spoke through the open space. "May I come in?"

Vana wriggled to a semi-sitting position. "Check your emails," I said. "We got the message from the consulate. They want confirmation if you're going or not."

"Are you?"

"Absolutely."

"Okay, then we'll go too. What about Cathy and Jerry?"

"They didn't get an email yet. Maybe they're working alphabetically or maybe it's because we registered with the State Department before we left home."

Vana also didn't find an email and neither did Mario. I forwarded them both mine and said they should respond individually. "I don't know if that's necessary, but these people are bean counters."

"Cathy must be relieved," Vana said.

I just nodded and decided to keep Jerry's meltdown private.

Phil filled in our passport details while Motoko and I emailed back and forth. Bobbie had warned me about thinking of the reporters too much as friends, especially Motoko. "They're nice people but their first priority is getting information. They want a reliable source. It's their job."

"Who's using whom?" I asked. "I've been down this road before—on both sides. I know we're never going to go out to dinner together, but they're getting our message out."

> **Motoko:** How are you feeling about this news, especially the 14-day quarantine?
>
> **Gay:** This is what we've been asking for because we never felt quarantine on this ship was safe. So far, our team's advice has been spot on…. But if this is necessary to protect other U.S. citizens, we will try to get through the time with good spirits and to be helpful to those who might be suffering far more. As my grandmother used to say, "Man makes plans; God laughs."
>
> **Motoko:** Where do you want to go?
>
> **Gay:** [Travis] is about four hours from our son…although maybe not a good idea to visit them…until we have not a single taint of this disease. What's a little spooky is it might not be that far from Manzanar [one of the camps where Japanese Americans were incarcerated during World War II].

So long as we can keep healthy, we'll be happy and if one of us should need medical attention, we're sure they have fine care at both bases.

Motoko: I am interested in whether you or Phil thought at all about *not* getting on the flight?

Gay: We are clear about going on the airplane *and* supporting the quarantine. Let us know if you want a statement.

Terry, who, we surmised, had been in touch with his own connections at the State Department and knew what was going down, wrote to suggest we might want to give a talk at the famous Explorers Club in New York, which I told him was most unlikely. He answered: "A talk, a book, a documentary—whatever you want. Just get back here safe and healthy. I think about you guys over and over again, each and every day."

Vana stopped by to say she was all packed except for her laundry. "I don't think I'll get it back in time. Are you missing anything?"

"I never sent anything out," I admitted. "I wanted to be ready in case of a miracle."

Phil signaled me. It was almost time for a live appearance on an MSNBC morning show.

"What's left to say?" Vana asked.

"We have to thank everyone," I said. The Reuters correspondent just wrote that she was happy our message was heard and the U.S. government acted on it. She said, 'Your positivity through our stories actually inspired many of our readers and your worries, reported by us, sent the right message to authorities as well.'"

Vana grinned. "Actually, she's crediting Reuters."

"Anyway, I feel as though a ton has been lifted from me."

"Tomorrow!" Vana waved as she closed the sliding doors behind her.

"Yes, we're going home!" I choked on the last word as tears streamed down my face, ruining my makeup.

"They're logging on," Phil called from our battle station.

"My face!"

"Tears of gratitude." Phil handed me a tissue. "This is exactly what they want!"

CARGO CULT

Sometimes you leave your house to go on vacation. And you gotta take some of your stuff with you. Gotta take about two big suitcases full of stuff.... You gotta take a smaller version of your house. It's the second version of your stuff... And even though you're far away from home...after a while you say, "All right, I got my nail clippers, I must be okay."

—George Carlin, *Monologue on Stuff*

Yokohama 16 Feb 2020

Updates from Phil and Gay Courter on the *Diamond Princess* Quarantine

Yesterday, the Courters and other Americans aboard the Diamond Princess received a letter from the US Embassy with more information about a planned evacuation of the US passengers aboard charter flights back to the USA.

The Courters have put in their request to participate in this evacuation and are awaiting more information. They are spending today packing and preparing for the trip and <u>will not be able to accommodate any interview requests at this time.</u> According to Gay and Phil Courter, "We currently have no details on boarding timing or where we will end up. We will supply our Boston-based team with details and they will be the ones disseminating information until we are settled in our new 'holiday home' on an Air Force base."

"We would like to thank the Japanese government for working with the US government to make this possible. We fully support the government evacuation, and honor and support further quarantine for the health and safety of all. Safety precautions like these are necessary when you are dealing with something that is still unknown."

This is what we'd been waiting for. The man at our door in the blue protective suit was wearing an unusual helmet and using what we later learned was a portable powered air-purifying respirator (PAPR). His tag identified him as Dr. Michael Callahan from Massachusetts General Hospital. The government had sent their A-Team. He asked if we felt well enough to travel and whether we had any medical issues.

"We've been doing wonderfully," Phil said.

"Maybe because we've taken Tamiflu prophylactically," I added.

"Have you had flu-like symptoms?" the doctor asked suspiciously.

I backpedaled, trying to explain about the doctor next door. Dr. Callahan said, "Stop taking it immediately. If you have the coronavirus, Tamiflu could make a definitive diagnosis difficult."

His words felt like a slap. What else had we done wrong? He told us to wear warm clothing because the plane would be cold. Also, there were no overhead compartments, which meant all carry-ons had to fit under the seat.

"Were you swabbed for the virus?"

"Yes, on the fourteenth," Phil said. "Do you have our results?"

"No," the doctor said. "You probably won't get them for a few days." He gave us some written instructions, then knocked on the Mendizabals' door.

I looked him up online and told Phil, "He's an infectious disease and disaster medicine doc who deploys to large-scale disease outbreaks."

"I don't care if he's Albert Schweitzer, as long as he approves us for the flight," Phil said. Then he waved his arms around the cabin, awash in open luggage on every flat surface. "Maximum of seventy pounds and two bags per guest. If you have excess baggage, use the Red-6 tags and they will be shipped separately," he read aloud.

"I'm not leaving bags behind!"

Phil didn't argue. "Disembarkation will begin at approximately 9 p.m. and all luggage must be placed outside the staterooms by 6 p.m. Your luggage tags indicate which plane you will go on. This has been decided by the U.S. Government and cannot be changed," he continued. "But there are no tags."

"I'll see whether Vana got theirs."

"No, *you* are packing, I'll go."

That reminded me I needed to put matters right with Jerry. I dialed their room. "Did you get baggage tags yet?"

"No."

"Jerry, I need to apologize for the email fiasco. It was entirely my fault. At first I thought it was coded to us." I listened to his objections. "You're absolutely right. We should have sent it immediately because you would have figured it out before we did. But Jerry, please know we would never, never, never have tried to keep you off the flight. It might have seemed like that at the moment, but it was not our intention."

"What have you decided to do?" he asked tensely.

"We're going on the charter flight."

"Did you hear that some Americans are planning to just walk off the ship in three days?"

"A bird in hand…" I said. "The State Department has made it clear they won't consider another flight until after March fourth. That's fourteen days from the nineteenth, which means that even if Americans stay, they could be quarantined in Japan and *again* in the U.S."

"I hope we end up in San Antonio—that's where my son lives."

"Our son lives closer to Travis."

"Have you noticed the food has gone downhill the past few days? It's almost all fish and rice and Asian sauces."

"At least it's not lobster," I said with a weak laugh, knowing of Cathy's allergy.

After I hung up, I told Phil about my attempted apology. "How'd it go?"

"Not that well, but we're all going to be edgy until—" I looked to Phil for the right word.

"How about forever?" he said.

✦　✦　✦

Phil still wanted me to put whatever we might not need in quarantine in our two extra bags, just in case they insisted we leave some behind. I paced between the closet and the balcony trying to figure out what I was willing to never see again. "This is a strategic nightmare," I muttered under my breath.

Phil looked up from the *New York Times* insert in that morning's *Japan Times*. "They're saying the planes are on their way to Tokyo Haneda and passengers should bring their own food and water."

"Really? Will they let it through security?"

"Maybe we'll be in a special terminal to protect the general populace."

"I'll be happy if they don't tattoo us with a scarlet C."

While I was debating about my hair dryer and curlers—would there be more media?—I looked up the American evacuation from Wuhan.

I held up my iPad. "This is what the inside of the charter plane might be like."

"Gay, I'm going to lose it if you don't start packing."

"It's hard. I just don't feel well. I'm having trouble figuring where to put everything."

"We're running out of time."

"Stop hassling me and I'll get it done. I'm trying to find a way to bring our own food."

"We can buy it at the airport." Phil looked at his watch. "It's after two and we haven't had lunch yet!" He handed me the last Coke in the fridge. "Low blood sugar," he said, pushing me to drink it.

Just then the desk phone rang. "Hello," I said curtly. "No, nobody's sick here. Yes, that was me. I didn't mean I was really sick. It's…emotional…. No, I'm fine. I'm just upset about everything that's happening. No, I don't need to see a doctor. Thank you."

"Who was that?"

"A woman wanting to know if anyone here is sick." We both looked up at the speaker. "Is this place bugged?"

"Speakers can work two ways. When they're switched off, they can act as a microphone to transmit."

"Do you think they can spy on everyone?"

"They probably have that capability. Obviously, they have a special interest in what we're saying. The crème brûlée signaled they were paying attention to our interviews." Phil went over to a shelf and held up the box that held the cell phone we had never activated. "This also could be a monitoring device."

"We never turned it on."

"It might work without power." He glanced at the desk. "For that matter, the handset's receiver could also work as an amplifier."

"I wish I had known that when I was writing *The Girl in the Box*. The whole ship is covered by cameras. They could have one up there too." I pointed to the ceiling. "Given the millions of people who cruise every year, there have to be bad apples and crazies..."

Just then, the lunch carts arrived. There were sandwiches, pasta salad, slices of fresh pineapple, and another of my favorites—lemon tarts. Our meal was interrupted by one of the last announcements from Captain Arma, who mentioned that he had a few more gray hairs but that a diamond is a piece of coal that does well under pressure. He slipped in that there were sixty-seven more cases, but we knew those were the figures from the previous day. The press had jumped ahead by reporting another seventy victims, now totaling 355. For the first time, the number didn't freeze my spine; I knew we'd soon escape the viral web. I wrapped half a sandwich and the lemon tarts in plastic baggies I had squirreled away—just in case.

✦   ✦   ✦

I packed. I showered. I dressed in the same comfortable outfit I'd worn on the flight from Houston. Two bags were reluctantly relegated to be forwarded. My carry-on had several changes of underwear and a few outfits I could layer. Phil put our medicine kit as well as a change of clothes in the extra bag he'd agreed to lug on the plane.

"Do you think they'll restrict us to three ounces of liquids?"

"Not if they said to bring water," Phil said, sounding more chipper since the closet was empty. "I doubt anyone's worried about terrorists on our rescue flight."

The afternoon wore on. Captain Arma announced that both Canada and Hong Kong were going to evacuate their citizens. We cheered. Phil called Katherine and Marlene to say goodbye. "See you in Oz," he said because, at that moment, we were still planning to visit them in a few months.

On Facebook, Bruce, the same guy who sent hate mail to Ashley, said he would rather take his chances in Japan than fly "coronavirus class" with "Hazmat astronauts." A few weeks later, the press chided him as an "Ugly American" when he bragged about touring Tokyo instead of quarantining at his hotel, potentially exposing Japanese citizens to the virus.

✦ ✦ ✦

Contrary to Phil's predictions, all the bags were ready before six. I have a history of being ready at the appointed time. Maybe not fifteen minutes earlier, but almost always on time. There was, however, no sign of baggage tags.

Jerry reported that he had checked with guest services and they were coming "momentarily." He asked if we'd received our "last supper" yet.

"No," I said. "Why?"

"It's a pathetic dry, tasteless fish. Cathy says to skip it and go right to the fruit crumble."

"Maybe they send military chefs to culinary school these days," I said, laughing nervously.

Our luggage tags weren't delivered until 8:30 p.m. Phil held up our Aqua-1 tags. "We're on the second plane."

I went next door. "Which plane are you on?"

"Purple. You?" Vana asked.

"Aqua."

"How did they screw that up?"

"Revenge?" I suggested.

"Probably alphabetical," Mario replied.

Their phone rang. "We're purple," Vana answered. "Cathy and Jerry are on your plane. He said both planes are supposed to land in California and then one plane will go on to Texas and the other to Nebraska." She hugged me. "That means we still might end up at the same place."

Phil was in the hall putting the tags on our bags. He put the Red-6s on the extra bags.

Vana joined me in the corridor. "They finally delivered the laundry," she said, stuffing it into one of their four matching suitcases. She pulled out a sweater for Mario. "I'll see if this is the one he wants."

Nobody was in the corridor. I slipped two of the leftover Aqua-1 tags on our excess bags and removed the Red-6s. Since this was a cargo plane, there wouldn't be any weight-and-balance issues. Besides, it was far easier—and cheaper—than having them shipped to Florida. After weeks of feeling like we were being locked up for a crime we didn't commit, I rationalized my little rebellion.

✦ ✦ ✦

Every half hour, I checked the corridor to see if any bags were left behind. Finally, a team from Japan's Self-Defense Forces wearing white Hazmat suits with blue seams began hefting the luggage. When it was silent, I peeked out the door. Everything was gone. Phil was snoozing on the sofa. Maybe there was time to see the rest of *The Goldfinch*. Shortly after 10 p.m., the call came for the Mendizabals to leave. I went out into the hall to wish them a safe journey. "See you in California."

I opened the mini-fridge and packed the half-sandwich, lemon squares, two apples, an orange, and Japanese crackers. I stuffed two water bottles in my backpack and the rest in a reusable nylon shopping bag I would carry over my arm. I crawled back under the duvet and continued to watch the movie.

"Will all guests on Emerald Deck port side please…" I startled, but after hearing it was not for us, I settled back to watch the film. The boy—now a grown man—was in an Amsterdam hotel and it seemed like he was contemplating suicide. "…Dolphin Deck port side, please make your way to the gangway on Gala Deck, Deck Four, forward…"

"That's us," Phil said.

"Port only. We have a minute." I made sure to use the bathroom, which turned into the best decision of the night. And then, finally, it was our turn. We donned our masks and ventured out.

✦   ✦   ✦

I tried, I really tried to give up all control and send our fates to the winds. If there ever was a time to be a paper boat bobbing in the stream, this was it. Dad's limbo. We shuffled along in a crush of sleepy, look-alike passengers. We were too hot in the

Passengers head to the ship's gangway to board buses.

Phil's selfie shortly after we'd boarded a bus on the first leg of our repatriation.

ship's corridors, then blasted with an icy chill the moment we approached the steep gangway. The long walkway covered in blue tarps that gave patients privacy on the way to the ambulances was now a dark, leaky tunnel pummeled by a drenching rain. The pace slowed, then came to an abrupt stop. Despite announcements to have passports in hand, an addled passenger couldn't find his. After his whole group had stood aside, we were directed to give ours to a Japanese immigration official. Without even opening them, he handed them across to another who said he was U.S. immigration. "You'll get them back when you get to the airport."

There was a line of Japanese military with their backs to the ship staring straight ahead as rain cascaded off their hat brims. I paused just before reaching the bus, turned toward the line of shiny faces, and bowed farewell.

The driver helped me up the high step to bus number eight. I took the window seat, Phil the aisle. I pushed aside the curtain, but my only view was of a staggered lineup of matching buses. "I don't think they've even moved the buses for the first plane." I glanced at my phone to check the time. It was almost one in the morning of February 17. It had taken more than an hour to snake through the ship. "The Mendizabals have been waiting for three hours already!"

I stood to remove my soaking wet jacket. The other passengers looked as if they had seen the same skeletal ghost. "Take a few pictures," I whispered to Phil. He twisted around and held up his phone discreetly, then turned back to show me his shots. For almost two weeks, we had been isolated from each other except for brief walks on deck—and even then, we had kept our distance. Now here we were scrunched together on a dank, overheated bus, with sweaty foreheads and sandpaper throats, wondering if the person across the aisle was infectious. Our eyes loomed over our masks as watchful as sentinels.

Everyone should have been tested because only people who were negative were going to be allowed to fly. We assumed the government received the results before we did. I felt sorry for those who might still be on board waiting to be removed by ambulance as well as the ones already hospitalized. And what had happened to their partners? Were they traveling with us or staying in Japan? I worried that I was so hot I'd fail a temperature check. Without considering the reduced airflow, Phil had insisted we wear surgical masks under the N95s for double protection. I stood up again, removed my fleece vest, and unbuttoned my cardigan. I fished a water bottle from my backpack, splashed some on the *tenugui* cloth in my pocket, and wrapped it around my neck. "I'm going to check email one last time," I said. "I'll tell the kids we're off the ship."

There was much more from the media than I expected. Motoko, who was fact-checking an article, had questions, but I couldn't confirm the details without the packed paperwork.

Gay: I'll let you know once off the plague plane.

Motoko: I just read your daughter's lovely essay about learning to trust you and Phil. Good luck tonight, and stay warm and safe!

Several other reporters were trying to reach me, including Ju-min Park with Reuters, who wanted to run a story that night. Crystal was keeping everyone apprised and said a Japanese news service had just announced our flights wouldn't leave until the "wee hours." At the bottom of her message she wrote, "Hang in there, Gay and Phil!"

I blind-copied Bobbie's media list and sent them Phil's best bus photo.

Motoko: Wow. You see fear there.

Gay: Silent. No chatter. Around ship lots of military. On quay photographers standing on camera-truck hoods. We did a passport hand-off from Japanese officials to Americans. Doctor on bus wearing blue haz-mat suit. Very tired. Clearing my throat sounds like thunder. Will the doctor send me to the wrong line?

An hour passed, maybe two. In any other travel situation, we might have asked questions, complained bitterly, or canceled the trip altogether. I tried to think of a time when we had been so devoid of power. Several people got off the bus because they needed a bathroom, not that there were any in sight. Much later were heard that the only option had been to pee in the rain.

At last there was some movement. Our bus driver came inside and closed the door at about 3:00 in the morning. We lined up behind a police car with flashing lights for a caravan. It took fifteen minutes to slowly make our way to the gates, the myriad lights of the *Diamond Princess* winking prettily through my rain-streaked window. My heart felt heavy and I had the odd sensation of feeling ashamed. Perhaps that's what is meant by leaving under a cloud.

✦   ✦   ✦

I held the curtains back with one hand and watched the cameramen who had been waiting in the frigid downpour for hours just for a few photos of the bus convoy, which seemed like one massive segmented organism slithering off in the night. I've seen our pale, masked, apprehensive faces in the stock images memorializing the moment. Where once we had been privileged travelers, we now looked like displaced persons, though our circumstances were not as dire. Like them, though, we were hungry, tired, confused, worried about our health, and fearful that we were paddling through a toxic soup that many—especially those our ages—might not survive.

At 4 a.m., outside the airport gates, the buses passed another assemblage of cameramen jockeying to get a shot that would make their uncomfortable vigil worthwhile.

And there they were! Two behemoth planes marked Kalitta Air.

"747s."

"They look bigger."

"That's because there are no windows."

There was no sign of a terminal. I resisted reminding Phil that there not only wasn't a food hall, there weren't any bathrooms, let alone metal detectors or security. The driver left the bus and was chatting with another driver under a nearby overhang. What were they waiting for? I leaned against my coat-and-fleece pillow and fell asleep. More than an hour later, cardboard boxes filled with passports arrived. An American voice called out names, then delivered them to those who responded. Only a few matched passengers on

One of the two cargo planes the U.S. government sent for Americans, viewed from our bus. We had no idea what was going on behind the scenes that would keep us on the bus for several more hours.

our bus. Soon another person with another box arrived. None of them were for any of us.

"I can't imagine what is taking so long."

Phil gave me a what-the-hell-do-you-expect-me-to-do-about-it look. "Something's not right. There's a mechanical problem or a governmental dispute or…"

"Maybe the president changed his mind. There's been a lot of nasty comments on social media about not letting us into the country."

I turned on my phone and received another email blast. The chutzpah award went to a Canadian journalist who wanted a "quick Facetime interview" from the airport. I wrote back one word: Impossible!

Bobbie seemed to know more than we did. "You're getting on the plane! Everyone here is whooping and hollering. Bon voyage."

I fell back to sleep with my finger in mid-reply and woke when Phil murmured, "Boarding" close to my ear.

"Wait! Did we get our passports back?"

"Yes, but it took a few hours."

I went into high gear, donning my backpack, slipping the food bag on my elbow, tucking the jacket and fleece under my arm, and extending the handle of my wheeled bag. The minute my feet touched the tarmac, I bounded ahead of Phil. Having lived through the free-for-all when we first boarded the ship in Yokohama, I knew that snagging good seats would be competitive. I pushed past the slow, the confused, the drowsy, and ended up in the first wave of passengers to crash through the doorway.

"Watch your step!" A man-in-white half-lifted me up onto a metal pallet covering the rails for sliding freight into place. The early birds had already commandeered the first rows of seats they came to without realizing they were adjacent to a nasty-smelling metal shed. I did a double take. Was it possible? Yes, they were porta-potties!

I kept pressing forward knowing Phil—always the gentleman—would be waiting his turn or assisting someone. All the seats were basic economy, upholstered in leather, vinyl, or cloth in various mismatched colors. The center section was mostly empty but too close to the chemical smell wafting from the toilets. The forwardmost section was filling quickly, but those seats were several feet from the side of the fuselage. If I can't lie down, I want a wall to lean against. The next group with rows of three seats had been bolted right against where a window on a normal plane would have been. The first row could be a problem if they required everything stowed under a seat. I pushed my bags into the second row and looked around for Phil, who was coming up the aisle. I perched my backpack on what would have been the window seat and tossed my coat to reserve the left aisle seat, which was perfect for Phil since he needs to stretch out his right leg.

"Don't worry about hogging the row," I said, anticipating Phil's concern. "We have to space for infection control." At least that's what it looked like in the Wuhan flight photos. "Hold the fort. I'm desperate to pee."

I passed Jerry and Cathy, who had a row to themselves in the center section. "Glad you made it!" I said. Jerry looked like he was still upset with me, but we were all stressed "to the max."

There was a long potty line. I turned to commiserate with the Nordic sweater–wearing woman behind me just as a man in a *Ghostbusters*-style hood connected to an air supply tapped her shoulder.

"Are you Mrs. So-and-So?" he asked. She nodded. "We've just gotten your results back from the Japanese Ministry of Health. You tested positive."

"I haven't been sick!"

"That's because you're asymptomatic. Don't worry. We'll take good care of you, but you'll have to sit in 'the Bubble.'" He clasped her elbow and steered her just forward of the potties, where an ersatz tent constructed from long sheets of what looked like white Mylar was hung on ratchet straps and duct-taped to the floor. He opened an overlapping door flap and maneuvered the stunned woman inside.

A potty door opened. Holding my breath, I ventured inside. There was a sink, but no water, only a dispenser of sanitizer, which I slathered to my elbows. As soon as I sat down, I further decontaminated myself with Sono wipes and wished there was a spray to fumigate my way-too-close encounter with the unfortunate Mrs. Nordic Sweater.

✦ ✦ ✦

Phil said, "They're going to check our temperatures twice during the flight. They've matched our names to our seats. We have the

Seating on the cargo plane, with the Bubble, where the infected passengers were isolated, at rear.

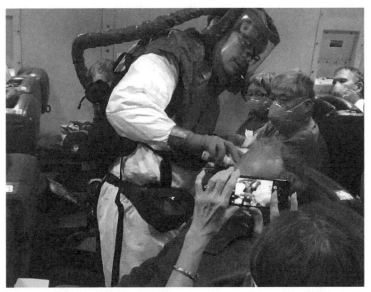

A temperature check by one of the Ghostbuster-like heath officials.

whole row." He stared at me. "What's wrong?" I told Phil about the woman.

"I thought nobody was allowed on the plane unless they were negative. Maybe they'll remove her before take-off."

"She's probably infected her whole bus by now and I was standing right beside her!"

I handed him some wipes and we swabbed the area the way we always do—even in first class. He turned to me with a crooked smile. "Well, dahling," he said in a snooty voice, "we're flying Cargo Class! How many people can say that?"

I laughed at the absurdity and then couldn't stop. "Not only that, it's even better than using points. It's free!"

A man with "Steve" written with a marker on his disposable suit and green hood held up a megaphone. "Welcome to Kalitta Airlines flight five eighty-one." He introduced himself, Rusty, and the doctor. Later we would learn this was Dr. James Lawler, an infectious disease expert who worked on pandemic preparedness for the two previous presidents. He had contributed to the critical "Red Dawn" email chain. In late January, when we—and most of the world—were oblivious to looming disaster, he had written. "Great Understatements in History: Pompeii—'a bit of a dust storm,' Hiroshima—'a bad summer heat wave,' and Wuhan—'just a bad flu season.'"

Steve told us we would be landing either at Travis Air Force Base in California or Lackland in Texas, but our destination was not yet known. "That's not true," Phil whispered, "they have to have filed a flight plan."

I was having trouble understanding muffled words through the megaphone, so Phil interpreted. "The airflow is from the nose to tail, so we're in a great position.... Don't go past those black curtains in the front, it's for crew only.... Mind the uneven surfaces and ratchet strap holders sticking out...Don't remove your masks….There aren't any oxygen masks, which is why we'll be flying at about twenty-seven thousand feet."

"Is it pressurized at least?" I looked around the cavernous plane. The uninsulated walls were marked with huge letters and numbers, probably for organizing cargo.

"Maybe not to the same standards as a passenger aircraft."

"I wonder if the pilots are getting hazard pay."

My phone vibrated just as the engines roared. I pounded out an answer to Motoko about Mrs. Nordic Sweater. A few minutes later, she replied.

> **Motoko:** The State Department confirmed what you told me about the asymptomatic but infected passengers on the plane and I would love your further thoughts on how you feel about flying…on the same aircraft.
>
> **Gay:** Hard to say. We are not in the porta-potty section at least.
>
> **Motoko:** There's that! Let me know when you land.
>
> **Gay:** Thanks. Go to bed! Sleep for us.
>
> **Motoko:** Safe flight!

I took a few minutes to peruse Facebook. Someone still on the *Diamond Princess* posted videos of our buses departing with the caption: "Rats jumping ship." I powered off my phone.

"Flying time is twelve hours and it's almost morning here," Phil said. "I'm going to pop my pill, you?"

"Maybe we should wait until we're in the air," I teased. "They're illegal in Japan."

"Actually, we're now under American control." He opened his sedative of choice and I did the same with mine.

"*L'chaim!*" I toasted with my water bottle. "And goodnight."

✦ ✦ ✦

"Wheels up" didn't come until almost 7 a.m. in Japan, six hours since we had disembarked from the ship. In that time we could have flown from Tampa to Seattle or driven to Atlanta. I leaned against the wall, but it had an icy sheen. I opened my suitcase in front of the middle seat. There had been no safety lecture beyond wearing face masks. Nobody cared that my egress was blocked or whether we were wearing seatbelts. Safety seemed to be the least of the authorities' concerns. I found my down coat, compressed to the size of a small book. Once it was unzipped, it could be used as a quilted blanket. I closed my eyes but the industrial-strength bright lights hanging about thirty feet above us burned through my lids. I located my sleep mask and felt around for my earplugs. Besides the roar of the jets, there was the ceaseless howl of an infinite wind tunnel.

Soon the swift-acting member of the benzodiazepine family began enhancing my gamma-aminobutyric acid receptors to transport me somewhere between the sky and the sea, the grass and the clouds, the hill and the valley…. My grandmother, the midwife, would be laughing at me. Didn't I tell you God punishes us by giving us what we asked for?

In my fugue state, I mused that this was the best flight of my life…. Like something bespoke. Rarer than a made-to-measure Turnbull & Asser shirt, precious in part because it can't be ordered by just anyone. Why else do we tell stories of mishaps and missteps?…the stories readers lap up because, there but for the grace of God, it didn't happen to them…. For the Africa trip, I was halfway through *West with the Night,* Beryl Markham's memoir about growing up in Kenya and becoming a bush pilot…She also had an affair with the ill-fated Denys Finch Hatton—a fellow pilot, also her good friend Karen Blixen's lover, all chronicled in *Out of Africa* and immortalized by Robert Redford—but was Beryl in the cast? No, that was Meryl....I wish I could hear the John Barry score. It's on my iPhone but that's way too hard to…

What was it Markham wrote about survival? She had mentioned the disadvantage in surviving a dangerous experience is that your story ends up being anticlimactic. If we don't get the virus, if we get home safe and sound…

Like when we were standing in the middle of the field telling the story of our plane crash to the firefighters, it can't have been all that bad…but people had to understand that if Phil hadn't spotted that field in the Pine Barrens….

The cargo plane hit an air pocket, startling me slightly awake. I should tighten my seatbelt…like I cinched it when there was that *bang!* and Phil said we'd lost the engine on our approach to Trenton for Blake's graduation from Princeton and we crashed-landed in the field with the sheep grazing…and then driving home to Florida we decided we were meant to do something else, something bigger than us…and ended up adopting Ashley.

Someone was tapping my shoulder. I pulled my sleep mask aside. A Ghostbuster waved a thermometer and I lent him my ear—like a good friend, Roman, or countryman…. No Chamber of Mylar yet. Good title for an Edgar Allan Poe short story with a modern twist. How hard could it be to write a collection of short stories…? I'd call it "Cargo Cult," a play on those Vanuatu islanders who began worshipping aircraft after seeing the first planes during the war….

I woke shivering. Nearby passengers were huddled under identical blankets. A few were eating sandwiches and drinking sodas. I untwisted myself from the nest I'd built against the wall and stepped over Phil as gingerly as I could.

The potties were ripening. I tightened my double masks. After a good dousing with sanitizer, I saw a man riffling through appliance-sized cartons, opening white lunch boxes, and deciding on three. I followed his lead. He reached into a gigantic plastic sack and came out with a handful of corn chips, handing me two bags. The song about a Teddy bears' picnic thrummed in my head as I picked out an icy water bottle and a ginger ale from a huge cooler. My arms were full when I passed open cartons of soft-looking Japanese Red Cross blankets. I cleverly dumped everything into the middle of one carton, lifted two blankets, and folded the corners to the middle to make a primitive basket. Without a free hand for holding on to the seatbacks, I stumbled a few times but managed not to fall. Later Dr. Lawler told me his greatest fear was that one of us would break a hip because of all the uneven surfaces.

I was starving and had no idea what time it was anywhere in the world, let alone what day. The crustless egg salad sandwich was luscious and the corn chips had the *je-n'sai-quoi-pas* sparkle of a post-cannabis munchie. I pampered my parched throat with my purloined Pellegrino…well, not purloined, but alliteratively perfect. There was a kerfuffle a few rows up. I stood to watch a passenger being stumble-walked by two Ghostbusters toward the tent of shame.

The right side of my head was pulsing with the prodrome of a migraine—always a risk on a long flight. I didn't hesitate to take the two miracle pills that always vanquish it. Maybe they might also dull the cricks in every joint. I did a reverse pretzel and lay down facing the aisle against the polka-dot bag covered with my jacket fuzzy-lining-side up. Phil's and my scalps were almost touching. The vast curve of the 747's ceiling was the perfect blank canvas for a modern Michelangelo…I'll write to NASA…Artists should decorate the space station…another government-sponsored mission…If I tossed the corn chips in the air, would they be weightless?

A foot cramp brought me to the surface long enough to turn back toward the wall and to zap me into another frequency. Why did they bother putting that guy in the Bubble…? or Mrs. Nordic Sweater…? Sometime soon…somewhere over the deepest part of the Pacific—the Mariana Trench?—a nuclear sub would fire a lone heat-seeking missile. And *Pow! Blam!* The infested plane would vaporize. That's why nobody cared about oxygen masks or seatbelts or sanitation. We were utterly expendable. Was there any way to tell the kids that it wasn't an accident? Should I let Phil remain blissfully asleep? My breathing became erratic. I ripped off the masks from my face and gulped air. I was awake—sort of—and maybe the surge of oxygen triggered the last of my lucid brain cells to have a rational thought: They could down one plane without too much blowback, but not *two!* Safety in numbers.

Steve was back on the megaphone. My watch said it was 6:10 at night in Tokyo. "Now we are permitted to tell you our destination is Lackland Air Force Base in San Antonio, Texas." That meant we were not going to change planes in California. I felt a frisson of loss. Maybe I relied on Vana even more than she needed me. Phil was stirring. I stroked his neck. "Landing in Texas," I said.

When Rusty announced that we were welcome to take the blankets, the aisles filled with people who wanted the ones still wrapped in plastic. I noticed others were eating bananas, yogurt, and packets of dried fruit. I had missed the breakfast carton! Even if I had wanted some, there was no way I could make it past the blanket scrum. A few weeks ago, we were dressed in gowns and tuxes and sipping Champagne with many of these cruisers. Now they looked like disheveled scavengers picking through flotsam and jetsam on a rocky shore.

The megaphone blared. "Due to heavy fog at Lackland, we've been diverted to Dallas."

Groans undulated through the fuselage like a stadium wave.

But minutes later…Bump! Wheels hitting tarmac. Bump! "Ladies and gentlemen, welcome to Kelly Field, Lackland Air Force Base, San Antonio, Texas. Welcome home."

Phil and I simultaneously said, "Huh?" and then joined the clapping and cheering.

✦ ✦ ✦

The fog was as thick as the proverbial pea soup. Haloed lights dotted the presumed airfield. Humans in white-hooded jumpsuits looked like larvae laid by the white-winged leviathan. As our species emerged, our leaders helped us navigate the treacherous stairs. We came laden with strange burdens—every one of us weighed down with more than we could safely carry.

I lugged my load, Phil shouldered his. "Shall we take one of these nice blankets?" I recognized his "last-straw" expression and dropped the idea.

I made my way down the stairs on my own power. This time Phil was several paces ahead. "Stop! Phil!"

He turned back. "You got a problem?"

"Just stop. Look at the plane. Look at the people. You have to shoot this." He ignored me. "Phil, this is the most amazing sight. It looks like *Third Encounters of the First Kind*—I mean *Close Encounters*."

"I *know* what you mean." His voice was crabby, tired, and slightly cruel. "How the hell can I get out my camera now?" I handed him my phone. He took a shot.

"A video. Please." He humored me for one more shot, picked up all the bags, and shuffled toward the glowing rectangle that was the opening to a vast hangar. All along the walkway, uniformed men and women were clapping. I looked around to see if someone had given a speech. Then I realized they were applauding us because we were Americans and we were now safely home. I burst

"Welcome to Kelly Field, Lackland Air Force Base, San Antonio, Texas. Welcome home."

into tears. Phil dropped his bags and put his arm around me and we hugged. A last vestige of purpose broke through. "Honey, take a video of that!"

✦ ✦ ✦

More than a hundred people in yellow personal protective equipment were on hand to "process" us back into the United States. Most were volunteers. We had fallen to the back of the line and were told to sit in the last row of folding chairs. While we waited, I removed the compression socks I'd been wearing since what seemed like last year and massaged the deep dents in my thighs. At last it was our turn for temperature taking and questions about our current state of health. "Crappy" was not one of the multiple choices. At passport control we were told to stand behind a line of black tape on the floor and hold up our documents, which they didn't want to touch even with gloved hands.

At the next station we were given our housing assignment, a key card, and a mobile phone coded to our quarters, all contained in a paper sack with the room number written in black marker. We moved on to the breakfast table but only slim pickings were left. The room was almost empty. Buses outside had their engines running. "We're keeping everyone waiting," Phil said. I gulped down a yummy pastry with orange juice and followed Phil to the bus.

After putting some of our hand luggage on the overhead rack, he opened a Coke and riffled through the paper sack. "The key card is missing!" Phil said. He handed me the soda can, which I placed in the aisle so I could help him find it. "I think I left it on the food table."

I stood up so he could move from the window seat, knocking over the Coke, which poured across the aisle. "Go!" I said to Phil before trying to blot the sticky mess with the napkins I'd stashed in my pocket.

Phil was back in a flash and reached over me for the paper sack. "They won't let me back inside. I have to turn this in and get a new assignment, phone…the works." He looked like he was going to cry. Nothing bothers him as much as feeling he's screwed up.

A few minutes later, he was back and apologizing to the busload of exhausted, disgruntled people probably blaming him for the further delay. Still the bus didn't budge.

I turned on my phone and up popped our provider's logo, banishing the ten-dollar-a-day fee. It registered U.S. Central Time. Almost twenty-one hours had passed since we'd left our cabin. We had been in the air for more than twelve hours of regular time and an infinity of hallucinatory time.

At last the buses were moving. I started counting the minutes until I could collapse and sleep the next two weeks away.

DON'T FENCE ME IN

There have been as many plagues as wars in history; yet always plagues and wars take people equally by surprise.

—Albert Camus, *The Plague*

U.S. Department of Health and Human Services
Centers for Disease Control and Prevention (CDC)

Order under Section 361 of the Public Health Service Act 42 Code of federal regulations Part 70 (Interstate) and Part 71 (Foreign): Quarantine.

Signed by Lisa Rotz, MD, Deputy Director
Division of Global Migration and Quarantine
Centers for Disease Control and Prevention
February 15, 2020

Section A: Subject Persons
All repatriated persons who were onboard the Diamond Princess cruise ship in Yokohama, Japan and arrived into the United States onboard a chartered flight...with subsequent forward

> *travel to and housing at Lackland Air Force Base in San*
> *Antonio, Texas*
> <u>*Penalties for violating the order may subject you to a criminal*</u>
> <u>*fine and/or up to one year in jail.*</u>

"I am *not* staying here!"

"We don't have a choice."

"I don't care. Just get me out of here! I won't spend a single night here. I can't even breathe in this room! It's...can't you smell it?...Mildew...mold...spores—everywhere!" I have a coughing jag. I run out of the room five minutes after entering it. I stand on the porch of a building that feels like the Bates Motel, gasping.

"Ma'am!" I hear a disembodied voice. "Ma'am!"

I look down from the second story and see a heavyset woman, full shield and face mask, head-to-toe surgical protective gear. She's waving at me. "Ma'am! You must get inside your room immediately."

I look around. Nobody's anywhere near me. "Why? I'm not allowed outside?"

"No, ma'am. You must remain in your room at all times!"

"Are you friggin' kidding me?" I'm screaming as I slowly do her bidding. "We can't go outside for two weeks?"

"That must be a mistake," Phil says, desperate to find a way to appease me.

"Call everyone we know. Now! There has to be somewhere else to put us!"

+ + +

As soon as we stepped off the bus, we were greeted by a corral of luggage. Front and center, all six of our bags—essential members of our traveling family—were huddled, waiting to be claimed. Someone had matched name tags to spare us having to forage through

Luggage and weary passengers as we arrived at Lackland.

a pile in our exhausted state. Not that I was able to feel anything beyond relief that one worry could be crossed off the list.

Yellow-clad men and women were waiting to help. Phil indicated which bags were ours and a woman grabbed two and led the way to the elevator. We had no idea that these aides included a rear admiral, several doctors, a pharmacist, a state disaster coordinator, a commander with the U.S. Public Health Service, and CDC executives.

Phil returned for a second load while I went to the bathroom. It was flooded! My sneakers were soaked. The shower drain must have been clogged because water was cascading slowly from the pan and trailing to the edge of the spartan motel room before it leeched into the carpet. While the bed was freshly made and the surfaces were dust-free, everything smelled as if it had been rotting from the inside out.

The minute Phil walked back in, I blasted him, saying I refused to stay there. He threw the two thin towels onto the bathroom floor, as useless as a sponge in a lake. I opened a door on the other side of the bathroom, which led to an identical motel room.

"What the hell? We have to *share* a bath!"

Phil's face flushed all the way to his bald spot. He sloshed into the bathroom and quickly determined that the leak originated in the showerhead. "I need tools!" He left the room to ask for help.

I sat on the bed to remove my soaked shoes and socks. It was rock hard. The coverlet was stained and my mind went to what thousands of lonely recruits had been up to.

Phil returned with the last of the bags. "Good news! We have both rooms to ourselves. And the other carpet is mostly dry so we can unpack in there."

"Get me out of here! I'm not staying here for a single night."

"Honey, we were some of the last people to be assigned a room. This might be the only one left."

"What about the one with the lost key card? That's probably still available."

"Okay, I'll ask. Also, they said they'll send a plumber, but they have to have one in full Hazmat gear, so it might take a while."

"There's got to be somewhere else they can put us. Officer's quarters or a hotel or…? This is unhealthy. Call Mario!"

My phone rang. "How's it going?" Vana asked. I didn't mince words.

"They're in officer's quarters," I said like a child jealous of a friend's new toy. "She says it's an apartment with a full kitchen, dining room, washer, dryer, and the weather's perfect."

"It's crazy hot in the sun. I've got to change." Phil opened his large suitcase and found shorts and a T-shirt. "You'll feel better if you get out some lighter clothes."

"I have no idea where to look."

Phil gently removed my long-sleeved sweater. There was a bottle of water on the dresser and he urged me to drink it. "It's eighty degrees outside and it must be ninety in here. Maybe I can get the air conditioner going."

He fiddled with the thermostats in both rooms, put on the bathroom fan, and found a portable one in the "closet" that was more of a wooden locker. He opened the front door to help with the airflow. "No doors may remain open," called a disembodied voice. He picked up the desk phone and dialed the operator.

Phil held on for a long time before it was answered. He asked for maintenance but was told that he could only leave a message. Phil was wilting but said, "I'll go downstairs again."

"It's complicated," he said when he returned, his head shiny with sweat, "but they explained that their system only provides heat this time of year and they don't convert it to AC till the summer."

I hadn't budged from the bed. "Did you ask to move?"

"They're looking into it."

"You don't get it. I won't stay here! My heart is pounding, my head is bursting, I can't stop coughing and it's not COVID, but they're going to think it is, which is fine with me. At least a hospital would have AC!" I finally stood up and staggered to the door, opened it enough to look down both sides of the walkway. "And what gives that bitch in yellow the authority to confine us to the room?"

Phil handed me our federal quarantine orders.

"Don't we have any rights?"

He lowered himself to the one upholstered side chair and repositioned his leg with the bad knee. "I don't know any more than you do. We're fenced in and there are armed federal marshals guarding the perimeter." Phil sighed deeply. "I have to lie down. He closed the drapes across the single window, switched off the lights, and aimed the fan at the bed. I stripped to my underwear, found my little pillow, and lay down beside him.

"I can't believe we're in the United States and the conditions are worse than on the ship," I said, my voice finally conceding defeat. Were we really in federal custody with armed guards preventing us from stepping outside? As I closed my eyes, my heartbeat increased. If this was fight or flight, I was ready to jump off the balcony or bust through the fence.

Some bad outcomes you half expect. This time the mammogram will detect an abnormality; this time the cop will notice you were ten miles over the speed limit; this time the IRS is serious about a total audit. But you don't expect that your luxury cruise will harbor a killer virus, resulting in your being returned to the U.S. in a cargo plane that lands at a remote Air Force base where you are ordered into federal quarantine for a minimum of two weeks, leaving you without rights, without agency, and on the wrong side of a heavily guarded fence in a room that smells like an outhouse. Maybe that's what I should write for *The Atlantic* if they really wanted a "slice of life." On the ship I had been too consumed with an exit strategy to recount my escalating dread, thus losing a sweet opportunity to write for them. But this I could describe because this was—intolerable.

✦   ✦   ✦

I stirred from my semi-sleep. "What's that noise?"

Phil also awoke. "A helicopter. We're on an Air Force base, remember?"

"Sounds like they're circling this complex. Probably the media" was the last thing I said as I crashed into the void of the "sleep of the dead." An hour later, I was upset to be roused by the door being banged a lot harder than the polite knocks on the ship. There we had been "valued guests." Here we were probably labeled "unruly inmates."

"Sir, please do not open the door again without first putting on your face mask," a woman chided Phil. She handed him a stack of paperwork, two brown bags stapled at the top, and four bottles of water. I stayed in bed with the splotchy coverlet pulled up to my chin.

Phil peeked into one bag. "Looks like lunch."

I overcame my inertia long enough to open my rollaboard, find fresh underwear and a black nightgown that could pass for a beach coverup. What I really wanted was a shower, but we'd used up the towels on the floor. Phil set his lunch out on the desk. I took the armchair beside the bed and tried to balance my Styrofoam box on the only other flat surface: the few inches in front of the lamp on the nightstand.

"I bet Jerry's loving this," Phil said facetiously after he tasted the food-court "Chinese" concoction with green peppers, maraschino cherries, and pineapple in a slippery pink sauce.

Another knock at the door. Phil put on his mask. He waved for me to do the same. A team of two nameless yellow Big Birds took our temperatures. "Do you need anything?"

"How about towels, a bathmat, someone to mop up the mess, AC, and a plumber—for starters." I am sure I sounded like an entitled brat. "Or how about moving us?"

I tried to fall back asleep, but the bed seemed to be rocking as if we were still on the ship. When I stood up, I had to grab for the wall to steady myself.

I propped myself up on the musty pillows and listened to television with my bleary eyes closed. Dinner was an attempt at Spanish rice and chicken. Both were cold.

"There's a microwave in each room. I'll heat these up."

"Don't bother," I said because it was as good as it was ever going to be. "Do you think this comes from the mess hall?"

"Probably. Supposedly, there are tens of thousands of people scattered around this base, so a hundred and fifty more plates shouldn't be a big deal."

"I don't think the heavy carbs they serve twenty-year-olds who drill off thousands of calories a day is going to sit well with this crowd of fussbudgets."

"I'll try to find out how to order from local restaurants."

My phone rang. Robin was calling, as she had done every day since our shipboard quarantine started. Any pretense of trying to make the best of a horrible situation shattered. "I'm not staying here for a single night!" I screeched. "You know people in Washington. Call them all. Call the Marines. Get me out of here!"

Not only is Robin a pediatrician, she also has a Ph.D. in child psychology, which was precisely what she needed to deal with my tantrum. I was as illogical and inconsolable as an overtired toddler who wants the blue cup instead of the red one.

"I'm sorry you're going through that," she said. "It sounds very hard. Do you have any ideas on what would make you feel better?" I couldn't come up with anything more lucid than "get me out of here." I was imagining a room like the one at the Prince Gallery hotel faintly scented with their signature blend of bergamot and citron, a pristine bathroom with fluffy towels and long-staple cotton sheets. Robin helped me narrow my demands to a dry room and cool air.

"Remember Doctor Schoomaker who helped get us medical advice from Doctor Fauci's team? He has close friends in San Antonio. Frank's a retired Army colonel and Wendy was the garrison commander at Fort Sam Houston, which is part of Lackland. If anyone can pull strings or get you resources more quickly, she can."

At that moment, Wendy sounded even better than Motoko and Sandi combined.

After a flurry of emails, Wendy called. She was in Ohio visiting family but would be home the next day. Frank, who had also held a high-ranking position at Lackland, would check with headquarters to see what they could do for us. As it turned out, the folks at Lackland had no authority over us because our quarantine was being run by the CDC. When she got home, Wendy and I talked for a long time about our families and her life in the military—nothing of any consequence—but she was warm, funny, knowledgeable, and only a few miles away. Wendy's ability to listen—and respond with sympathy while explaining limits—eased my free-floating apprehensions. She knew that our housing unit hadn't been used in quite some time (we would figure out the reason much later) and apologized for the lack of amenities. She'd probably spent a good part of her career talking distraught soldiers "off the roof." Our plight was not that much different from a young recruit away from home for the first time and trying to adjust to military discipline. They were under orders; we were under orders.

Wendy wrote or called daily. She sent us a care package and helped interpret various military traditions. When I asked why there were no bath mats, she said, "Soldiers are required to wear flip-flops in the shower, so they're not needed." All day long, we would see long lines of soldiers drilling and asked what they were chanting. "Those are the 'cadences' that help them keep in time. Most are made up by the group—it's a bonding thing—but there are famous ones too. You can look them up."

I did. Like limericks, many have locker-room themes, and just being forced to chant along might be onerous for women soldiers. Some of the marching rhymes—thank goodness—are more funny than smutty:

Birdy, birdy, in the sky
Dropped a whitewash in my eyes
I'm no wimp, I won't cry
I'm just glad that cows don't fly

Now I realize that my "tantrum" was a classic panic attack. I had held my anxieties in check for weeks, kept my frontal lobes occupied with the media campaign, and sublimated my fears by presenting a brave front for the family—and the cameras—while trying to be tough for Phil and logical for Vana. Now on American turf, I felt safe enough to let my primal emotions gallop out of the stable bucking and kicking.

The quarantines rekindled the value of networking—or in this case: degrees of separation. From Robin to her colleague to Wendy was only two degrees, which was the same distance from Terry to head honchos in the State Department as well as Summer to the Oval Office. We were even closer to journalists and producers. Thanks to social media and email, making those connections is easier than ever. With the most generous spirit, Robin's friend of a friend determined that what we needed was to be heard by someone. Robin was my first "horse whisperer." Wendy was the second.

✦   ✦   ✦

That first night I had only enough energy left to find my toothbrush. Phil aimed a fan so the air circulated over the bed. The minute I lay down, I felt as if a solar flare had knocked out the power grid that kept my body in motion.

I slept late on February 18, which was counted as the second day of our second two-week quarantine. Phil had been awake since 5:30 a.m., when a trumpet playing "Reveille" blasted over the loudspeakers throughout the base. The bathroom floor was dry. Clean towels hung on the rack. He had taken over the sink in the first bedroom and had hung my cosmetic bag over the one in the second. He'd organized items from our food bag on the other dresser and made me a cup of tea in the microwave. Our water and drinks were in both mini-fridges. The carpet was no longer soaking.

"But…how…?"

"I woke up in the middle of the night and heard a relentless dripping sound. I got out my flashlight and found the plumbing problem. I almost woke you trying to dig out my Leatherman tool, but you just turned over. Anyway, I found the problem—the valve packing in the shower handle was loose. I used the pliers to tighten it, then took a shower and whatever was blocking the drain must have washed down. It's decent and there's plenty of hot water."

"How did the carpet dry out?"

"When I put my clothes away, I found two brand-new dehumidifiers. They know they have a problem. But they put out heat, so I've staged the fans to suck most of it through the other room and—What's wrong now?"

I was crying, which came out more like snuffling and blinking. "I don't know…. It's…okay…just…" I was flooded with a muddle of unsorted feelings. I stumbled to the shower and turned it on. I had some hotel-sized bottles of shampoo, conditioner, and body wash from the Prince Gallery. Soon the dank bathroom was wreathed in the scent of bergamot, juniper, and patchouli. Talk about your yin and your yang. If a soothsayer had told me where I would be in February 2020, I would have called him a charlatan. But here I was in some form of house arrest ordered by a federal court, forbidden to leave these rooms. I reject the inane concept that "everything happens for a reason." If there are any laws of the universe, then the opposite is true. I do see substance in "what doesn't kill us makes us stronger." In adversity, it's natural to search for meaning. How bad was this really? Phil was here…more than here…he was trying second by second, minute by minute to make this easier on me. The least I could do was to try to repay him in kind…with kindness.

"Don't flip out when you see the emails," Phil warned when I showed up in a fresh outfit and gave him a kiss. "We're in for a busy day."

Without checking, Bobbie had booked us on the BBC, CNN, ABC's *Good Morning America*, and MSNBC. She had held everybody off the day we arrived, but now they all wanted to know what the cargo plane had been like.

"I guess these are paybacks," I said, "but maybe we can wind the publicity down."

"I'm sure they're going to ask about the quarantine here, but let's not complain or we'll sound like whiny brats. At least we're a lot safer now."

Motoko was one of the first who reached out to me the day we arrived, but I hadn't even checked email. Once I looked, the barrage was led by her and Bobbie. I told her about Mrs. Nordic Sweater, the Bubble, and the other person I saw escorted into it by a Ghostbuster during the flight.

> **Gay:** Three people went to the hospital from here [Lackland] this morning. And they weren't [the ones] behind the screen [the Bubble].
>
> **Motoko:** Oh boy. I'm sorry. You must be really scared.
>
> **Gay:** To be fair, it was the most interesting flight of my life.
>
> **Motoko:** Love your attitude!
>
> **Gay:** Any new numbers from the ship?
>
> **Motoko:** 99 new cases. How's Lackland?

Gay: Getting panicked, not allowed outside at all, moldy room, making me sick, no other available rooms, guards everywhere, fences up, poor ATT connectivity, feeling out of control…otherwise chipper.

Motoko: Oh no! Hang in there.

Phil and I were still piecing together the story about the infectious passengers. Thus far we knew only that while we were delayed on the buses in Yokohama, the Japanese Ministry of Health revealed that fourteen of the Americans who had been tested on February 14 were confirmed to be positive for coronavirus. There had been eleven buses, so it was fair to assume that almost every one of them had been contaminated. The long delay was due to a dispute between the State Department and the CDC over whether to let them fly.

"It was the worst nightmare," said a senior U.S. official involved in the decision, speaking to the *Washington Post*. "Quite frankly, the alternative could have been pulling grandma out in the pouring rain, and that would have been bad, too."

The State Department won the argument, resulting in a decision that nearly doubled the number of known coronavirus patients in the U.S. at that time. Most Americans were not concerned about the few cases that seemed remote from their lives, but nobody knew better than us how quickly these could multiply. The epidemic on the *Diamond Princess* began with one man from Hong Kong, then spread to ten people, then twenty. Two weeks later, numbers on the ship surged from 355 to 454, including 33 crew. Then the next day's total rose by 88 to 542—more than any country in the world except China. And Motoko wondered if we were scared! Of course, we were petrified. After the long delay on the bus, we knew our risk had risen incrementally, especially after my close encounter with Mrs. Nordic Sweater. Our only comfort was that if we became ill, we would be cared for in English-speaking health facilities; and considering the media spotlight on the evacuees, we might receive super-vigilant care.

✦ ✦ ✦

I unpacked. The second bedroom became my dressing room, my office, and the food pantry, which was well stocked with the left-over CUPNOODLES that I confess I stuffed into our suitcases. The other bedroom was reserved for sleeping and our media set-up. We called Wanda, who was managing our office and caring for Willoughby, and Michelle, who takes care of our house and coaxes our garden to thrive, and gave them a list for an overnight package: Phil's laptop, various cables and computer accessories, checks to pay the overdue bills, bath mats, washcloths, large towels, shorts and summery tops, a bathrobe, the latest *New Yorker*s, some medications, and personal items. They packed everything into a big "Who Gives a Crap" cardboard box—we order their toilet paper because they donate half their profits to build toilets in the developing world. Packages that arrived at the base had to be inspected before being sent to our quarantine area and then delivered by appropriately protected personnel. Later we heard the printing on the box had been the subject of many jokes.

The computer made it easier to manage the media and keep up with emails. Of course, as soon as lighter clothing arrived, the weather normalized for that time of year—and do not underestimate the comfort of a bath mat.

The media hadn't vaporized in the contrails across the Pacific. Requests continued to pour in, especially from the Tampa Bay broadcasters, who wanted frequent updates. At least being on U.S. Central Time was far easier than Japan time. Surprisingly, we had more trouble with the internet and cellular calls on the base than on the ship, so every set-up was nerve-racking and took longer

Even though we had achieved our goal, the media interest in our quarantine continued at Lackland. Bobbie sent a tripod, which made Phil's job easier.

than expected. Thankfully, we still had Bobbie, Crystal, and their team to sort everything out.

> **CNN:** We would like to interview Gay and Phil Courter, the parents of Ashley Rhodes-Courter, about their experience being quarantined in Texas. 9:00 pm EST, 5 minutes via Skype.

> **Bobbie:** Don't think tonight can work, what about tomorrow?

> **CNN:** Darn. They really wanted to do a segment on them tonight.

> **Bobbie:** There's no way tonight could work.

> **CNN:** Promise it will only take ten minutes of their time!

> **Bobbie:** We reached out to Gay and Phil on your behalf for tonight. They said OK.

> **CNN:** Can we use photos from their son or daughter's Twitter feed? Also, John Vause is our anchor tonight. He's fascinated by their story and the detailed accounting. He wants to

know how they are coping; especially as new cases are being announced. What are their biggest concerns?

Bobbie sent us our login instructions and their questions for the "ten-minute" interview.

- The experience on the ship and then the trip to Lackland
- How you think the Japanese govt handled everything
- How did you spend your time, etc.
- The experience being quarantined in Texas

The most pressing question was how we felt about the State Department's insistence—over the CDC's objections—on the fourteen people who tested positive traveling with everyone else. We said that once they were on the bus, most of us already had been exposed. However, a few days later, at a State Department press conference, the managing director of operational medicine insisted that the people in the Bubble had been completely isolated during the entire flight. We knew that to be untrue because they were using the same porta-potties as the rest of us!

The journalists also wanted to hear if we believed the additional quarantine was justified. "It's hard," I said, "and we wish we did not have to be here. But we do. This is what we asked for. We wanted to come home where we would feel safer. It's our civic duty to keep everyone else safe too. We don't want to infect our friends, family, or community. Sometimes doing what's right isn't necessarily pleasant."

We felt like air show daredevils knowing that the story would be much more exciting if we crashed by turning positive. So far, we didn't have the results from Japan but assumed that the CDC would have been notified if we had been infectious. Still, there was always a breath-holding moment in the few seconds between when our temperature was taken and the number was read out where we thought: "This is it! This is when our luck runs out."

Everyone in our quarantine received throat and nose swabs on February 21. Four days later, on February 25, two of the health workers who regularly took our temperatures twice daily reported our results: Negative in both Texas and Japan, with the paperwork to prove it! Jerry and Cathy also had good news, but Mario's came back "inconclusive." Vana assumed the worst until he received the results that cleared him two days before they returned home.

We also had been pessimistic. Without sharing our fears, both of us had been under the assumption that at least one of us was likely to have COVID-19, we just weren't symptomatic…yet. We not only were high risk by age and pre-existing conditions, we had been exposed by the "miasma" on the ship plus the proximity to infectious people on the buses and plane. Once we had been "incarcerated" at Lackland, though, we knew the chances of a fresh exposure were infinitesimal. We exhaled and hugged. If we could hold it together for five more days, our nightmare might be over.

Ichigo Ichie

And the world cannot be discovered by a journey of miles, no matter how long, but only by a spiritual journey, a journey of one inch, very arduous and humbling and joyful, by which we arrive at the ground at our own feet, and learn to be at home.

—Wendell Berry

At first there was no easy way to get information on what was happening. There was "us" on one side of the chain-link fence and "them" on the other. Upon arrival we had been told to dial one number to reach our "case manager" to explain what we needed. Every time we did this, the discourse was polite but not a single question was answered. Because I had trouble hearing on the official phone (my hearing aids are paired only with my iPhone), Phil made most of the requests. The first day he politely asked, "May we please have two sets of towels tonight?" He explained that the others had been used to mop a wet floor. The reply, "Yes, sir, I'll make that request," was always the same.

Further queries like "Could we have them tonight? Within an hour? When?" were useless. The question went out into the ether.

Surprisingly, the skimpy Motel 6 towels were delivered; eventually, they found some washcloths. Bath mats? The housekeepers, who did not speak English, and could not clean our rooms, gesticulated that they would try.

At that point, I had zero knowledge of how the chain of command worked, and the process looked both laborious and inefficient. It would take a dramatic illustration to prove me wrong.

✦   ✦   ✦

Phil and I pride ourselves on being self-sufficient. Anyone in quarantine, though, is dependent on the outside world for everything. Specialists in public health understand that if you isolate people, you must care for them. The group quarantines for the Wuhan and cruise ship groups were more drastic than even the lockdowns during the flu pandemic a hundred years earlier. Not that there is a modern rulebook for managing a quarantine, because this was the first quarantine in the United States in more than fifty years—except for the ones routinely run by NASA. The first of those took place after the moon landing in 1969 with Neil Armstrong, "Buzz" Aldrin, and Michael Collins in case they had been exposed to "dangerous lunar microorganisms." The last public health quarantine began in July 1963 when a sixty-nine-year-old American visited Sweden, which was undergoing a deadly smallpox outbreak caused by an international traveler. She was stopped at the airport in New York because she didn't have proof of inoculation and was quarantined in a government hospital on Staten Island. Her daughter, a lawyer, took the matter to court and lost. That decision stood as the only federal court battle over the government's quarantine powers since that time—until the one that would take place in San Antonio two weeks after our arrival.

✦   ✦   ✦

There was hardly a moment when Phil and I weren't restless, tense, or apprehensive. What cheered us most were the FaceTime calls with our grandchildren, all too young for real conversation, and so we watched them playing in parks, eating meals, petting animals, singing songs. A cute video was the highlight of our day. We'd not only view it repeatedly but comment on it as if the four-year-old's version of "Twinkle, Twinkle Little Star" or the first grader reading were breaking news.

When our door was open, we could see through the second-floor walkway's iron railing. At least we were facing the parking lot where the action was taking place. Though we never occupied them, our "lost-key-card" rooms overlooked the perimeter fence and the road, with federal marshals in unmarked cars situated so they could view each segment of the Gateway Villa "prison" compound. From time to time, we observed a fellow detainee strolling by. The second day, I asked the temperature-taking crew, "How do we apply for permission to walk outside?"

"Officially, you are not allowed to leave your room. However, we cannot legally stop you."

"In other words, you won't shoot us," I said, trying to sound lighthearted, but received no response.

After lunch, I had indigestion after "chowing down" a chicken-fried steak with white gravy, mashed potatoes, and beans also in beige sauce—at least a month's worth of Weight Watcher points.

"We need some exercise," Phil said. "Let's blow this place." The temperature was in the fifties and it felt good to put on a jacket. I still was slightly unsteady and carried my walking stick, which helped on the stairs. We peered through a fence where uniformed people entered and exited a single-story building without a layer of protective gear. To the right was the Q-gate, which could be opened only by an armed federal marshal. Anyone walking or driving to "our" side had to be covered from head to toe. I dubbed the housekeepers and maintenance workers in the hooded white full-body suits our "white knights." The temperature takers and meal deliverers were "yellow birds." There were no name tags or other identifying badges to indicate who they were. Eventually we learned that many of them were MDs, high-ranking government officials, and executives who staffed disasters as part of the Department of Health and Human Service's Incident Management Team under the Assistant Secretary for Preparedness and Response.

We observed—from at least six feet away—as the white knights, their hoods not unlike medieval helmets, sorted plastic bags for pickup. We had been given blue bags for linens and towels, white for personal laundry, and red for trash—a lot more hygienic than dumping everything in the corridor outside our cabin! On the "safe" side of the Q-gate, there was a "donning" area with a checklist of precisely the order in which to put on protective clothing. The "doffing" area was on our side of the fence, where portable sinks were set up. The rules for removing gear were stringent. The six-step instructions for just the gloves specified:

1. Outside of gloves are contaminated!
2. If your hands get contaminated during glove removal, immediately wash your hands or use an alcohol-based hand sanitizer
3. Using a gloved hand, grasp the palm area of the other gloved hand and peel off first glove
4. Hold removed glove in gloved hand
5. Slide fingers of ungloved hand under remaining glove at wrist and peel off second glove over first glove
6. Discard gloves in a waste container

We continued our walk along the edge of the temporary fence, noting that it was held in place with only twist-ties and sandbags. Escape from the compound would be easy; eluding the marshals— not so much. "Now, now grandma," I imagined the dashing black-belt officer saying, "time for your milk and cookies" as he coaxed me back.

We recognized several of the couples walking in the same vicinity. We'd been on at least one other cruise with Marcia and Rich and they had joined our seaplane tour of Ha Long Bay. On the ship we would have stopped to chat. Now we barely nodded and moved on. Tyler and Rachel, newlyweds from Dallas, smiled and waved. I'd seen them huddled together under one of the gray blankets on the plane and had sympathized with them about their extended honeymoon. Rachel had said, "We started our cruise after being married five months, and now we feel like we've been married fifteen years." She even managed a luminous smile and I wished I'd said, "If you get through this, the rest of your life will be a breeze," but my quiver of quips had been empty.

It was a few days before we figured out the building where Jerry and Cathy were staying, though we had been comparing notes on the phone. At one point, when neither Phil nor I could figure out what we were eating, we called Jerry for clarity. "Why, any Texan worth his salt would know that was a breaded fried pork patty," he said in a playful drawl. Then, more seriously, "The raw bacon at breakfast yesterday was the last straw. And, if I see another scoop of white rice with mystery fish and brown sauce—" When his professionally written complaint letter made it up the command ladder, he let us know. "They called to tell me they've changed caterers."

"Caterers are turning out this slop? I'd assumed it came from a mess hall."

"We might see an improvement tomorrow," Jerry replied, not sounding hopeful.

✦ ✦ ✦

Sometimes Phil and I walked outside together. Mostly, though, one of us just had to escape the room and would leave whenever we couldn't take it any longer. Besides, Phil walked much faster and needed to expend energy; I did more of a stroll-and-stop, if for no other reason than to rebalance. My dizziness hadn't decreased. For the first week I blamed it on sea legs, then I began to worry that something was amiss. Inside it seemed as if the walls were tilting toward me, and I did find some relief outdoors. I consulted with Dr. Google and learned that claustrophobia can be caused by a fear of losing control or being confined. Well, hadn't I lost control; wasn't I being confined?

Every now and then I saw someone on the other side of the fence talking to "one of us." Was that allowed? Both were wearing masks and they were more than six feet apart. One afternoon I noticed a man watching me watching him. "Hi," he said. I moved closer to the fence, like a curious—yet wary—zoo creature.

"Hi," I replied. "What do the initials DMAT on the back of your shirt mean?"

"Disaster Medical Assistance Team."

"Thanks. I'm acronym impaired."

"Where are you from?" he asked.

"A small town on the west coast of Florida. You?"

"Ohio."

"Are you a doctor?"

"No, I'm an emergency health specialist. In Ohio, I work for the state Emergency Management Agency, but I go on leave if our team is deployed for federal disasters." He mentioned that he'd responded to a few hurricanes in Florida, then added, "My name's John. But they call me Woo." He pointed to a man behind him wearing a similar shirt. "The guy with the ponytail is my boss, Tony."

I told him my name and said, "We're the folks talking to the media all the time, but you probably knew that."

"That's your right as an American. We realize that none of you want to be here."

"Actually, we're thrilled to be off the plague ship and accept that being quarantined is the price we have to pay. Still, it's difficult being so restricted."

"How did you like the Freedom Flight?" I did a double take. "That's what a guy in your group called the extraction."

"A unique experience!" I said with a laugh. "I feel better now that we know our test results. I had anxiety attacks just thinking about them."

"You and everybody else. We've talked about putting out Valium salt licks!"

That cracked me up as I imagined us coming out at twilight like deer in a meadow to get our daily dose in the parking lot. Just then, a jumbo aircraft thundered overhead, its angle of attack indicating it had just taken off. John pointed skyward. "You don't see those too often."

"What is it?"

"That, ma'am, is a C-5 Galaxy. It can carry more cargo farther distances than any other aircraft. They're used to carry the president's motorcade. The limo the president rides in is called 'Stagecoach,' and the backup is 'Spare,' plus all the other specialized vehicles."

We chatted for a few more minutes before Tony called John away and I headed back to our cell. I felt like I did when I'd run home to tell my mother that I'd made a friend on the first day of school.

✦ ✦ ✦

"Stressed, depressed, or need to talk?" was written at the bottom of our daily newsletter.

"Maybe I should call that number."

"Why?"

"My dizzy spells could be caused by PTSD."

"I thought that only surfaced after trauma—not in the midst."

"Let's find out."

After a bit of coaxing, Phil called and we had a joint session with the counselor. He clarified why people suffer from post-traumatic stress and suspected that many in our group would experience it to some degree. He encouraged us to talk to a counselor after we returned home. However, in terms of my dizzy spells, he thought a doctor should rule out a physical problem first.

Ashley runs a counseling agency, so when she called, I asked her to line up teletherapy appointments for us. She said, "Oh, thank goodness you brought it up first!" she said. "Josh and Blake and I were trying to decide which one of us should broach the subject with you."

One afternoon I had just finished a Skype interview and started to stand up. Everything blurred and then flickered to black. I sat down fast and lowered my head between my knees. A few minutes later, I tried again to get up, but the swirling sensation was relentless. "Ask for a medical check," I said. "This is the worst one yet."

Phil called our case manager, who—as usual—took the message without comment. In the meantime, I checked my blood sugar, which was fine.

"What do you think it is?" Phil asked.

"A brain tumor?"

"Not funny."

"There's also labyrinthitis or Meniere's disease—both are inner ear disorders. Maybe it's a rare symptom of the coronavirus or psychosomatic vertigo."

I couldn't believe that the doctor who examined me was also one of the "yellow birds" who delivered our meals. She took my blood pressure, asked about my medication and any other issues. I was open about my anxieties and described the sensation of the walls moving closer and tilting. My blood pressure was lower than my usual. She suggested cutting back on my hypertension meds. I called Mario and got his opinion. "Try that," he said, adding he could run tests when we were all home, which would be in just over a week…if all went well.

✦ ✦ ✦

On February 20, we learned that two people from the *Diamond Princess* had died from the coronavirus. Both were Japanese citizens in their eighties. I remembered a few interviews where I had said that if people start dying, nobody would come to the Olympics. I also remembered the happy families who were celebrating the New Year with a lavish trip; now they were attending funerals. My remark had been flippant; now I felt as if I had been doused with a cold bucket of truth.

I opened Phil's computer to a blank document to see if I could organize my tangled thoughts. Sometimes I find it easier to write about my feelings than think. Was this a zero-sum game? Could someone else's death be my gain? Better them than us? The very real possibility of dying from COVID-19 was the question mark at the end of every sentence. Yes, it made me dizzy even to consider it for a fraction of a second. Now I had typed it: Is this what will kill one of us?

The words…thoughts…emotions started splattering on the page. I was writing for the first time in a month—a very different process from pecking into my iPad or talking into my phone. If I'd had the computer, I probably could have unwrapped my bundle of shifting moods and come up with something for *The Atlantic*. On the ship I had been so busy campaigning to be rescued, I hadn't focused on my feelings at any given moment. I paused. Now it is about "us" and "them." On the ship we kept saying we were all in the same boat. Here at Lackland everyone on the other side of the fence was in uniform. If they crossed over to interact with us, they dressed in full protection regalia. When we opened our door, they backed up, taking our temperatures with an outstretched arm.

How did I feel? I felt dehumanized, like a pariah, scum, an outcast. Would someone want to read what it's like to be a carefree cruiser one moment, then held hostage by a foreign government, and finally repatriated into an even harsher environment?

I emailed *The Atlantic's* editor to see if she still wanted an article. Her response was polite, but she was miffed because she thought I'd written the op-ed for the *Washington Post* instead. I explained that the purpose of the op-ed had been to persuade those in power to bring us home and was nothing like what I'd write for her. She responded graciously, saying that she understood that I had been in "an extremely difficult and unusual situation" and welcomed my submission.

I never appreciated a keyboard more than at that moment as I sorted the panoply of emotions brought on by forced confinement. I could freely express whatever came to mind, then double back to carve the words more artfully.

> I used to think that if I carried the right accoutrements, I would have something on hand for any emergency or change of plans. I had something for almost every need, even anti-anxiety meds in case of a crisis—which indeed this was. But I had forgotten the ruby slippers. There was nothing to click to send us home. My debit card, which works in

any ATM in the world, cannot unlock the fence around the perimeter of this stockade. All the airline points in the world cannot purchase a single ticket home. Technically, we are not allowed out of our rooms. After seeing some other cruisers in their N95 masks walking outside, we asked how we could win the same privilege. "We do not recommend you leave your room for your own safety," the yellow-suited guard with no name tag said, "but we can't stop you."

So here I stand, against advice, gulping fresh air through the mask's fiber, watching soldiers in Army drab and Air Force blue drilling and chanting. I wake to the bugle playing reveille at 5:30 a.m. and hear taps at what must be a soldier's bedtime. At precisely 5:30 p.m., there's another bugle alert called "retreat." We open the door and see members of our "support team" on the better side of the fence. They have stopped in their tracks and placed their right hands over their hearts while the "Star-Spangled Banner" is played. Everyone stares in the same direction, where presumably a flag is being lowered. Every day a few more of us quarantined cruisers put on our face masks and do the same. They brought us home for one reason only: Because we were Americans in harm's way. Someday—hopefully—we will be on the same side of the fence.

The article was well received. Then, when the *Post* wanted a follow-up op-ed, it seemed as if I had emerged, if briefly, from has-been, over-the-hill status and was now a boomer with a second chance.

A few days later, Blake caught me at a low moment. "Everything seems much more difficult, like swimming in slime."

"Nice simile, Mom, but don't you realize you're living every writer's dream?" When I didn't have a ready comeback, he said, "Doesn't every writer wish she could be locked away without anything else to do and have a great story to tell?"

"It *is* an amazing story," I admitted, as the disparate elements from the glamorous trip formed into a flip book taking us from the lavish hotel's expansive vistas of Tokyo to the Peak in Hong Kong to the ship's bow dipping and rising as it cut a path through the Pacific, all the while being stalked by a vicious virus.

Blake encouraged me to outline the narrative while it was still fresh. He was right. I discarded my victim cloak and made the only sensible move: I contacted my literary agent, Joëlle Delbourgo.

She said, "There's room for one great book on the *Diamond Princess*, but you will have to move quickly." I told her that my *Atlantic* story and second *Post* op-ed were about to be published. "That's great. Momentum is vital because I expect that some well-known journalists may also be shopping book ideas."

At the same time, media curiosity about the military quarantine increased and Bobbie was keeping us busy with interviews. She even sent Phil an iPhone tripod to make his job easier. But I knew better than to put off Joëlle. I'd almost blown it with *The Atlantic* and understood that if I didn't try to sell a book at this crucial time, I'd regret it forever. I could do this…but I needed help and knew where to turn. I contacted Sarah Flynn, who had edited three of my bestselling novels. We sent drafts back and forth and, miraculously, we were able to deliver a twenty-two-page proposal for a book—tentatively titled *The Deadly Diamond*—in four days!

The timing couldn't have been better. I was on a writer's high, not unlike the first time one of my books made the *New York Times* bestseller list. On Sunday, February 23, Motoko's comprehensive story "'We're in a Petri Dish': How a Coronavirus Ravaged a Cruise Ship" appeared on the front page of the Sunday *New York Times*, accompanied by a photo of me in our cabin wearing a mask, with a credit to Phil, and including several more of his pictures.

A few days later, on February 27, my *Atlantic* article was published. One of the first people to compliment me was Motoko.

Phil wriggled his arm through the fence to take this picture of me, which *The Atlantic* used to illustrate my dispatch from the Lackland quarantine.

"What an excellent piece of writing!" The piece stayed on the magazine's "most popular" list for a while and the *Times* also mentioned it in their "What We're Reading" feature: Lara Takenaga, a staff editor, recommended it for "the quirky details about locked-down life at sea."

My mood peaked the next day when my second op-ed was published by the *Post*. I had tried to give a different flavor of the quarantine.

Poorly fueled by biscuits and gravy and mystery meat, a rebellious spark flared this week as we strolled along the fence. Phil noted its zip-tie fastenings and the sandbags holding it upright.

"Why don't we stage a coup?," I said, imagining marshaling our fellow boomer cruisers. "We could use our walking sticks as swords, walkers as battering rams, the wheelchairs as cavalry. In the film, the soundtrack could be 'Do You Hear the People Sing' from 'Les Mis'!"

Even if the proposal didn't sell the book, I was content that I'd been published by people I admired. I even accepted that being called quirky—for the second time—could be considered a compliment.

✦ ✦ ✦

They called us Cohort II. We weren't sure why until a few days into the quarantine we received a notice about a conference call with the Incident Management Team. The invitation listed forty names on an organizational chart and featured a photo of their meeting room, which looked like a mini-version of NASA's mission control. Our fearless leaders included Commander Mark Byrd of the U.S. Public Health Service, working out of Dallas. He has been on active duty for more than twenty years as an environmental health officer and deployed more than thirty times in disasters. In command of the CDC's portion of our quarantine was Rear Admiral Dr. Nancy Knight, director of that agency's Division of Global Health Protection and assistant surgeon general of the U.S. Public Health Service. She had spent more than ten years in Africa and was a leader in the Ebola outbreaks.

Commander Byrd's classy Texas accent was more Southern Comfort than twang as he clarified that Cohort I included the Wuhan evacuees, who were billeted in Lackland's officer's housing—nice family apartments like the one the Mendizabals were assigned at Travis. The group had done well and was scheduled to leave in less than a week. He explained the complexities of living on a military base, especially in terms of ordering anything and why so many of us were frustrated. A relative had tried to send us a gift from Edible Arrangements but they were not allowed to deliver. No takeout food deliveries, except from the pizza company on the base, were approved. We could order groceries (and a modest amount of wine) only from H-E-B, the official purveyor. Anything else would take several days to be inspected, so nothing perishable was permitted. If it seems like a good portion of the meeting was devoted to food, it was!

Rear Admiral Knight introduced a brand-new concept: social distancing. Way back in February 2020, the rules of infectious disease control were unfamiliar; within weeks they would be hammered into a good portion of the world's population. Admiral Knight was relentless in repeating instructions for hand washing, avoiding touching the face, and covering coughs and sneezes with tissues, which should be tossed immediately, after which we were supposed to wash hands again. We had to wear masks—correctly—whenever we left the room and remain at least six feet apart from everyone else. We were issued gloves and special blue masks to be used during room cleaning, plus various sprays and wipes, and encouraged to scrub all surfaces, especially in our bathrooms, because nobody else was permitted to service our rooms.

Several families had not received their luggage. To me the idea of being without any possessions was downright horrifying. We all cheered as various bags showed up, especially when the last of the missing pieces were located at Travis and "repatriated" to Texas.

The most important news was the health status of our fellow shipmates who had tested positive. Thus far, Cohort II had seven confirmed cases, all of whom had been transported to a local "health care facility." Much later I learned that they had been sent to the Texas Center for Infectious Disease, the only hospital of its kind in the United States, which is probably why San Antonio was selected as a quarantine site. It specializes in the treatment of tuberculosis and has a Hansen's disease—leprosy—clinic. Many of the rooms had specially designed air-handling systems to prevent the spread of infection.

Best of all, nobody in our group was seriously ill; their symptoms ranged from none to mild, like a bad cold. "For some unknown reason, Cohort II seems to have a higher rate of transmissibility than the Cohort I from China," we were told.

"Maybe because they weren't on buses or planes with infectious passengers," I whispered sarcastically to Phil.

At the question and answer session, someone asked how long it took for someone to be released back to the base. Rear Admiral Knight said they didn't yet have an average time it took to "clear the virus," but that the patient had to have two negative tests twenty-four hours apart.

A woman wondered whether she could go with her husband if he became ill. The answer was no. "If a partner or roommate tests positive, the clock is reset for the person who is still asymptomatic," the admiral explained. "That means that the fourteen days starts all over again."

To end the meeting, Commander Byrd announced the dinner menu that made everything sound "finger lickin' good." He seemed like a genuinely kind person.

We began to look forward to the daily conference calls and found them the surest—if not the only—way to get definitive answers to our questions. Our "management team" tried their best to meet our needs even beyond shelter and sustenance. They sent treats to honor birthdays and anniversaries, tried to accommodate special dietary needs, and offered inspirational services led by a base chaplain. Catholics could order ashes for Ash Wednesday and communion was available by request.

Many of the daily questions involved rumors in the media and online. Someone heard that all quarantines would be doubled to twenty-eight days and had heard that "the CDC was recommending twenty-one days for 'high-risk groups.'" We were told that was not true.

I'd read that we were being blamed for the rising positive cases, even though on February 24, the beginning of our second week in

Texas, there were only fifty-three cases in the whole country and that included the evacuated Americans from the *Diamond Princess*. Two days later, it was reported that President Trump was furious that he had not been briefed before the people who tested positive were allowed on the extraction flights.

"Your quarantine ends on Monday, March 2," Commander Byrd said to reassure us. "We are already planning your demobilization—what we call de-mob—for that date." He chuckled. "To prove it, we're planning a special meal and you can vote on the menu."

There was a flurry of questions about making plane reservations and getting to the airport, but we were told to hold off until they had more information. "Based on how long it took to process Cohort I, don't plan to fly out before three in the afternoon."

There was an odd rhythm to these sessions. Just when the questions were winding down, someone would ask about a topic the staff had already covered. The disaster team taking care of us was accustomed to the problems faced by people in extremis, many of whom had lost loved ones, homes, their whole world. They realized that we also were suffering from a group psychosis and so they did not seem to mind the repetition. The morning after our meetings, we received a printed follow-up with the headline "Your daily access to accurate and updated information is our priority!" Everything was repeated in a bullet-pointed memo at the front of the daily newsletter. Even so, the same questions would be asked the next day and answered with gentle equanimity.

The day after my *Atlantic* article appeared, a woman with a reedy voice called into the meeting and said, "I was very disturbed that someone here wrote an article criticizing this quarantine. She said she felt like an outcast and dehumanized. We are very happy to be here and realize you are doing everything possible to provide for us. I just wanted you to know because that woman doesn't represent all of us."

I felt as if I'd been slapped. There was a long silence. Admiral Knight answered first. "Thank you for telling us that. Not everyone reacts well to isolation and we have to respect everyone's feelings."

I was heard and she understood. The admiral was my hero! Not only that, but the next day Commander Byrd apologized for calling us a "cohort" because it sounded too impersonal. "We're all friends here," he said, "and from now on, we'll refer to each other as friends."

In my second *Post* op-ed I gave the admiral a shout-out: "Rear Adm. Nancy Knight, director of the Centers for Disease Control and Prevention division leading the medical side of our quarantine, has drilled us so much about 'social distancing' and 'proper hand washing' that her dictums about infection, prevention, and control measures are lodged in my mind. The admiral has kept us safe. On the ship, cases escalated into the hundreds in a few days. Here, only single digits have shown symptoms or tested positive."

✦   ✦   ✦

I received an email from someone named Karen that began "Do I have a story to tell you!" Since at least four Karens are important in my life, it took a few seconds before I realized this Karen was my *Diamond Princess* trivia team buddy. She had spiked a fever on the fourth day of quarantine in Yokohama and asked to be tested. A few days later, she was taken by ambulance to the National Center for Global Health and Medicine in Tokyo.

"Phil!" I called out. "Karen from trivia has coronavirus! I can't believe it. I was with her several times on the last few days of the actual cruise!" Scenes flipped through my mind: bending over the tiny tables scribbling our guesses…celebrating our "big" win with high-fives…drinking Champagne while laughing and toasting each other. The last we'd been together was February 3, twenty days earlier. Quarantines were set at fourteen days, but did anyone really know the true incubation period for COVID-19?

I wrote Karen asking more about how she was feeling and how sick she had been. An only child of Chinese American parents, she was traveling with them for the holiday. When she tested positive, she was told to bring all her luggage to the hospital because she would not be returning to the ship. Her mother helped carry her luggage to the gangway, sobbing the whole way. At the last moment, the formidable older woman climbed into the ambulance and refused to leave. The Japanese medics understood tiger moms and let her ride along.

Karen and her mother stayed together at the National Center for another eleven days. After she was discharged, American officials required an additional health clearance to comply with CDC requirements before she could return to the U.S., but the Japanese declined to do the additional testing, saying it was an "American problem" because she was cleared by Japanese standards.

"What's your status now?" I wrote Karen.

"I can't get any answers," she replied. "It's been quite the ordeal."

"I've got to find a way to get Karen home," I announced to Phil.

Phil swept his arm around our room as if to say, "How are you going to do that from here?"

I wrote and asked permission to use her name and share her story with the American press. She said, "Give my information to anyone who might help." I put Karen in touch with Motoko, figuring she might appreciate the irony of the story and/or have useful contacts.

"I have a few connections in Japan," I said to Phil, but I doubt they can help because if there's anything that defines that culture, it's rule following."

"You could never live there," Phil said, kidding me, "because instead of asking for permission, you ask for forgiveness later."

He was right about that. "Nobody has autonomy. If the hospital doesn't want do it the American way, no amount of pressure will change their minds."

"But that's not going to stop you, is it?"

"Well, I have one idea!"

I called our case manager and told him I needed to ask Admiral Knight a question that only she could answer. The next day there was a knock at the door. I reached for my mask but forgot to take my glasses off first and they fell on the floor. I picked them up, but when I pulled the upper elastic into place, out popped one of my hearing aids. I bent to locate it and tucked it safely into my bra. Finally, I opened the door, but as I tried to pinch the mask to my nose, I realized it was upside down. During the phone meeting the night before, the admiral noted that some of us were wearing our masks incorrectly and she was instructing the staff to re-educate any miscreants. "Whoops! Upside down…." I closed the door, flipped my mask, and opened it again.

"I'm glad you are getting the knack of it," she said.

I had only heard the admiral's voice over the phone and so was taken aback by her appearance: She was petite, with silver hair in a stylish bob. Every inch of her commanded respect. Feeling a bit foolish for wasting her valuable time, I hurriedly explained about Karen. "All I wanted was the contact information for your counterpart in Tokyo."

"That sounds sensible." I asked her to wait while I wrote out Karen's information. Admiral Knight shook her head. "Give it to your case manager."

"But…" I stopped myself. Since I was asking a favor, I had better do as she directed. I thanked her again, but figured I'd hit a brick wall.

Three days later Karen wrote, "I'm not sure if your contact pulled some magic but I'm at the airport now and almost on my way home. Thank you for doing this for me."

"Thanks," I wrote, "but I really didn't do anything."

Karen was the first in her family to arrive home. Her father went to Travis for two weeks and her mother had to complete an additional quarantine in the Japanese hospital. Just before we left Lackland, our case manager called and asked, "How is Karen doing?" After I figured out to whom he was referring, I said that she was grateful to be home. He said he would pass the news to the admiral. Had the admiral helped Karen or was she just curious whether the issue had been solved?

In the early stages of writing this book, I contacted Andrew, who became one of my "fence buddies." He's a pharmacist who was the deputy lead for the quarantine's Service Access Team. He told me he was on leave from the FDA for this special assignment. I had been curious about where all the people who were staffing our quarantine came from and how he could do both jobs. "In Lackland, I worked as an assistant to Admiral Knight."

"I talked to her about helping a friend named Karen get out of Japan, but I never heard what happened."

"Really?" he said. "Since you said the name, I can tell you the admiral assigned Karen's case to me."

"Did you contact the CDC in Japan? Because suddenly she was cleared and she never knew how or why." He confirmed that the admiral's counterpart had been happy to help eliminate the impasse.

The chain of command might have seemed incomprehensible, but it had worked.

✦ ✦ ✦

We had adjusted. The stages of acclimating were not unlike those of grief, perhaps because we felt as helpless as anyone facing a crisis over which they had no control. We went through denial, anger, bargaining, depression—perhaps not in that exact order—until we reached a truce that could be called acceptance. The days had a rhythm and, much like the quarantine on the ship, meals marked the time more than clocks. Most days followed a familiar pattern. "Reveille" woke me long enough to pee and then I cuddled next to Phil, grateful that I didn't have to rise and shine, salute and march. In the evening, "Taps" had a lonesome sound. I felt a maternal pang for the young women and men far from home being trained to risk their lives in wars, which are becoming an outdated means of human conflict resolution. There are many more fruitful ways to use our human capital, like making life on earth more livable for all.

And, as I had mentioned in the *Atlantic* article, there was that bugle call at 5:30 every afternoon, followed by the national anthem. I asked Wendy, my interpreter of all things military, what was going on. She said it was called "Retreat," which signified the end of the workday and was a signal to salute our flag. The next time I heard it I went to the door. Everyone in the parking lot area, which was more like our community commons, was frozen in place facing in the same direction, though no flag was in sight. Some saluted, others stood at attention, the majority put their right hand over their heart. A few from our group stopped in mid-stroll and did the same. And so did I.

Until that moment, I've never felt an overwhelming sense of patriotism, even though I've often marveled at the brilliance and wisdom of the founding fathers who drafted the Declaration of Independence and the Constitution. Considering the innate selfishness of human nature, it amazes me that the principals of democracy work as well as they do.

I started timing my walks to be outside for "Retreat." By the second week, there was a well-worn path close to the edge of the perimeter fence, as if we all wanted to be as close to freedom as possible. When the bugle sounded, I also turned to face wherever the flag was supposed to be. I've stood respectfully for the national anthem many times, but until now it had only been out of courtesy.

As the anthem ended, I would say under my breath: "*Ichigo ichie*." In Japanese it means "one time, one meeting" and refers to a situation that has never happened before and will never happen again. Supposedly it originated as part of the tea-drinking ritual. Phil and I took a class in the classic tea ceremony, in which every movement is both deliberate and meaningful. It's painstakingly done with care to be as flawless as possible because the past can never be repaired. We cannot fake it. We must participate with sincerity. It's no longer good enough to "phone it home" and perhaps can best be understood as being "present" or "mindful." You can go on vacation and die from a disease you never heard about before you left. You can plan to fly home in luxury and end up grateful for a bottle of water and a portable toilet. You could order from a menu with a hundred items or accept a bowl of rice with equanimity.

This is seizing the moment, holding it close, your hand feeling that your heart is still beating. You are not in an ambulance, on a gurney in a foreign hospital, or on a ventilator. You are standing in a spot as exceptional as the deck of a Vietnamese dragon boat, a seat on the Kowloon ferry, a cabin on a ship making lazy circles off the coast of Japan, floating naked in an *onsen*, sleeping in a glass tower overlooking the lights of Tokyo, or celebrating the Lunar New Year in a Chinese temple. In this moment, in this *ichigo ichie*, you are right here—in the land of the free and the home of the brave.

DEUS EX MACHINA REDUX

*A deus ex machina will never appear in real life so you best
make other arrangements.*

—Marisha Pessl, *Special Topics in Calamity Physics*

"Something's gotta go, Gay!"

It was Sunday, March 1, and packing time—again. Phil had
covered our bed with everything we'd acquired at Lackland. Since
friends and family couldn't send us fresh food, they deluged us
with gourmet snacks, specialty teas, a fancy fruit basket, a jigsaw
puzzle, a coloring book and pencils, and other ways to occupy
what they assumed was our free time. A business associate in Belgium sent my favorite chocolates and a seasonal assortment of
Easter treats. Our niece Laura, who lives on a Wisconsin dairy
farm, had baked poppy seed, snickerdoodle, molasses, and cran-
berry-white-chocolate-with-pecan jumbo cookies. A few days earlier, a team from Princess arrived to assist with our departures and
delivered two goodie bags filled with mugs so we wouldn't have to
drink from Styrofoam cups, gum, mints, a puzzle book, pens, and
logo water bottles. Inside each was a heartfelt letter from a Princess

team member. We also received letters wishing us well from citizens of San Antonio and charming drawings from a local primary school. On top of the pile was the fuzzy throw from Princess, the Red Cross blanket—well, two actually—and everything that had been sent from home.

At first we contemplated renting a car and taking a leisurely drive around the Gulf of Mexico, but after two months away, we were too eager to get home. I had already ordered an extra suitcase online, but Phil complained, "Even with it, everything is not going to fit. You just have to leave the blankets—or whatever else—behind." As Phil predicted, we were one bag short. Reluctantly, I made a leave-behind pile on the unused bed.

"I promise I'll sort it out after the call from Paris," I said, because that morning I had a phone interview with Olivier, a journalist from *Paris Match*. I love all things French, but nothing as much as a man with a Maurice Chevalier accent. Olivier didn't disappoint and I rode a high for a few hours afterward.

I had made some packing progress when Bobbie called. We were trying to wind down the media requests just as our local stations were revving up to greet us at the airport. "Bobbie, as much as we owe it to them, we don't yet know which airport or flight."

"Don't worry. We'll arrange an event at your house a few days after you're settled."

But the vision of satellite trucks and a microphone bank wasn't our idea of what we needed most: to reclaim our own space without being beholden to anyone.

✦   ✦   ✦

This time I was anxious to get plane reservations. Southwest Airlines had only one direct flight to Tampa daily and another to Orlando. Tampa is a bit closer and a far more user-friendly airport. Princess said they would reimburse us for the cost of the tickets as well as excess luggage, which I hoped would appease Phil. Though we usually purchase the cheapest fares, we decided to get a refundable one in case there were more glitches. Though we never said it aloud, we still worried that one of us might be positive at the last minute.

Vana and Mario were leaving from Sacramento the next morning. Their support staff rarely held conference calls, so they knew even less than we did. Jerry's son, Ross, who lives in San Antonio, had flown to Houston to pick up Jerry's car and drove it to his home so it would be ready for the Giambalvos to drive to their home outside Dallas.

Planning our "de-mob" had invigorated our Incident Management Team. They labeled it "Operation Return Home." One of our fellow detainees dubbed it "Freedom Day." The team thrived on complex scheduling, organization charts, and color-coded schematics and sent out a directive that made a simple walk to the bus seem like a military obstacle course. We would receive our official clearance papers rescinding our federal quarantine orders on the morning of March 2. Like most homesick campers, we couldn't wait to leave Camp Corona in the dust.

We had been told that our "Departure Day Schedule" would start with a 6 a.m. final temperature check by the CDC and then we would proceed from our rooms to luggage-tagging and other out-processing events before being bused to the airport. We had a diagram showing the precise path we would walk from the "Q-Zone" through the quarantine fence to pick up various forms at tables. Finally, we would march like well-trained soldiers to the "freedom zone" and the airport-bound buses.

At least theoretically.

When we arrived at the airport, Princess reps would escort us to the airline counters, cover our excess baggage fees, and then take us through a private area to clear security.

"The full celebrity treatment," I commented. Some of this was to avoid being accosted by the press, but there were also concerns some San Antonians might stage a protest against us "radioactive zombies" contaminating their airport.

"Seems ridiculous to me," I said.

"Don't forget we're in Texas, lady," Phil said in his best cowboy accent, "where everyone packs heat."

✦   ✦   ✦

As much as I like to plan trips, this minute-by-minute precision seemed excessive. We were all world travelers, not teen recruits. They had thought of everything—or had they? We had given our case manager our flight schedule. Late in the day he said that even if we were on the first bus the next morning, we probably wouldn't arrive in time. I logged into our Southwest account, found a later flight that arrived in Orlando instead of our preferred Tampa, and had the new seats instantly. "We even saved three dollars."

Shortly after our last high-carb lunch, we received a newsletter with the updated bus schedule and the welcome news that there had been no new positive cases in the past twenty-four hours. Our certificate of quarantine completion and medical clearance letter would be delivered after we passed the Monday morning temperature check. "With our luck we'll turn positive at the very last second," I said kiddingly to preempt Phil from his usual pessimistic quip.

We had our final conference call at 4 p.m. so we could participate in our final "Retreat." The team reminded us to let our case manager know if we needed extra luggage because Princess would provide whatever we needed. I raised my hands in a silent cheer and put in my bag request as soon as the meeting ended.

The group had voted to have Texas barbecue for the last supper—not my favorite—but Phil loved the brisket, sausage, and pulled pork. Commander Byrd had waxed poetic about the special beverage: a root beer float made with local Blue Bell vanilla ice cream.

"They really know what we boomers like," Phil said. "Is there going to be a sock hop tonight in the parking lot?"

Princess delivered a hard-sided rollaboard bag after dinner, which was the perfect size to fit all the excess items, even the six remaining CUPNOODLES. Everything was ready long before "Taps." While Phil watched the late local news, I went into the other bedroom and typed up notes I had scribbled with contact information from new friends on both sides of the fence. I sent our updated flight information to Michelle, who was picking us up, and the kids. Then I wrote thank you notes to Wendy and our other San Antonio friends.

"Gay, come see this!" Phil called from the other room. I wrote a final line and hit Send.

"You missed it!" Phil was pacing.

"What happened?"

"The mayor of San Antonio just gave a press conference. I didn't hear the whole thing, but apparently, someone from the Wuhan group who had tested positive was released from the hospital after two negative tests. Then a third test came back weakly positive—whatever that means—and the city is freaking out. They've closed the mall she shopped at for fumigation and the mayor is blaming the CDC for the screw-up."

"That shouldn't affect our plans."

"I have a bad feeling."

"Look, we've completed our quarantine. We're getting proof of that tomorrow, and besides, we've never tested positive."

"I hope you're right," Phil said, clicking through the TV channels and rejecting all the choices, even *The Curse of the Bermuda Triangle*. "Next they'll be showing *Curse of the Diamond Princess*."

"Do you think that would make a better title for my book?" I asked. I snuggled beside Phil and fell asleep with the delicious thought that tomorrow we'd be in our own comfy bed.

✦   ✦   ✦

"Reveille" woke me from a sound sleep on Monday, March 2. As much as I hate an early wake-up call, I was as ready as any kid on Christmas morning. I made a show of marking the final X on our second jailbreak calendar denoting twenty-six days of detention by two governments.

"Freedom's just another word for nothin' left to lose." I sang the Janis Joplin song off-key as I put on the clothes I'd laid out the night before. "What the hell was that supposed to mean anyway?"

"It means…" Phil said with a twinkle in his eyes, "that if you lose all your things—all your (cough cough) baggage—then you are truly free."

"What if you have all your baggage and have lost your freedom?"

"You still can have a free spirit, free thoughts, free—ah—love." He punctuated the last with a sweet kiss on my mouth.

"Hea-vy…." I said in my coolest sixties voice.

I opened the door but didn't see any "yellow birds." The only people around were the marshals at the Q-Gate. "Nothing's happening. Nobody's set up the tables yet." I pulled back the bedcovers. "I'm going back to sleep until they come for our temps."

The knock on the door came just before 7 a.m. "What's going on?" Phil asked while they took his temperature. I slowly rose, put on my mask, and presented my forehead.

"There have been some changes to the schedule. There's a conference call at eight-thirty that will explain everything. Oh, and breakfast will be delivered to your room."

"Are we still leaving today?"

"I don't have any more information. Sorry."

"What the—?" Phil said, splotchy red wicking from his neck toward his scalp. "Damn chain of command! Nobody will tell us anything! It's like on the ship. All news came from the captain. Now it's the commander or the admiral. If we've learned anything from this, it's that if they are controlling the message, no news is definitely not good news!"

I stepped outside to see what—if anything—was going on. "They're leaving! The buses. Two are already gone and I think they were empty."

Phil dialed into the meeting. Right off, they mentioned that the call would be short so they could "work out some urgent issues." My heart was beating so hard I caught only snatches: There will be a delay in departures.... They are committed to keeping us informed and safe....There would be more conference calls.... No hard information at this time about when we could be released.... Some discussions with the "government" due to some "late-night issues."

We scrambled to the internet for news and also tuned into a local TV station. There had been an emergency hearing in federal court first thing that morning between the CDC and the City of San Antonio. U.S. District Judge Xavier Rodriguez denied the city's request to keep the quarantine in place, noting that the federal government's current determination that a fourteen-day quarantine and two negative tests for the virus were "sufficient to prevent transmission or spread of COVID-19." The court, Rodriguez wrote further, "has no authority to second-guess those determinations even though the court also shares the concerns expressed by the [city]."

However, the court did not have jurisdiction over the mayor's public health emergency declaration forbidding travel through the city by anyone who had been quarantined, and this was backed up by the Bexar County judge.

At our second conference call of the day, there were only guarded answers to the barrage of questions: *Were we still leaving today?* We don't yet know, but don't change any flights yet. *Is this a problem with just the city?* No, the governor is now involved. *What's the situation with the woman from Cohort I?* Her clinical course was longer than usual, but at the time of discharge she met all the criteria. Admiral Knight admitted that "we don't yet fully understand the novel virus."

Someone from our group announced, "They may have crossed the line on habeas corpus to illegal confinement. I have retained a Washington law firm willing to represent everyone in this quarantine pro bono."

Just then Vana called and I told her what was going on. She said, "Our buses are late, but it looks like we're still going," she said. "I hope you get out of there!"

"We're watching the news and the governor is going to be making a statement soon. Text me when you're on the way to the airport. I doubt we're leaving today. The mayor wants us to have more tests and stay twenty-one days."

"Don't you have your release paperwork?"

"We were supposed to get everything just before we got on the bus."

"Don't worry," she said in a role reversal. "See you at home."

Just before noon, Governor Greg Abbott held a press conference and announced, "The other patients scheduled to be released from quarantine at Lackland Air Force base will be held until the CDC can guarantee they have no trace of the coronavirus in their system."

"We're not patients!" I yelled at the television.

I checked my email. "Everybody in the world knows more than we do! Motoko had already heard that 'the Texas governor's office is blocking your departure'—with two question marks."

Lunch was a depressing reprise of chicken-fried steak with papier-mâché-paste "gravy," creamed corn in another gluey sauce, and bow-tie pasta salad to complete the all-beige motif. I wasn't hungry anyway.

We had kept the door open and heard a lot of yelling. One of our fellow evacuees was trying to scale the chain-link fence, which bent against his weight. Several of the marshals' cars surrounded him and he backed down. We headed to the parking lot where everyone was gathering. Most had discarded their masks and were freely fraternizing. One man was handing out slips of paper with the phone number of the law firm. "Call them and say you want to participate and give them your email."

This would have been the perfect moment for the real *Les Mis* uprising to commence and to sing about "the people who will not be slaves again"—and for us boomers to start battering the barricades with the wheelchair brigade.

Slowly our fellow former cruisers began retrieving their luggage that had been tagged for their assigned bus. Several women were sobbing. Another man kept running up to the fence, circling back, pulling at his hair, all the while screaming incoherently and swearing. "My thoughts exactly," Phil said. The man suddenly rushed the fence but it didn't yield. He bounced back and tried again. The marshals on the other side didn't react.

"I hope they have aerosol cans of Valium to spray the crowd," I said aloud.

The woman standing next to me laughed and asked where I was from. "Oh, my cousin lives in The Villages and we've been boating in Crystal River."

"You're from Long Island," I said, recognizing the accent.

She introduced herself as "Alice" and answered, "Now retired in Delray Beach."

This was typical shipboard banter, but now the sudden camaraderie felt unsettling.

"Did you change your flight yet?" Alice asked.

"I completely forgot!" I excused myself and hurried back upstairs. On the Southwest page I had two choices: "Choose another flight" or "Cancel." Since I had no idea whether we'd be released in a few hours or a few weeks, I canceled. A few minutes later, Vana texted that she and Mario were at the airport but their flight had mechanical problems and they were being rerouted. At least she was in the freedom zone; we were in political purgatory.

✦   ✦   ✦

All. Too. Much.

I felt as if I'd been hit with a blow to my head and was being sucked into a black hole. I collapsed on the bed fully clothed and never made it under the covers. The television blared. Sunlight streaked across my face. I lay flat on my back and Phil claims I was loudly snoring. My dream involved black-winged creatures, like a headless Pegasus, clashing swords, somewhere that looked like London during the Blitz. Phil's voice seemed far away, "Another conference call." He sat on the bed with his phone in speaker mode.

Commander Byrd apologized for not getting back to us sooner. He said there were some "shifts" with the state of Texas. The situation as of that moment was that Ron Nirenberg, the mayor of San Antonio, had declared a public health emergency and issued a restraining order prohibiting anyone who had been quarantined to travel in or through the city. In the meantime, our federal quarantine order would legally expire at midnight. Admiral Knight then asked us to "hold on a little longer" until they had a solution.

"If we chartered a plane, it could land on the Air Force base," said a man with a slight British accent. "That's out of the mayor's jurisdiction, right?"

"We're looking into that possibility," Commander Byrd said. He thanked us for our patience. "You're safest spending the night here and all meals will be provided in your rooms. However, you are free to leave after midnight, except for those few who have further quarantine orders." He went on to say that they would execute the same plan as they had for today starting early Tuesday morning. "We're going to try to run an early bus, since several people now have flights first thing in the morning. Only thing different is there won't be temperatures and you won't need masks. Think of it as Groundhog Day."

We ate cheeseburgers and potato salad while switching channels to catch the latest news. The mayor was demanding another fourteen-day quarantine for "everyone's safety." The next knock on the door was the "yellow birds"—without masks. For the first time we could see their smiling faces. They handed us envelopes with our medical clearance forms and a letter from the associate director for Policy and Regulatory Affairs, Division of Global Migration and Quarantine at the CDC saying: "The CDC has determined that you have successfully completed your federal quarantine as of Monday, March 2, 2020, 14 days after your arrival in the United States following your departure from the *Diamond Princess* Cruise. You are now able to complete your travel home. Thank you for your patience and understanding while under federal quarantine. Your cooperation increased the U.S. Government's ability to contain this novel Coronavirus within the United States."

Jerry phoned to say Ross was coming to pick them up as soon as possible. They were heading out to the Q-Gate to get a ride to the Valley View gate. Phil told him we'd come down to say goodbye.

We walked to the fence and saw Jerry and Cathy on the other side. The marshal on duty opened the gate for us too. I hesitated only slightly before crossing the imaginary line.

"Are you going all the way home?" Phil asked.

"I'm too wound up to drive that far tonight."

"That's an understatement," Cathy added. "We'll find a motel about fifty miles north of this insanity."

"What are you going to do?" she asked.

"Don't know yet," I said, and hugged her. "Good luck!"

As we walked back upstairs, Phil turned to me. "What *are* we going to do?" I shrugged. "How about trying to get the same reservations for tomorrow?"

"Sure. They seem to have plenty of seats for those full-pay tickets." I didn't say that I wanted to check other options first. Maybe renting a car very early in the morning made sense to get the hell away from here as soon as possible.

There was no clear path to a decision. Two of our friends in San Antonio had volunteered to take us to the airport—but that was before the mayor's orders. One had a permit to drive onto the base. We would have to meet the other at one of the gates. I called both, hoping for an invitation to spend the night. Both apologetically said they would not break the law. To me this felt more in the line of civil disobedience—what we did all the time in the sixties. I'd never been arrested, but even friends who had been jailed during sit-ins and peace demonstrations suffered few consequences. Would I have broken this unjust law for a friend? Of course, you never know until the situation presents itself, but the answer was most likely affirmative, especially if it was someone who had been in quarantine more than a month and never been sick.

"Phil, what if we are arrested? How bad would it be? One call to Bobbie and it would blow up in the international press and the mayor of San Antonio would become a laughingstock. Blake would call Summer and Terry, who would 'make it a federal case.' We'd get some hot-shot Texas lawyer to take our case pro bono for the publicity. Besides, wouldn't it make a great chapter in the book?"

"Please don't go manic on me, honey. I think this has been the most stressful day of my life."

"Worse than our wedding day?"

"Nothing as bad as that," he said as we both recalled the moment he caught sight of his family arriving and felt so faint he had to lie down.

At this moment, Phil didn't look all that different than he had fifty-some years earlier, albeit with less hair. His face had blanched and he looked dazed, on the verge of collapse. "I'm sorry, so sorry…. This is so bizarre. Here I am going off about playing Bonnie and Clyde—weren't they from Texas?—and whether the feds will protect us from the evil mayor of Metropolis after escaping from the clutches of our Japanese jailers! Help, we're stuck in a B-movie again—and we can't escape."

I passed him his bottle of water. "It's my turn to fix the shower head," I said. "I'm going in the other room and make new reservations. You go to sleep and let me sort it out."

Phil sighed and began to undress. I almost felt like helping him remove his shoes and socks the way I did when our children were too tired to do it themselves. Phil would never have been one of the guys trying to scale the fence or swearing at the world—at least not outwardly. Inside, though, the upheaval was just as real. He might have gone on passively for another week or so if that had been part of the original plan…but not now, when we had been so very close to leaving. For more than a month we had no control over our destiny, and once again our ability to go anywhere we wanted had been appropriated in a brazen political move that had nothing to do with whether we were a threat to the community. In fact, our cohort was probably the healthiest in the state. For more than two weeks we had been tested and retested and quarantined and had no contact with anyone who had not been covered from head to toe in protective gear. The mayor was more likely to be a vector than we were.

I put on the nightgown I had packed away in the last open bag this morning, brushed my teeth, and prepared the pillows on my side of the bed so I wouldn't disturb Phil. I kissed him goodnight. "Be back soon."

✦   ✦   ✦

I sent a text to Wanda and Michelle that we did not yet have new plane reservations and would get back to them in the morning. I then wrote the kids and told them not to worry, before I checked incoming messages. There was one from Motoko: "I am gathering that between the Texas governor and the San Antonio mayor you are still trapped? What a nightmare."

I was getting tired of having the rug pulled out from under us over and over. If you've gotten this far in my story, you know I don't like feeling trapped. The man on the conference call had mentioned getting a plane to land on the base, but what was he thinking? Charter a plane to take us to the San Antonio airport a few miles away and then transfer to commercial flights? How much could that cost? Maybe Princess would cover it? Or what about a military plane? There must be dozens in hangars all over this base that could take us to a friendlier facility, although that was unlikely because there were always political repercussions to fistfights between local and federal interests. Besides, it would take too long to organize. I thought back to when we had landed and Steve said, "Welcome to Kelly Field, Lackland Air Force Base." I Googled "Kelly Field" and learned it had been in use since World War I. Now it supported the Air Force Reserve Command's operations for the Lockheed C-5 Galaxy—the huge planes that carried the president's motorcade—and also the Texas National Guard's

F-16 Fighting Falcon. Then I looked up: "Kelly Field and FBO," which means "fixed base operator," and refers to a company that runs a service for general aviation—private and corporate airplanes. Yes! There was one: Atlantic Aviation.

I tiptoed into the bedroom and found the slacks I had laid out for the next day. My black nightgown could pass for a tunic in the dark. I slipped out the door in the other room, ran down the stairs, and hurried to the Q-Gate. A marshal headed over to open it. I waved him off. "I just have a question," I said, hoping I wasn't violating the sacred chain of command.

"Yes, ma'am."

"So, this is an Air Force base, right?" I pointed to where I thought the runways were. "When we arrived from Japan, we landed at Kelly Field." He nodded. "Then we got on buses and followed a military vehicle across the runways—I assume they had permission from the tower—and then got on a road that led us here."

He nodded and grinned. "I like the way you're thinking, ma'am."

"Theoretically, then, if someone with a private plane landed at Kelly, we could hitch a ride across the same runways without violating the mayor's jurisdiction."

Two more marshals who had been listening in approached the fence. The man I'd been talking to introduced one of them as his superior. "I just want to say that I think what the mayor and all have done is a disgrace!" he said. "You folks have done everything required and don't deserve this foolishness."

"Thank you, sir," I said. "If a plane did come for us, could one of your men drive us to the FBO at Kelly Field?"

"You a pilot?"

"No, but my husband is."

"Might be hard to get permission, but it's not more than a couple of miles from here on Route 90."

"Is that a federal highway?"

"Yep, it's called US 90, but I don't rightly know about driving across the airfield."

"You own a private plane, ma'am?" the boss asked.

"Used to, but we crashed it."

"Anybody hurt?"

"Nope. My husband's a brilliant pilot. It was the same type of plane that John Kennedy went down in, but he was over water and we landed in a field. The magneto assembly fell off."

"Well, good luck to you, ma'am. Hope you can get a flight."

✦ ✦ ✦

I almost flew up the stairs. I found Buzz's twenty-four-hour emergency hotline and dialed him.

"Sorry to wake you," I said, though I wasn't sorry in the least.

"No problem, Mrs. Courter, I'm still up on the West Coast. I hope you're calling to report you are home safely."

"No, we're not, and that's why I'm calling, Buzz. We have another type of emergency." I filled him in on the mayor and the governor and where we were.

"That's terrible, ma'am."

"We just don't know what to do. But I was talking to the federal marshals and they said private planes could land right here at Kelly Field. So, I was wondering if you might be willing to come for us and fly us home to Crystal River."

"Yes, Mrs. Courter. We can do that."

I was speechless.

"Absolutely. I'll start working on it right away. We should have a flight booked in a few hours. What time can you be ready to leave?"

I told him we had all our papers and luggage—a lot of luggage—and could be ready with an hour's notice. He said he'd be in touch with all the details and hoped I could rest up until then.

✦ ✦ ✦

I was too excited to go to bed, so I went back to my email. I answered Motoko's latest query.

> **Gay:** Lots happening. Looks like our [evacuation] insurance has paid off.

> **Motoko:** Are you getting that medevac at last?

> **Gay:** Not counting our jets until they land, but it looks like another *deus ex machina*.

Of course, there were further complications. Buzz called in the middle of the night to say he couldn't get permission for us to depart from Kelly Field. We had to get to an FBO at the San Antonio airport. Nor could he send a car to pick us up at the Lackland gate because his company could not violate the mayor's orders. When Ross brought Jerry's car to the gate, he'd returned home in an Uber so they could get out of town as quickly as possible. Apparently, there was a "don't ask, don't tell" policy at the exit gate. I was too exhausted and peeved to figure out the next step before I fell into a restless sleep.

At "Reveille" Phil stirred beside me. "Honey," I said. "We're going home."

"What?" he said, still half asleep.

"Buzz is sending a plane for us."

"That doesn't make sense."

"Let's call it reparations."

After Phil showered, I explained about the transportation conundrum. "I'll go down and see what's going on," he said in as chipper a voice as I'd heard in a month. He returned so fast I was certain he had reached another dead end. "Everything's taken care of. We're on the first bus." He misread my confusion for distrust. "It's being run by the CDC and they think they can get us to the airport."

"But—"

"Our plane will wait till we get there. Don't worry. The admiral's got this."

We—well, mostly Phil—dragged all *twelve* bags to the bus. I packed a shopping bag with beverages, yogurt, fruit, and snacks, leaving behind a decorative basket that I hoped one of the white knights would be allowed to take home. The Q-Gate was wide open and, as we walked through, people were tossing their masks in the air. The whole Incident Management Team was out and clapping. Tears flowed again. The tables were staffed with people in Princess t-shirts. I thanked them for the blanket, the gifts, the suitcase, and for taking such good care of us under the circumstances. Handshakes and hugs were distributed freely. We turned in our key cards and official phones and were given more documents. Admiral Knight stepped forward and gave me a bear hug. I thanked her for everything and she handed me her calling card. I waved to John, Andrew, Tony, and all the "yellow birds." The problem with masks is that you don't see expressions, I thought, realizing that might have been why I felt hostility at first when just the opposite had been true.

We got on the bus. And waited.

Nobody spoke. It felt like a flashback to the dreadful hours on the buses in Japan. A man named Rich Stinson briefed us on the procedures at the airport. We later learned he was an airport executive and a veteran who had served in tactical and operational units with six combat tours in hot spots including Iraq, Afghanistan, Africa, and Bosnia-Herzegovina. Now he was transporting the world-weary Cohort II to the airport through another sort of "enemy" territory. Once everyone was past security, Princess staff would handle any issues, especially if passengers were harassed by anyone. Rich said he would be in the SUV leading the caravan and the route they had selected would take longer than usual.

Rear Admiral Knight spoke last. "It has been a pleasure to take care of you and your health…. If you have questions, get in touch with CDC. Please help your friends and neighbors to prepare. This is not the end of coronavirus in the United States: It is the beginning. So safe travels and I won't say that I hope to see you again. But if you ever come to Atlanta, we've got a great museum at CDC, and you can come by and visit us and say hi. I would love to see you again—but not in this situation!"

Everyone laughed and cheered. I felt a pang. This accomplished woman had touched my heart.

✦ ✦ ✦

I waited at the curb while Phil ferried all the bags. We were planning to take a taxi to the FBO, which was somewhere on the other side of the airfield. But this wasn't the regular airport entrance and no taxis were in sight. Parked just ahead were several police cars and vans, with officers standing beside them facing the street. I walked up to Rich and pointed them out. "Are we safe waiting here for a taxi?" Phil rolled two bags past me.

Rich recognized Phil. "You're going to Signature Aviation, right?" Phil nodded. Rich went over to another man and tapped him on the shoulder, then pointed to me. He introduced himself as "Tom" and said he'd take us there himself. A few minutes later, he pulled up in an SUV and helped load our bags, happily without comment. When we thanked him, he handed us his card. Once inside the FBO, I looked at it. "Guess who gave us a lift? Tom Bartlett is the Deputy Director of Aviation for the airport."

The world of private aviation was an indulgence I missed. Even when we had our first plane, which cost less than a luxury car, we were treated as well as any president or potentate—well, almost. Now our luggage was whisked away. We relaxed in buttery leather armchairs. They offered free beverages, snacks, stations to plug in phones and computers. There was a room for pilots to plan their trip, a lavender-scented ladies' room, even a fresh bowl of water for traveling pooches. "Your plane is ready," a woman announced and she walked us through a hangar and out to the tarmac where a Beechjet 400 was waiting for us.

Phil's eyes sparkled. "This...is...unbelievable."

We were introduced to "Jeff" the pilot and "Justine" the co-pilot, eventually learning they were a couple. While Jeff did his

When the mayor of San Antonio declared a public health emergency and issued a restraining order against the release of *Diamond Princess* passengers, our evacuation provider sent a private jet to take us home.

preflight check, Justine was sanitizing every surface with wipes. "Can't be too careful," she told us. "There's a lot of people with coronavirus who've just been discharged from the Air Force base."

"Really?" Phil said.

"Do you mind me asking where you're going?" She didn't say "with all that luggage," but the question was implied.

Phil had prepared an answer. "Crystal River is our home. We're documentary filmmakers returning from a long trip."

After a quick safety briefing, we took off. "This is a rocket," Phil said to me. "It's faster than most commercial airliners." Unspoken was the fact that, in the end, we could have taken a Southwest flight. He leaned his seat all the way back, stretched his legs, pulled his Tilly hat over his eyes, and promptly fell asleep.

I stared out the window, drop-jawed all the way across the Gulf of Mexico. From the ANA plane to the extraction flight to this unbelievably cushy ride. *Ichigo ichie...ichigo ichie,* I chanted silently. Don't forget a single second of this...the clouds, the sea... the smell of leather and disinfectant...this incongruous, unbelievable, magical gift.

Soon we were flying over a familiar landscape, which we knew well from the air. Then the turn for final approach, the whoosh of descent, the floaty moment of ground effect, the bump of the wheels.

The plane pulled up right in front of the "Welcome to Citrus County" sign.

A celebrity-style black SUV was waiting with a nattily dressed driver in a three-piece suit. The man had driven two hours from Tampa.

"I expected Michelle would pick us up."

"Buzz insisted we have security," I answered. "He was worried we might be harassed by the media."

Phil laughed but was perfectly content to let the driver and the pilot stow our belongings.

Two miles and five minutes later, we were home.

✦   ✦   ✦

Updates from Passengers Phil and Gay Courter on the *Diamond Princess* Quarantine
Crystal River, Florida, 3 March 2020, 4:00 PM EST

Phil and Gay Courter have returned home after completing their quarantine at Joint Base Lackland in San Antonio, TX. The Courters were in quarantine aboard the *Diamond Princess* and at Lackland for a combined 28 days.

On February 17, 2020, the Courters were part of the evacuation of more than 300 American passengers and crew from the *Diamond Princess*. Gay and Phil continue to appear virus-free and are thrilled to be home with their Cavalier King Charles spaniel, Willoughby.

Today, Tuesday, Lackland-quarantined *Diamond Princess* passengers are returning home. The released "cruisers" were bused from the base either to the airport or to other local locations for onward travel.

The Courters want to thank everyone for all their help in getting them home, "especially our friends in the media. We believe the media coverage was key to the decision to retrieve the Americans in quarantine.

"We will need some time for recovery and will try to make ourselves available as soon as possible."

"For many of us, today is a homecoming," said Gay. "We are thrilled to hear that the last of the crew, including Captain Arma, are off the ship. Still, many have yet to return home. We have friends in medical facilities in Japan, Australia, California, Nebraska and Texas. We are also still mourning the loss of seven of our shipmates, the most recent in Australia."

"We'd like to recognize the effort our friends, family, and professional colleagues put into getting the word out and improving the outcome for the passengers and crew on the *Diamond Princess*," added Phil.

"While the quarantines for us were difficult—especially putting our lives on hold for a month—we couldn't have been cared for better. The Princess organization has gone far and above anyone's expectations in terms of care and making sure nobody suffers any financial burden. We received personally written notes from Princess employees, gift bags, and had frequent calls from their care team. They assisted in travel arrangements and are paying all return travel expenses—even delivering extra luggage for items we have accumulated. Nothing that happened was their fault and they have acted as though we are family members—not customers.

"The team assembled to care for us has run an excellent quarantine designed to keep us all as safe as possible from the disease and to care for our every need: Food, comfort, physical and mental health. So many agencies worked together, starting with the Assistant Secretary for Preparedness and Response, who is responsible for overseeing all disasters and public health emergencies. Medical management was handled by their Incident Management Team and the National Disaster Medical System Team. Many of our needs were tended to by their Service Access Team and they were supported with tents, equipment, and supplies by the Logistics Response Assistance Team. The US Public Health Service, which includes doctors, nurses, therapists, and pharmacists also looked after us. And that was just half the team!

"The Centers for Disease Control (CDC) came with their Public Health Response Unit, who are studying this very new disease and provided epidemiological surveillance, testing, and, most importantly, infection prevention and control for both the evacuees and the support staff. Their

Epidemiological and Surveillance Lab team monitored us to see who might be at risk. The Global Migration and Quarantine team supervised isolation measures and monitored us during the potential incubation period. Finally, the US Marshals Service provided security. This was a huge effort and designed to keep us safe and the community healthy."

Epilogue

And the plague gathered strength as it was transmitted from the sick to the healthy through normal intercourse, just as fire catches on to any dry or greasy object placed too close to it. Nor did it stop there: not only did the healthy incur the disease and with it the prevailing mortality by talking to or keeping company with the sick—they had only to touch the clothing or anything else that had come into contact with or been used by the sick and the plague evidently was passed to the one who handled those things.

—Giovanni Boccaccio, *The Decameron*

July 10, 2020 at 4:29:47 AM EDT

Farewell message to U.S. Citizen *Diamond Princess* passengers and crew from Chargé d'Affaires Joseph Young and the American Embassy Consular Team

The U.S. Embassy and the Department of State have no higher priority than the welfare and safety of U.S. citizens abroad. My team and I are pleased to let you know that the final U.S. citizen passenger, of the nearly 80 who were hospitalized in Japan, has returned to the United States.

> We are extremely happy to report that all 430 U.S. citizens who were aboard the *Diamond Princess* have now made it back to the United States or their homes abroad. Our team at the U.S. Embassy in Tokyo has been honored to get to know many of you and your family members over the past several months, and we have been inspired by your resilience and courage. To those of you who may have lost loved ones during this pandemic, we extend our heartfelt condolences.

Nobody knew.

Even as I write in mid-July 2020, six months after we embarked on the *Diamond Princess*, with more than four million cases in the United States and almost sixteen million worldwide, there are no definitive answers as to how COVID-19 spread on the ship. In the end, out of the 3711 people on board (2666 passengers and 1045 crew), 712 (567 passengers, 145 crew) tested positive and fourteen died (all passengers, the last one reported in mid-April). The median age of the crew was thirty-six; the median age of the passengers, sixty-nine. The passengers were 55 percent female and the crew was 81 percent male. Of those who died, nine came from Japan, two from Hong Kong, one from Australia, one from Canada, and one from the United Kingdom. Three were women, nine were men, and the gender of two is unknown. Four of the deceased were in their eighties, six in their seventies, one in her sixties, and the ages of three are unknown.

In retrospect, it is obvious that the novel coronavirus identified in December 2019 spread through the ship with impunity. The Japanese government had control but no experience with an unstudied infection; Princess Cruises had to follow their orders and do its best to placate customers amid an evolving political and medical crisis.

The day we returned to the United States for quarantine in Texas, there were approximately 73,000 cases worldwide, 72,000 of them "confined" to China and the rest scattered around the globe, with *fewer than twenty* in the U.S.

While China used authoritarian measures to lock down the disease's epicenter, each country was writing its rules in real time. Phil and I, our traveling companions, and our shipmates were guinea pigs in a botched experiment to control the pestilence on an artificial island. Almost every country on Earth would be faced with the same problem within a few weeks. The other countries we visited have fared much better. Japan is the worst, with more than 30,000 cases and almost 1,000 deaths. Hong Kong has fewer than 2,500 cases, Taiwan and Vietnam have fewer than 500 each. The cases worldwide are exploding, and we must assume that in a few months the statistics cited here will long since have been surpassed.

During our Lackland quarantine, there were approximately nine positive cases in our group, but there were more at Travis. This does not count the ten or so who went directly from Japan to be treated at the University of Nebraska.

Somehow, we stayed safe, as did Vana, Mario, Cathy, Jerry and all our shipboard friends and acquaintances—except Karen. Even her parents didn't get sick. Most of us are still isolating at home—an excellent time to write a book, it turns out. Dr. Mario has returned to his medical practice. We all follow the CDC sanitization and social distancing protocols scrupulously, wear masks when outside our homes, and require our infrequent visitors to wear masks in our home.

The *Diamond Princess* will go down in history as the first but not the worst contagion on a ship in modern times. Unfortunately, its lessons were not learned in time to prevent the outbreak on the *Grand Princess* (which departed San Francisco for Hawaii on February 21, while we were at Lackland) that resulted in 103 positive cases and two deaths (the majority of passengers refused testing, so the true number of positives is unknown). The *Ruby Princess* (which departed Sydney, Australia, five days *after* we returned to Florida) ended up with 850 cases and twenty-five deaths—a total of forty-one deaths on Princess alone. Shamefully, Princess, along with eight other cruise lines, allowed more than twenty-five additional ships to sail even after the *Diamond Princess* was quarantined.

Epidemiologists have calculated the *Diamond Princess* outbreak at an R_0 (R naught) basic reproduction of 14.8, much higher than the usual 2 to 4 for COVID-19. (One of the most infectious of all diseases, measles, has an R_0 of 15.) They calculate that an earlier evacuation of our ship could have reduced the number of cases to *only seventy-six*! That's about 10 percent of the final total! Research on the *Diamond Princess* outbreak indicates that 72 percent of the positive cases (about 410 people) were asymptomatic. Scientists are uncertain whether these people were as infectious as symptomatic patients. Yes, we really feel as if we dodged a volley of bullets that could have been coming from any direction.

On March 11, 2020, eight days after we returned to Florida, the World Health Organization characterized COVID-19 as a pandemic. On March 24, Japan postponed the 2020 Summer Olympics.

As we had hoped, almost all the countries with more than a few citizens aboard followed the lead of the U.S. and made plans to repatriate them within a few days of our extraction. The president of South Korea sent his own plane for nine passengers and five crew members. Canada rescued 129 passengers, Britain came for thirty-two, Australia 180, and Hong Kong sixty-eight. Most of these countries had done the same for their citizens in Wuhan, which helped them formulate plans quickly. The other countries also arranged two-week government-supervised quarantines on military bases, in hospitals, or at other facilities.

Repatriating crew proved far more difficult. In response to the rapid spread of COVID-19 on cruise ships, the CDC published a

"No Sail Order" on March 14, in effect shutting down the world's cruise industry. Four months later, there were as many as two hundred thousand crew waiting to be repatriated, including a few pregnant women. At least ten suicides—and a few unexplained deaths—have been reported among crew, two of them on other Princess ships.

We consider our media campaign to enlighten the world about the predicament of everyone "held hostage" on the *Diamond Princess* successful. Within a few days it was obvious the quarantine had failed, so every case—and every death—after that could have been avoided by placing us in a more secure quarantine—like the ones run by the CDC—on shore. The Olympic Village was an available resource that was ignored for political reasons.

Can we take credit for the American repatriation effort? Absolutely not! Nor can anyone else on the ship. Many people contacted their congressional representatives and the State Department did pay attention to their input. We were hardly the only people—passengers and crew members—appealing to their countries to repatriate them. The international media was able to sustain contact with people from many countries who remained healthy and also some who were hospitalized in Japan and later in their home countries. The coronavirus story has been leading the news ever since.

While it might seem simple to fill a plane with several hundred people and fly them from Japan to the United States, evacuating us from the ship was a massive diplomatic, public health, and humanitarian operation that benefited from the blueprint developed for the extraction of the Americans from Wuhan. As it turns out, the U.S. State Department had been working with the Japanese Ministry of Health on a strategy for repatriating Americans from Japan in the event of a disaster such as an earthquake. Incredibly, they had an exercise planned for March; instead, they instituted the real deal in February.

A high-ranking official with the State Department described how their task force worked around the clock with the White House and the National Security Council. The decisionmakers were "paying close attention to public opinion," I was told, including the reports we were filing through our international media connections. We are honored to have this verification that our voices were heard.

Because of the urgency, at least twenty-five U.S. government staffers accepted double shifts cheerfully; hundreds more assisted in various stages of the operation. Some slept only a few hours a day without leaving their stations. There were officers from the Bureau of Consular Affairs checking passports and flight manifests, experts from the Japanese desk of the State Department coordinating with their counterparts in Tokyo, and liaisons from the departments of Health and Human Services and Homeland Security, all crammed into a narrow room on the State Department's top floor, a short walk from the offices of Steve Biegun, deputy secretary of state and a member of the interagency Coronavirus Task Force. Our planes were staffed by members of the State Department's special crisis medicine unit who were in direct communication with their Washington counterparts as they monitored our temperatures and health status.

The task force followed our progress minute by minute from the time the planes went wheels up in Atlanta en route to Japan until wheels down in California and Texas. While we sat in limbo on the buses, they were privy to the dispute between CDC and State Department officials about the newly positive passengers. Some were just as jubilant as us when they were told our aircraft doors were closed, we were taxiing, and our wheels were finally up. All of them were working overtime to bring us home.

I am chagrined that Phil and I so cavalierly insisted that "they" come for "us" without any understanding of the effort, let alone the cost. While in Texas I learned how expensive it was to keep just one of the disaster units on site for a single day and realized the price tag of our very safe and secure quarantine was well beyond anything I could imagine.

Dr. Michael Callahan from Massachusetts General Hospital, who accompanied the plane to Travis, wrote me that we were part of "the largest international repatriation of infected people anywhere. It was much harder than all the Ebola, Marburg, and High Path flu outbreaks I have responded to."

We were disappointed to discover that the story about Australians receiving wine via a drone delivery to their balcony was a hoax promulgated by some bored, wine-loving cruisers. Not only did we buy into it, we heard a rumor that the story got a lot of chuckles in the White House, with some staffers saying, "Hey, if the Australians are sending wine, we should be able to liberate our Americans." No matter the intent, the spoof may not only have been good for laughs—it might have provided the spark that set the wheels in motion.

My tantrum about the moldy quarters at Lackland wasn't all in my fevered imagination. In 2019, photos of ceiling electrical fixtures leaking water, moldy showers, pillows, vents, fans, floors, and walls were posted on social media and investigated by journalists. Inspectors eventually found "the presence of mold in 14% of the rooms across Joint Base San Antonio," of which Lackland is a part.

Phil and I have canceled all nonessential forays outside the house. Most of our dinners are supplied by meal delivery services, which cuts grocery shopping to a minimum. Phil runs most of the errands—with a mask—and with a sanitation routine in his car and at home. We have kept only a few medical appointments and have deferred the rest.

As of July 2020, the *Diamond Princess* is located off the coast of South East Asia (coordinates 4.78556 N/99.99893 E), cruising in international waters. Carnival has announced that it is selling or scrapping thirteen ships in its fleet. So far, we don't know if the *Diamond Princess* is on that list, but it has canceled its Asian sailings at least until April 2022.

Everyone asks: Would you ever take another cruise? We would expand the question to when or how we would travel again, whether to see our grandchildren in another state, return to Japan, or cruise internationally. The answer is that of course we want to and we will. As of May 2020, more than forty cruise ships have had positive cases of COVID-19 on board. The industry will have to reinvent many aspects of the cruise experience, including better air filtration, modified buffet dining, and fewer passengers to allow for more social distancing. To us, though, the crucial factors will be that effective vaccines, antiviral medications, and routine supportive care are in place. We expect that most cruise lines as well as countries will require proof of coronavirus vaccination, just as they once did to eradicate smallpox, polio, and other infectious diseases that could prove fatal. Besides, Princess has offered us a free cruise and we hope the time will come when we can accept their offer happily—especially if Captain Arma is at the helm.

Phil and I both suffered from traumatic stress. Some of the initial indicators were nightmares and our inability to think clearly or understand what others were saying. Our anger at being forced to quarantine was a natural response to having no control of the situation. Instead of burrowing in bed for the duration, we mobilized our media campaign. Even if it hadn't been effective, it distracted us from our predicament. Later, at home, we had difficulty concentrating and sleeping soundly. My dizziness—a known side effect of PTSD—continued, especially in confined spaces like the shower, where the walls sometimes seemed to move. For safety, Phil installed a grab bar, which I especially needed when I closed my eyes. For a while I considered a neurological workup, but the symptoms slowly faded. I assume it was a psychosomatic reaction to confinement.

The PTSD symptoms that first appeared on the ship and worsened in Texas did not miraculously evaporate once we were home, so we each began tele-counseling, which we found helpful and restorative.

While I do take insulin, my diabetes has always been well controlled and I am permitted to have some sweets, in moderation, including green tea ice cream and crème brûlée.

Philip, my brilliant, loving, saint of a husband, can build, design, craft, sculpt almost anything—including (but not limited to) plumbing. Once, during a family party, someone asked, "If you were stranded on a desert island, who is the one person here you'd want with you?" Everyone said "Phil," because he would have built a seaworthy boat.

But once a filmmaker, always a filmmaker. You won't be surprised, then, that while I was writing this book, Phil discarded the notion of a family "home movie" and instead produced a documentary: *Quarantine! How We Survived the* Diamond Princess *Coronavirus Crisis.*

✦ ✦ ✦

We embarked on a much-anticipated Asian holiday in mid-January 2020 with not a care in the world; we returned home in early March in the throes of a pandemic, the likes of which had not been experienced in a century. Our expectations of returning to life as we knew it were crushed because the rest of the planet was also beginning to isolate, learning about social distancing, wearing masks, sanitizing, and disinfecting. We were home, we were free, but our daily routine barely changed. Yes, we could go out—but there was no place more secure than our house.

If I were to have imagined a dystopian novel, I could never have envisioned that the streets of New York, Paris, Rome, Washington, London, or Tokyo all would be photographed devoid of people. We once thought of face masks as surgical gear—not what anyone would wear in public unless you were immune-compromised or in the Tokyo Metro. Travel, one of the delights of life and a frequent indulgence in our semi-retirement, is a dormant industry. The pandemic has decimated cruising, crippled the airlines, and threatens hotels, restaurants, museums, and entire countries that depend on tourism. What good are credit card points if there is nowhere to spend them? Our extended family would be alienated if it were not for all the ways to communicate electronically. Hugs, cuddles, holiday meals, story time, and just being able to help each other are off limits. Singles and the elderly are more lonesome than ever. Unemployment is soaring, the medical system is stretched to the breaking point, and most bizarrely…how to protect yourself and others from becoming sick has jumped from being a public health issue to a political one.

COVID-19 is a disease. Eventually there will be a vaccine for prevention, antiviral medications, and better therapies to relieve symptoms during recovery. Countries like New Zealand, Taiwan, Iceland, and Greece, with alert, competent heads of state and respectful citizens, have been able to protect each other by flattening the curve. We have no respect for leaders who believe the bottom line is more important than human lives. Magical thinking—if we wish hard enough, a pony will appear, or the nasty illness will vanish into thin air—has not succeeded.

Those of us who have been on the frontlines must speak up to fear, ignorance, and complacency. Everyone is hurting but we are not helpless. The world is going to be markedly different when this plague passes—as they all eventually do. How will we create a new, more vibrant reality, that will make life more meaningful, safer, and healthier for all humanity?

When Phil and I returned home to find that the "miasma" has reached the most remote corners of our planet, we discovered that now our shipmates are every citizen in the world. We are all sailing on the same boat with the same destination: health and safety.

Our quarantine never ended.

P.S. To date, we have not viewed the rest of *The Goldfinch*.

ACKNOWLEDGMENTS

She could imagine a world in the not-too-distant future where they actually could be friends, like how in postapocalyptic worlds ruined by plagues and zombies you could be best friends with someone you would never otherwise encounter.

—Emma Straub, *All Adults Here*

For the six months from mid-January through July 2020, I have been either touring Tokyo, on an Asian cruise, quarantined on the *Diamond Princess*, quarantined at Lackland Air Force base, or at home in Florida isolating from COVID-19 while writing this book.

Thanks to my perceptive longtime agent, Joëlle Delbourgo, who encouraged me to write the proposal while quarantining at Lackland as much for therapy as for sale, but then turned around and placed it the first week we were home! Consulting editor Debra Englander and Post Hill Press had the flexibility and nimbleness to publish the book on a fast-track schedule with the help of managing editor Heather King and other PHP staffers. We all had hoped the COVID-19 pandemic would be petering out by the end of 2020. With no end in sight, the *Diamond Princess* will stand as the canary in the coal mine.

When I began this project while cooped up in our dingy digs without my usual computer, I wrote to Sarah Flynn. She and I have been friends ever since she worked on my first three novels as a manuscript editor at Houghton Mifflin in the 1980s. Those were the old days, when publishing company copy editors might sit side by side with an author for a week at a time, which we did both in Boston and in Crystal River and Sarah did with other authors such as Pat Conroy and Jimmy Breslin. For the last thirty-odd years, Sarah has been a developmental editor, helping many distinguished journalists, academics, and other writers shape their books. When I asked Sarah if she would team up with me, her immediate answer was "Sure!" The speed and exigencies of the writing and editorial process in a compressed time period would have been daunting for a mere mortal, but Sarah has been both brilliant and steadfast. Sarah, who brought a lifetime of editorial prowess to this project, is the sweetest taskmaster anyone could have. She is the very backbone of this book.

And especially much gratitude to David Prosten for being the editor's editor and one of the writer's first readers.

Our son Blake insisted that I tell this story if only because he thought the project was the best way for me to process the bizarre situation. In fact, he chronicled the campaign to get us home before I did in a fine piece of writing called "The Ten-Day Cause," which became my blueprint for writing about the media campaign. Our three amazing children and their remarkable partners contributed significantly. I can't thank them all enough: Blake and Amber, Josh and Giulia, and Ashley and Erick. Their support, effort, and affection bring us the greatest happiness. Home for us is not a place. It is all about them and our seven grandchildren.

Catherine and Jerome Giambalvo and Vana and Mario Mendizabal proved their mettle as intrepid travelers and steadfast friends. We'd go anywhere with them, but they might not want to take a chance on us. We remember Mary Lou Dowd through the love of her daughter, Cathy.

This book has relied heavily on Jerry's exhaustive and accurate travel journal, detailing where we went, what we ate, the times of events—including the captain's announcements—and how many people developed the virus and when. He kept accurate reports of what we each had spent, in which of the five currencies, calculated the exchange rates, and who owed what to whom. I tried to stump him with the scent of the Prince Gallery's bath amenities, but Cathy had the label!

Terry Balderson was with us every step of the way—and went far beyond friendship to bring us home. Next time we will take his sagacious advice.

Bobbie Carlton and her associates at Carlton PR & Marketing, especially Crystal Woody, Sarah Barsch, and Kerry Fristoe, micromanaged our quarantine lives through the maze of time zones and communications apps so we could let the world know that everybody was at risk on the ship. Indeed, they may have saved lives; it felt as if they saved ours—if only by scheduling rest days and prioritizing where we should focus our energy.

The novel coronavirus was virtually unknown when we departed in January 2020. We, along with the rest of the world, were always eager for the most up-to-date medical advice. Special thanks to our traveling doctor, Mario Mendizabal, MD; my sister, Robin Madden, MD, whose top-notch network was at the forefront with accurate information; Kenneth H. Rand, MD, Professor of Pathology and Medicine at the University of Florida's College of Medicine; Anthony Fauci, MD, and H. Clifford Lane, MD, National Institute of Allergy and Infectious Diseases; Eric

Schoomaker, MD, forty-second Surgeon General of the United States Army; and, perhaps most significantly, Summer Decker, Ph.D., Vice Chair for Research, Department of Radiology, Morsani College of Medicine, University of South Florida.

We cannot praise the media enough. Everyone we dealt with personified the tenets of ethical journalism: accuracy, independence, impartiality, accountability, and most of all—humanity. A huge thanks especially to Motoko Rich, the *New York Times*; Autumn Brewington, *Wall Street Journal*; Sandy Sidhu and Will Ripley, CNN; Molly Hunter, NBC News; Jon Meyersohn, A&E; Erin Burnett, CNN; Louise Connelly, NBC; Mitch Mansfield, BBC5; Zena Olijnk, CBC; Clare Hiler, MSNBC; Briona Arradondo, WTVT-Fox 13; McKenna King, WFTS-ABC, Tampa; Crystal Harper, WTSP-CBS, Tampa; Justin Schecker, WFLA; Tim Wronka, Bay News 9; and Mike Wright, *Citrus County Chronicle.*

The *Diamond Princess* was our home—by choice and by fiat—for twenty-eight days. Despite the frightening circumstances and a situation with no precedent in modern times, the officers, crew, and staff did everything in their power to take care of all the guests at the risk of their own lives. Simple gratitude is inadequate. Captain Gennaro Arma's ship was hijacked by Japanese authorities who had the legal right to quarantine us but lacked experience with a previously undiscovered enemy—a viral invader with no known antagonist. We hope Captain Arma will again be at the helm of a vessel that will be "the happiest ship on the seven seas."

Special thanks to Natalie Costa and Mikiko Ikemoto, who, under perfect conditions, are terrific cruise directors. Under duress they earned every medal for heroism, creativity, charisma, and compassion. As far as I am concerned, they have earned four stripes on their epaulettes.

Also best wishes to the whole crew, but especially to Edwin, Jorge, Michael, and Faith.

We have so many friends-by-sight from the *Diamond Princess* who we hope are healthy and home. Thanks for the friendship of Katherine Jones, Marlene, Shannon Vo and family, Marcia and Rich Goldstein, Tyler and Rachel Torres, and Karen Lau. *Arigatou gozaimashita* to our Japanese guides and assistants Aki Tenaka, Kyouko Uemura, Masumi Tsuha; Inside Japan Tours (Amy Tadehara, Philip Ledford, Andrew Sinclair, Halley Trujillo, Lauren Handlon, Kristen Elrod); Heather Hopkins Clement, CEO, Cruise Port Navigation; Mike Holland; and Shoki the Demon Queller, for his protection from plagues. Huge thanks to our other Asian guides: Amy Overy in Hong Kong; Tom Lee in Taiwan, Jerry Ngo in Vietnam.

The American Embassy Consular Team in Tokyo did more behind the scenes that most will ever realize. The American Citizen Services, our consuls worldwide, are always available for citizens in crisis in foreign countries. We would like to thank Chargé d'Affaires Joseph Young and his team for more than six months of supporting the American passengers and crew. Also, thanks to the State Department and White House task forces that worked so hard to repatriate us and to the few friends of friends who kept us in mind.

Thanks to everyone on Kalitta Flight 581, especially Steve, Rusty, and James V. Lawler, MD, Co-Director of the Global Center for Health Security; the State Department's Operational Medical Staff; and Michael V. Callahan, MD, Infectious Disease Specialist, Massachusetts General Hospital, who flew on the plane to Travis Air Force Base.

We arrived at Lackland as anonymous members of Cohort II; we departed as friends grateful for the tough love that kept us healthy. A great big socially distanced hug to Rear Admiral Nancy Knight, MD; Commander Mark Byrd of the U.S. Public Health Service; all the "yellow birds" and "white knights" who tended to us; and our many new friends, especially John R. Woycitzky and Andrew Kim.

With much appreciation to Wendy and Frank and Bev Levy for your friendship and kindness. A Texas-sized thanks to our hosts at Joint Base San Antonio, Lackland. We will miss waking up to "Reveille," going to sleep with "Taps," and, most of all, our meaningful pause during "Retreat." We won't forget the last-minute assistance of Rick Stinson and Tom Bartlett.

We also want to recognize Stephen Oxman for his encouragement.

We can only leave home in the first place because Wanda Shelley and Michelle Delosh take such perfect care of us, our home, and Lady Willoughby of Pax, and know what we need sometimes before we realize it ourselves. Thanks for all!

I could accomplish nothing without Phil: for better, for worse, forever.

Author's Note

Nothing ever happens unless the whole world is watching.
—Blake Courter, "The Ten-Day Cause"

Quarantine! is a memoir and thus is mostly a reconstruction of memories. Memory, of course, is selective and biased: No two people recall shared experiences the same way and nobody can repeat a conversation verbatim, which is why dialogue in nonfiction may be suspect. Since I mainly write fiction, my writing style is a combination of description and "representative dialogue," which provides the gist of a conversation. It's probably not verbatim unless there is an audio- or videotape to refer to. In this case, I do have accurate records of the captain's announcements, some broadcasts by Princess staff, and transcripts of television and radio interviews and news about the ship.

Most of the time, though, I have recreated what was discussed. Although most writers choose not to do this, our travel companions have read the manuscript to make sure they do not have a different memory or are portrayed inaccurately. It may not be what journalists do; it is what friends do. As for Phil, he and I not only know each other well enough to complete each other's sentences, we sometimes don't even have to speak aloud.

Quarantine! was never meant to be the definitive work on the complex medical, political, diplomatic, public health, and epidemiological aspects of the deadly outbreak of the disease that wasn't even named until almost the end of the shipboard quarantine. It is the report from our cabin, Dolphin-401, and is personal, subjective, and filtered through our perceptions and prejudices.

I have been in touch with Princess public relations, management, and their senior communications advisor. They declined approval of using the ship's name in the cover photograph. Nobody from Princess agreed to be interviewed and none of my questions or requests for corroboration have received any response. Therefore, none of the facts or statistics about Princess have been verified by Princess Cruises, Carnival Corporation, or any of their representatives or employees. We have cruised ten times with Princess and three times with Carnival. I have owned a hundred shares of stock in Carnival Corporation PLC (CCL) since 2012.

Names and details about some of the people, relationships, job descriptions, and companies in the book have been altered for reasons of privacy and security.

Gay Courter is the author of five bestselling historical novels, with over three million copies in print, and *I Speak for This Child: True Stories of a Child Advocate*. Gay did research for *The Girl in the Box*, a medical mystery set on a cruise ship, aboard the *Diamond Princess* in 2017.

Philip Courter (photographer), Gay's husband, is an Emmy-winning documentary filmmaker, author of *The Filmmaker's Craft*, and designer/builder of innovative film devices. Now semi-retired, he designs and builds musical instruments, furniture, and sculptures. He's also a bluegrass musician.

Sarah Flynn (editor) was at Houghton Mifflin in Boston when she worked with Gay on her first three novels. An independent editor since the late 1980s, she is also co-author of *Voices of Freedom*, a companion volume to the Emmy-winning documentary series *Eyes on the Prize*.